NEW ENGLAND INSTITUTE
OF TECHNOLOGY
LEARNING RESOURCES CENTER

Progress

# Progress
## Fact or Illusion?

Edited by Leo Marx and Bruce Mazlish

*Ann Arbor*
THE UNIVERSITY OF MICHIGAN PRESS

Copyright © by the University of Michigan 1996
All rights reserved
Published in the United States of America by
The University of Michigan Press
Manufactured in the United States of America
⊚ Printed on acid-free paper

1999   1998   1997   1996     4   3   2   1

No part of this publication may be reproduced, stored in a retrieval system, or transmitted in any form or by any means, electronic, mechanical, or otherwise without the written permission of the publisher.

*A CIP catalog record for this book is available from the British Library.*

Library of Congress Cataloging-in-Publication Data

Progress : fact or illusion? / edited by Leo Marx and Bruce Mazlish.
    p.   cm.
  Includes bibliographical references and index.
  ISBN 0-472-10676-7 (hardcover : alk. paper)
  1. Progress.   I. Marx, Leo, 1919–   .   II. Mazlish, Bruce, 1923–
HM101.P895   1996
303.44—dc20                                                 95-50970
                                                                   CIP

# Progress

Is it then certain that the hope of perfecting the human species and of improving its lot must be regarded as chimerical? Ah! Far from us the men who amuse themselves by repeating that there is nothing to be done for the happiness of humanity; let them be content with excusing themselves from working for it, without bringing discouragement to the souls of those who still dare to hope for this happiness or intend to work for it! If hoping for the happiness of the people is an error, it is the only useful one, and the only one that must not be taken from the human race.
—Marquis de Condorcet, 1776

A Klee painting named "Angelus Novus" shows an angel looking as though he is about to move away from something he is fixedly contemplating. His eyes are staring, his mouth is open, his wings are spread. This is how one pictures the angel of history. His face is turned toward the past. Where we perceive a chain of events, he sees one single catastrophe which keeps piling wreckage upon wreckage and hurls it in front of his feet. The angel would like to stay, awaken the dead, and make whole what has been smashed. But a storm is blowing from Paradise; it has got caught in his wings with such violence that the angel can no longer close them. This storm irresistibly propels him into the future to which his back is turned, while the pile of debris before him grows skyward. This storm is what we call progress.
—Walter Benjamin, 1940

# Acknowledgments

Many of the essays in this volume had their origin in a conference, "The Idea of Progress Revisited," sponsored by the Dibner Institute and by the School of Humanities and Social Science of the Massachusetts Institute of Technology, December 6–7, 1991. We are grateful to Philip Khoury, Dean of the MIT School of Humanities and Social Science, to Evelyn Simha, Executive Director of the Dibner Institute for the History of Science and Technology, and to the Burndy Library at MIT for their support of the conference and their help in making this volume possible.

We thank Kenneth Keniston and Neva Goodwin for their acute critical reading of several contributions; Judith Stein of the MIT Program in Science, Technology, and Society for her help and advice; and we owe a special debt of gratitude to Judy Spitzer, also of the STS Program at MIT, for her unfailing good sense, humor, and industry in cajoling contributors, meeting deadlines, averting electronic pitfalls, and overcoming chronic institutional inertia. The editors at the University of Michigan Press have been unfailingly helpful.

In addition to the contributors to this volume the participants in the conference included Hayward Alker, Roberta Brawer, David Bucksbaum, Robert Cohen, Greg Crowe, Marcos Cueto, Ronald Dore, Susan Emanuel, Deborah Fitzgerald, James Fleming, Richard Fox, Decima Francis, Bernard Frieden, Elizabeth Garrels, Owen Gingerich, Neva Goodwin, Mark Harvey, Bill Hubbard, Richard Hudson, Robert Irwin, Jean Jackson, Arthur Kaledin, Kenneth Keniston, June Kinoshita, Brigitte Lane, Miriam Levin, Najwa Makhouc, Frank Manuel, Fritz Manuel, Gary Marx, Barbara Masi, Anne McCants, Louis Menand, Louis Menand III, Everett Mendelsohn, Philip Morrison, Janet Murray, John Myer, Brian O'Donnell, Scott Paradise, Lisa Peattie, Peter Perdue, Barbara Rosenkrantz, Harriet Ritvo, Lloyd Rodwin, Vernon Rosario, Nancy Rosenblum, Wade Roush, Bish Sanyal, Martin Sherwin, Merritt Roe Smith, Frank Sulloway, David Thorburn, Jessica Wang, William Watson, Timothy Weiskel, Sara Wermiel, Rosalind Williams, Everett Zimmerman, and Muriel Zimmerman.

# Contents

| | |
|---|---|
| Introduction<br>*Bruce Mazlish and Leo Marx* | 1 |
| Science and Progress Revisited<br>*Gerald Holton* | 9 |
| Progress: A Historical and Critical Perspective<br>*Bruce Mazlish* | 27 |
| Medicine and the Idea of Progress<br>*Leon Eisenberg* | 45 |
| Rousseau Redux, or Historical Reflections on the Ambivalence of Anthropology to the Idea of Progress<br>*George W. Stocking, Jr.* | 65 |
| The Economic View of Progress<br>*Robert Heilbroner* | 83 |
| A Political Assessment of Progress<br>*Alan Ryan* | 95 |
| Feminist Views of Progress<br>*Jill Ker Conway* | 111 |
| The Nature of Progress: Progress and the Environment<br>*Richard White* | 121 |
| Particular, Universal, and Infinite: Transcending Western Centrism and Cultural Relativism in the Third World<br>*Zhiyuan Cui* | 141 |
| "Progress": Illegitimate Child of Judeo-Christian Universalism and Western Ethnocentrism—A Third World Critique<br>*Ali A. Mazrui* | 153 |
| Denying the Holy Dark: The Enlightenment Ideal and the European Mystical Tradition<br>*John M. Staudenmaier* | 175 |

The Domination of Nature and the Redefinition of Progress  201
*Leo Marx*

Contributors  219

Index  223

# Introduction

*Bruce Mazlish and Leo Marx*

This book is about the idea that history is a record of improvement in the conditions of human life. Variants of this gratifying notion have been advanced here and there since remote antiquity, but only in the West, during the modern era, did it come to dominate the worldview of an entire culture. What gave credence to the Euro-American belief in an endlessly improving future was the rapidly accelerating expansion of knowledge of—and power over—nature achieved, during the last four centuries, by Western science, technology, economic innovation, and overseas exploration. Eighteenth-century thinkers like Turgot and Condorcet, Priestley and Paine, Jefferson and Franklin incorporated the idea in what is now often referred to, with varying degrees of retrospective skepticism, as "the Enlightenment project." That project was aimed at nothing less than the creation of a new kind of universal culture: secular, rational, humanitarian, republican, or, in a word, "progressive." Indeed, it may be said that in the period between 1776 and 1914, the chief European and American elites saw the world from the perspective of their belief in progress.

Since then, however, confidence in humanity's ability to realize the promise of the Enlightenment—of history as progress—has gradually waned. The most obvious explanation for this loss of confidence is the calamitous record of organized tyranny, oppression, and mass murder compiled by humanity since 1914. In the face of this blood-drenched history, the very idea of progress strikes some as obscenely complacent. "After the Holocaust," many have asked, "how is it possible to take seriously the idea of progress?" Or, if the reality of Nazi genocide is insufficient to dispel progressive optimism, we also could invoke such other appalling chapters of contemporary history as the two devastating world wars; or the buildup of humanity's capacity, exhibited at Hiroshima, to accomplish nuclear devastation; or the uncontrolled expansion of population in the undeveloped world and its consequences—extensive mass poverty and an ominously widening gap between the rich and poor nations; or the recrudescence of religious fundamentalism and ethnic nationalism; or the discovery, on an unprecedented global scale, of new forms of environmental degradation that threaten the biological stability of the earth.

2    Progress

As if this dismaying record were not enough, several important, not unrelated, intellectual developments of the recent past also have weakened the plausibility of the belief in progress. One is a growing skepticism about the validity of the very scientific knowledge that has been a major source of that belief. Both the Kuhnian notion of the history of science as a sequence of historically grounded paradigms and the more inclusive conception of the social construction of all scientific knowledge have challenged the claim of science to objectivity and to providing humankind with an ever closer approach to a permanently valid, context-free truth about external nature. Even on theoretical grounds, then, and quite apart from such manifestly negative results as nuclear explosions, a central bulwark of the idea of progress—a vivid sense of the benefits of scientific knowledge—has been weakened.

Another challenge has come from the tide of postmodernist and deconstructionist thought with its critique of modernism and modernization. In retrospect we can see that while modernism was closely bound up with positivist assumptions about linear progress and the rational accumulation of knowledge, it also bore within itself the seeds of antimodernism and, as it were, its own destruction. As early as 1863 Baudelaire, in his seminal essay "The Painter of Modern Life," wrote that "Modernity is the transient, the fleeting, the contingent," and then added, capturing the close affinity of modernism with the foundationalist aspect of progressivism, "It is the one half of art, the other being the eternal and the immutable."

By the 1960s the fleeting aspects of modernism were being treated by its postmodern critics as "privileged," and its commitment to foundationalist ideas—the "eternal and the immutable"—was vehemently attacked. Postmodern skepticism came into prominence. Whatever the locus of its origin (whether Latin America, North Africa, India, or Europe), its rise now may be seen as having marked a major shift in the dominant "structure of feeling," a shift away from the hitherto Eurocentric white male viewpoint. Thus the modernist vision of the world, with its strong universalizing, positivistic, technocratic, and rationalistic bias, has appeared to yield to a postmodernist embrace of difference, heterogeneity, fragmentation, indeterminancy. That change has been accompanied by a distrust of all universal, or "totalizing," kinds of discourse and a preoccupation with the validity and dignity of the hitherto marginalized "other." In this new climate of opinion, inhospitable to any sort of all-encompassing explanations, or "metanarratives," the progressive spirit has withered. For many intellectuals, the instabilities of particular "discourses" have displaced the reassuring and predictable "dialectic" of historical progress.

The discrediting and possible demise of Marxism (a major metanarrative) is another of these intellectual developments concurrent with the waning of belief in progress. It is now customary to see Marx as a groundbreaking modernist. Thus Marshall Berman describes *The Communist Manifesto* as "the first great modernist work of art"; it embodies a conception of capitalism as an ever dynamic, expansionary system that dissolves all established forms and brings into existence a society in which, as Marx and Engels put it in the *Manifesto*, "all that is solid melts into air." Although Marx hated capitalism, he saw it as a necessary stage in humanity's advance toward socialism and communism. A strong millennial note runs through this Marxist conception of history as an evolutionary ladder that humanity must climb toward true communism and an everlastingly peaceful, prosperous, and harmonious existence. The driving force behind this succession of improved social systems was, in Marx's view, humanity's steadily increasing productive power. At bottom, the advance of science-based technology was the key to his distinctively materialist version of historical progress. By now, as the events of 1989 imply, one major effort to realize the Marxist version of progress has failed. Perhaps, some would say, all such efforts are doomed, but in any case orthodox Marxism, as a program for realizing the progressive hope, is in danger of being swept into the dustbin of history.

The approach of the year 2000, the end of both a century and a millennium, also reinforces skepticism about the idea of progress. Interestingly, it was only in the seventeenth century, as the concept of progress was beginning to take hold of the Western imagination, that the very concept of "century" was adopted as a means of creating a periodization of history. To divide historical time into decades or centuries, like marking segments of a line on a graph, is a typically Western notion. Dividing history by millennia is a much older and more universal practice; it appears in Islamic as well as Christian cultures.

In the 1990s the millennial sense of an impending end of an epoch has been intensified, especially in the West, by the quincentennial celebration of the discovery of America by Christopher Columbus. In fact, both the words *celebration* and *discovery* became focal points of an international controversy. Some historians thought the event, which initiated so much suffering, should be denounced rather than celebrated, and that to call it a "discovery" exemplified an arrogant Eurocentric obliviousness to the existence of other peoples. So far from seeing the voyage of Columbus as a positive achievement, many scholars have interpreted it as having initiated the decimation of indigenous peoples by European diseases; the irresponsible devastation of American plant and animal life, perhaps of entire ecological systems; and the imposition upon the indigenous peoples of virtual slavery by cruel, tyrannical colonial regimes (though often the indigenous regimes being replaced also were tyrannical and cruel). Indeed, the skepticism directed at the voyage of Columbus, which traditionally had been surrounded by the optimism of the European myth of new beginnings, is closely akin to the skepticism directed at the larger belief in progress.

Century, quincentennium, millennium—more often than not these terms, along with fin-de-siècle, are invoked to mark the end of an epoch. The prevailing mood of the 1890s, for example, frequently is characterized as one of enervation, effete sophistication, and incipient nihilism. However it is characterized, the fin-de-siècle cuts against the optimistic grain of the progressive belief system. For true believers, however, progress will never end, and of course a century, a quincentennium, or a millennium can as plausibly be interpreted as a beginning. But of what? With what will these empty containers of the future be filled? Are we "progressing" into them, or are we sliding into decadence and dissolution? How might a knowledgeable believer in progress, aware of the melancholy history of this century, envisage the far side of the year 2000?

Writers of several of the essays that follow defend the "Enlightenment project," and the idea of progress, but in distinctively modified, late-twentieth-century vocabularies and conceptual frameworks. They regard the stock arguments of nineteenth-century ideologues of progress as naive or complacent or both.

Gerald Holton expounds the classical arguments from a rational and scientific perspective, while Bruce Mazlish discriminates among three kinds of progress—in knowledge, morals, and material life—and assesses their relative salience in the light of contemporary evidence and criticism. Looking at medicine, Leon Eisenberg makes a thorough survey of recent discoveries and their use in health-care systems, and he compares the resulting gains and possible drawbacks. The economist Robert Heilbroner and the political philosopher Alan Ryan put aside the usual cant about the progress of society and bring subtler, more complex current concerns to bear on the possible meanings of economic and political progress today. The historians Jill Ker Conway and Richard White examine the significance of progress within the context of two distinctive late-twentieth-century preoccupations: the unprecedented transformation of women's lives and the rise of a popular environmental ideology.

Much of the recent work of anthropologists, with their espousal of postmodern relativism, has been a major source of antagonism toward the idea of progress; in his chapter, George W. Stocking, Jr. traces the origins of current thinking in the earlier history of anthropology. John M. Staudenmaier, who approaches the subject from a religious—and more specifically, Jesuit—vantage point, is highly critical of the excessive regard for rationality entailed by the belief in progress. Of all the contributors, the most hostile to the idea of progress probably is Ali A. Mazrui, who contrasts the paradoxical universalism of the Western claim of progress with its actual Eurocentrism; writing from a third world perspective, he vigorously sets forth a number of noteworthy, highly controversial criticisms of the progressive ideology. His chapter tacitly raises the issue of what alternative vision to that of development and "progress" is available to the non-Western world. Zhiyuan Cui, also writing from a third world perspective, takes up the same question, but he seeks a way of transcending both currently prevailing views of development (he calls them "Western centrism" and "cultural relativism"), and he offers, as a way of transcending them, the emerging Chinese mode of rural ownership and production: the Shareholding Cooperative system. Leo Marx argues that the prevailing Western concept of progress assumes society's endlessly expanding dominion over nature, but that Thomas Jefferson, drawing on the heritage of pastoralism, recognized the need to repudiate the primacy of economic criteria in setting social goals and to replace them with environmentally oriented, quality-of-life criteria, and he thus envisioned an alternative concept of progress.

Should we in fact abandon the idea of progress as a view of the past and a guide to the future? If so, how would we redescribe history? Is the alternative a cyclical account or does it entail a return to a presumed state of greater simplicity and harmony? Or can we learn to dispense with all master narratives and inure ourselves to the idea that the course of events is merely random and disorderly?

In spite of the horrors of the recent past, many cogent arguments remain available to those who hold that history may yet prove to be a record of progress. One set of arguments, implicit in what already has been said here, would begin by examining the record within particular sectors of human experience. If it can be demonstrated that genuine progress occurs within the bounded realm, for example, of economic, scientific, technological, or political practices, and if a reasonable case can be made for the special determinative efficacy of those particular practices, then the idea of general progress in the long term retains its plausibility. Several of the chapters that follow contain such an implicit argument.

Another way of looking at the subject, implicit in some of the chapters that follow, focuses on the distinctive achievements of modernity. At the outset this approach insists on the differences between (1) transient events and long-term trends, and (2) relatively superficial and fundamental kinds of change. If we compare circumstances today with the rosy expectations of the more fervent advocates of progress, today's prospect admittedly looks bleak. But if we take as a baseline the actual conditions of life of most Europeans in, say, 1700, and compare them with conditions today, the picture may look altogether different. Or consider the changing situation of half the population: the women. Is there any doubt that the status of women has improved markedly in European and other "advanced" or "developed" societies—societies that have adopted the Enlightenment project?

Isn't it in fact presumptuous, the argument runs, to offer final judgments about that project at this early date? Judged by any realistic sense of historical time, after all, it was initiated only yesterday. A span of three centuries hardly provides much scope for testing the viability of such an ambitious project. Besides, even during that relatively short time, the accomplishments of political democracy and science-based technology have been stunning. They have effected a radical transformation in the conditions of life for most citizens of "advanced" societies. This statement may well be indisputable, but what remains at issue is whether that massive change, all things considered, has been for the better.

By now the usual method of settling this argument—drawing up a balance sheet of gains and losses—seems intellectually bankrupt. Those who say no, the change has been for the worse, are likely to offer an inventory of modern horrors like the one introduced earlier. But those who say yes contend that such transient events are incommensurate in the depth, scope, and persistence of their ultimate consequences, with a variety of long-term processes of change (progress)—demographic, technological, or structural—set in motion by the advances of the Enlightenment. Thus, for example, the wars of our century have taken a terrible toll of human life, yet in the long run that fact may be overshadowed by such demographic achievements as the success of advanced societies in combating disease, increasing longevity, and lowering the birthrate. Or take, for another example, the many kinds of power with which humanity has been equipped by advances in science-based technologies. Even if we grant that those powers often have been grossly misused, they nonetheless belong among the permanent assets of humanity and presumably will be available to future—and possibly wiser—generations.

This line of speculation suggests that it may not be possible to assess adequately the significance of modernity, the secular form of life toward which many would say that "progress" has been leading us, by evaluating its components in piecemeal fashion. That is because such characteristic features of modern society as political democracy, technologically advanced economies, universal education, ethnic and cultural diversity, and scientific rationalism are in fact parts of an interrelated, long-term, foundation-building program, hence their value must finally be assessed as parts of that putative whole. Until recently, moreover, it was possible to attack this kind of society as a product, perhaps a dangerously Eurocentric and imperialistic product, of the Western Enlightenment. But the apparent success of non-Western adaptations of this style of modernity—in Japan, Taiwan, South Korea, and even Singapore—has given new credence to its claim of potential universality.

The idea of progress is a protean concept. It can be, at one and the same time, a philosophy of history, an ideology serving the interests of different social groups, and a millennial-like faith. (And that is to name only three of its more conspicuous embodiments.) The idea of progress may be proposed either as a statement of evident fact, supported by evidence, or as a hypothesis, increasingly discredited by recent developments. It may serve as an obvious, almost unavoidable, way of ordering time, of lending meaning to events, or of projecting a deceptive vision that unrealistically throws an optimistic coloring over nefarious activities.

There are in fact no simple formulas for reconciling opposed views on the subject. Indeed, the chapters that follow indicate that the debate about the idea of progress raises virtually all of the fundamental intellectual issues of our time. Our aim is not to provide either a resolution of the debate or another history of the idea, though versions of that history undergird all the positions taken in this book; rather, our purpose is to reexamine, from a historical perspective, the concepts that accompany the arguments for and against, and the actualities behind, the idea of progress.

The essays in the chapters that follow fall broadly into two categories: one set emphasizes the concept, or vision, of progress, the other the presumed "fact" of progress as a historical actuality, realized or potential. The essays on progress as a concept reconsider the origins of the idea of progress as an aid to reevaluating its validity. The essays on progress as an actuality address the question: Assuming that the idea is intellectually viable, are the practical consequences of the progressive belief system desirable? Of course the two categories—progress as concept and progress as actuality—overlap at many points, and we distinguish between them chiefly for purposes of expository convenience. Indeed, we hope that this volume will suggest ways of resolving the implications of the idea of progress, in its absracted form, with what can be learned from an analysis of various efforts to make progress a societal reality.

# Science and Progress Revisited

*Gerald Holton*

**Prologue**

Writing at a time when the idea of progress was still triumphant, it was quite reasonable for J. B. Bury, the Regius Professor of Modern History at Cambridge, to dedicate his classic and still relevant book, *The Idea of Progress,*[1] to Saint-Pierre, Condorcet, Comte, Spencer, "and other optimists mentioned in this volume." And although, by present standards of scholarship, he rather slighted the role of science, Bury found for it a key place in the origins of the concept of progress, which he traced in part to the proposition of the thirteenth-century Franciscan friar Roger Bacon. For in his *Opus Majus,* Bacon had declared such sciences as mathematics, astronomy, physics, and chemistry not only to be interconnected in a "solidarity," but also to be knowledge essential both for the intelligent study of theology and for its intellectual reform. Thus, Bury thought, advances in science would help furnish the needed weapon for the most important and cataclysmic event Bacon and all of Christendom saw looming—the appearance of "Anti-Christ and his forerunners" (27).

It is therefore ironic that as we come to the end of this millennium, the idea of progress is in some quarters held to be "an idea whose time is past because it is no longer intellectually defensible" and "an idea in crisis," as the invitation to the writers of these chapters asked us to consider. Indeed, a spreading fin de siècle fashion turns Bury's idea on its head and assigns precisely to science the role of the Antichrist. Consider, for example, the following passage from a fairly recent publication:

> Modern science, constructing its universally valid image of the world, thus crashes through the bounds of the natural world which it can under-

---

I am grateful to the Andrew W. Mellon Foundation for partial support for research on this essay.

1. J. B. Bury, *The Idea of Progress: An Inquiry into Its Origins and Growth* (London: Macmillan and Co., 1920).

stand only as a prison of prejudices from which we must break out into the light of objectively verified truth. The natural world appears to it as no more than an unfortunate left-over from our backward ancestors, a fantasy of their childish immaturity. With that, of course, it abolishes as mere fiction even the innermost foundation of our natural world. It kills God and takes his place on the vacant throne, so that henceforth it would be science which would hold the order of being in its hand as its sole legitimate guardian, and be the sole legitimate arbiter of all relevant truth.

This passage deserves some careful thought because it comes not from some New Age fanatic but from the pen of the poet, playwright, and statesman, Václav Havel.[2] He elaborated it as follows in sketching what he claims to be a "spiritual framework of modern civilization and the source of its present crisis":

[Ours is] an epoch which denies the binding importance of personal experience—including the experience of mystery and of the absolute—and displaces the personally experienced absolute as the measure of the world with a new, man-made absolute, devoid of mystery, free of the "whims" of subjectivity and, as such, impersonal and inhuman. It is the absolute of so-called objectivity: the objective, rational cognition of the scientific model of the world. . . .

Modern rationalism and modern science, through the work of man that, as all human works, developed within our natural world, now systematically leave it behind, deny it, degrade and defame it—and, of course, at the same time colonize it.

More recently, Havel published an address before the World Economic Forum, again as one-sided and uncompromising as some of the defenders of scientism have been on the opposite side. In it, Havel expanded his broad charge against science and objective, rational cognition from the personal to the geopolitical arena. Under the ominous title "The End of the Modern Era,"[3] the essay looks back on a century that a Central European might be expected to characterize first of all by brutal irrationality and bestiality, in which the fates of millions were sealed by the whims of Kaiser Wilhelm, Hitler, Stalin, and

---

2. Jan Vladislav, ed., *Václav Havel, or Living in Truth* (London and Boston: Faber and Faber, 1987), 138–39. Since portions of this paper were given in my talk at the MIT Conference in 1991, passages of these materials were incorporated in my other writings; for the passages that follow, see Gerald Holton, "The Value of Science at the 'End of the Modern Era'," in *Ethics, Values, and the Promise of Science* (Research Triangle Park, N.C.: Sigma Xi, the Scientific Research Society, 1993), 115–31.

3. Excerpted in the *New York Times*, 1 March 1992.

their henchmen. But Havel finds the chief source of that legacy of horror to be the very opposite of irrationality and inhumanity, namely "rational, cognitive thinking," "depersonalized objectivity," and "the cult of objectivity." As to the role of science in furthering progress, Havel has only contempt: "Traditional science, with its usual coolness, can describe the different ways we might destroy ourselves, but it cannot offer us truly effective and practicable instructions on how to avert them."

After listening to such sweeping condemnations—of which Havel's serve only as an example of an increasing chorus of similar writings—one's thoughts return to the volume by Bury, who had ended his book with the certainty that the history of the idea of progress had been connected "with the growth of modern science, with the growth of rationalism, and with the struggle for political and religious liberty" (348). This journey toward the promise of "earthly happiness" had been, in his view, a victory of "the majesty of the immutable laws of nature" over the prestige of Providence, a "reinstatement of the kingdom of this world" against the otherworldly dreams of the manipulators of mystery and dogma.

But there Bury added a startling and prophetic epilogue. Must not the idea of Progress, the child of the Enlightenment, itself "submit to its own negation of finality? Will not that process of change, for which Progress is the optimistic name, compel 'Progress' too to fall from the commanding position in which it is now, with apparent security, enthroned? . . . A day will come in the revolution of centuries, when a new idea will usurp its place as the directing idea of humanity. . . . Or [he concludes] will it be said that this argument is merely a disconcerting trick of dialectic played under cover of the darkness in which the issue of the future is safely hidden . . . ?" (352). It was as if he had foreseen what in our day is being pressed upon us by Havel and his epigones—and what, in this very volume, some are hailing as a return to what they call the "Holy Darkness."

To a historian, these swings of prevailing worldviews are not surprising. Every generation asks old questions in its own way, thereby revealing its particular preoccupations. If we go back no further than to the mid-nineteenth century, we find Hermann von Helmholtz proposing the goal of science to be unlimited progress leading to the unification of its theoretical base, and he ended the same speech with an enthusiastic endorsement of the prospect of the unification also of the German states. Herbert Spencer called progress "not an accident but a necessity," and stretched it over all fields. During the 1870s, the German physiologist and polymath Emile Du Bois–Reymond, in his famous essays "The Limits of Natural Knowledge" and "The Seven World Riddles," launched a counterattack with his assertion that scientific progress must come to a halt at least with such questions as the nature of matter and of consciousness; before these, we can only say "ignorabimus" rather than "ignoramus." That called into question the ontological position of science itself, and this in turn brought the reaction of positivists and pro-"Unity of Science" scientists and philosophers such as Ernst Haeckel and Ernst Mach. The controversy resonated for half a century. As late as 1936, the seminal historian of science and Duhemian positivist George Sarton repeated his earlier assertion:

> *Theorem:* The acquisition and systematization of positive knowledge are the only human activities which are truly cumulative and progressive.
> *Corollary:* The history of science is the only history which can illustrate the progress of mankind. In fact, progress has no definite and unquestionable meaning in fields other than the field of science.[4]

But during the years of the Great Depression, scientific and technological progress was widely identified as the cause for an increase in workers' unemployment. Related sentiments were expressed in Franklin Delano Roosevelt's second inaugural address and again in 1937 in his letter to President Karl Taylor Compton of MIT, where he wrote that the engineer's responsibility should include considering "social processes," "more perfect adjustment to environment," and designing mechanisms "to absorb the shocks of the impact of science."

By the end of World War II, the mood had changed again, symbolized by the editorial in the *New York Times* on the day after Hiroshima, which eulogized the event as the crowning achievement of scientific progress. In the afterglow, Vannevar Bush's vision of science as the "endless frontier" persuaded the nation that disease, ignorance, and unemployment would somehow be conquered if basic science were supported on a large scale, that this would bring in its wake "a fuller and more fruitful life."

By the mid-1960s, the counterculture reaction began to swing the pendulum again mightily the other way throughout the industrialized West. The Dionysians and other "Reenchantment-of-Nature" sects captured the stage, announcing that scientific progress had converted our culture and our society into a malignant megamachine. Soon the loudest talk was about various "limits of scientific inquiry." In the 1980s, this trend was joined and made much more visible by a variety of parallel movements originating from within different constituencies, each with prominent spokespersons, but pointing to very similar objections to previous ways of thinking about, or even tolerating, progress in science. (For example, Mary Hesse: Science is a "social myth," albeit a useful one.[5] Bruno Latour: We must "abolish the distinction between science

---

4. George Sarton, *The Study of History of Science* (1936; reprint of revised edition, New York: Dover, 1957), 5.

5. In *The End of Science? Attack and Defense,* ed. Richard Q. Elvee (Lanham, Md.: University Press of America, 1992), 57.

and fiction."⁶ Sandra Harding: Physics today "is a poor model for physics itself";⁷ before science can really progress, we need "a more radical, intellectual, moral, social, and political revolution than the founders of modern Western culture could have imagined."⁸) The challenge of various strands of fundamentalism to modernism, and particularly to evolution in all branches of science, is another force to be taken very seriously.⁹ And it is almost inevitable that these recent currents—which might be identified by the phrase "the Rust of Progress," the title of Robert Nesbit's sensitive essay on the equivalent nineteenth-century discussions—will have been at work in motivating this volume.

Most bench scientists today, I believe, would not agree with these recent characterizations of the authority of science and its place in our culture. What impresses them most is not a careful refutation of these charges, but simply the patent fact that throughout this whole period, and despite the occasional attacks, scientific knowledge itself has advanced greatly, and on occasion spectacularly, by almost any criterion. The significant exception was that at times and in certain specialties, political authority (as in Nazi Germany and Stalin's USSR) imposed ideological strictures on scientific thought. Scientists and science policy planners seem to have learned that the constriction or expansion in the rate of scientific advance is markedly controlled by the action of the legislative and executive branches of government, hence their intense lobbying for resources, on the one hand, and the fear-driven activities against proposals to control progress through political and social institutions that impose limits from above, on the other hand.

What scientists think about too rarely is not only the kind of challenge symbolized by Havel's attack, but also the question whether in modern science and culture itself there are inherent limits on whether scientific progress can continue into the foreseeable future or, on the contrary, there are internal mechanisms that will propel scientific advance in more or less the way we have seen it occur in the modern era. These are the questions that are worth selecting from all possible variants of the interactions between science and progress; they are appropriate to be considered here, for they concentrate on a topic of concern to all scientists: progress *within* science.

---

6. In *Knowledge and Reflexivity: New Frontiers in the Sociology of Knowledge*, ed. S. Woolgar (London: Sage Publications, 1988), 166.

7. Sandra Harding, "Why Physics Is a Bad Model for Physics," in *The End of Science? Attack and Defense*, ed. Richard Q. Elvee (Lanham, Md.: University Press of America, 1992).

8. Sandra Harding, *The Science Question in Feminism* (Ithaca, N.Y.: Cornell University Press, 1986), 10; see the trenchant reviews of this issue in Miriam Levin, *American Scholar* 57, no. 1 (1988): 100–106.

9. This portion of my chapter is expanded in chapter 6 of Gerald Holton, *Science and Anti-Science* (Cambridge: Harvard University Press, 1993).

The notion of the eventual end of progress and with it the decay and death of science is neither a contradiction nor a novelty. The idea has been proposed many times in the past, and we can count on the recurrence of this fascination. Therefore, our chief task here is to learn how best to think about this topic as a whole, how to think about the possibility of an eventual end to science. Here history will help us, for with very few exceptions, virtually all proposals to this effect are driven by just one or the other of two fundamental thematic ideas.

One of these ideas represents science as evolving essentially along a meandering, but on the whole rising, line. It recognizes the existence of occasional plateaus, temporary downturns, and sprints of exponential growth. So on the average there is a more-or-less steady increase in the state of scientific knowledge, in its width of coverage of phenomena, in its internal coherence, in its accuracy of predictions, in its refinement of the values of the natural constants. All these hint at the distant possibility that this evolutionary development tends in time more and more closely to approach the kind of unified *Gesamtwissenschaft* that inspired Ernst Mach's circle and its successors.

The adherents of this view, whom one may call the "linearists," tend to come out of the background of having actually done research in natural science. They see science as largely an autonomous activity, not primarily driven by external forces. A typical image that emerges from their writing is science as an advancing river system, branching and combining again, as it makes its way toward some total, holistic understanding of the natural world.

The opposite view is that of scientific understanding rising for a time, but then falling and decaying, thus behaving in a cyclical manner. These "cyclicists" tend to think of science not as a goal-directed, progressive, cumulating activity. They are apt to invoke the image of a biological organism, based on the metaphor of the cycle—run through once or repeatedly—from childhood and youth to old age and death, or the closely related political metaphor of periods of revolution, followed by a normal state, followed by yet another revolution, leading to yet another incommensurable state—a sequence of paroxysms or changes of sentiment that leave no certainty for certifiable progress. These cyclicists come more often from among social scientists and historians, and, contrary to the linearists, they see science as driven largely by social processes. In the extreme case, they think of science as just one expression of some general spirit of the time—a by-product of it, as it were—or even chiefly a matter of "social construction," not essentially different from the game of chess.

As is generally the case with thematically opposed positions, one cannot expect to decide for one and against the other by some simple test. Moreover, they correspond to and may result from quite opposite types of fundamental visions about the destiny of mankind itself—on the one hand an acquiescence in the inevitable decay of material identity, on the other hand an assertion that there is transcendence, a "way out" of the cycle. It is not the purpose here to pursue such an analysis. Instead, we shall try to set forth these two scenarios by presenting in turn the arguments for each as expressed by its most eloquent proponent. This encounter with two interesting minds may help one to understand better what to do, at the intellectual level, with the question of the putative end of science.

**A Cyclicist Theory of Science and Progress**

Perhaps the most direct insight into the intellectual base of the cyclicist school of thought of the fate of science can be reached through what remains to this day one of the most fascinating and outrageous books, a book completed after ten years of labor by an obscure and impoverished German high school teacher, then in his thirties, with a doctorate in Greek mathematics and an encyclopedic ambition. His 1,200 pages, much of it written by candlelight during World War I, offered a grand Teutonic theory of both the past and the future course of all history, interspersed with dramatic predictions, a good share of absurd-sounding speculations, and some shrewd insights. But the arresting overall conclusion of his book was revealed even by its original title, *Der Untergang des Abendlandes*—the sinking away, the annihilation of all Western civilization, including its science. The subsequent English translation gave the title of the book only inadequately as *The Decline of the West.*[10] The author's name was Oswald Spengler.

His enigmatic work, published in July 1918, just as the terrible war was grinding to its bitter ending, was an immediate sensation, an irresistible challenge. The debate about it, in which scientists also joined, continued for decades.[11] In his critical study of Spengler, the historian H. Stuart Hughes observed that despite all its shortcomings, and even because of them, "the book remains one of the major works of our century, the nearest thing we have to a

---

10. This portion of my chapter is presented in expanded form in chapter 5 of my book *Science and Anti-Science*. I am basing my analysis on, and quote from, the following works by Oswald Spengler: *Der Untergang des Abendlandes: Umrisse einer Morphologie der Weltgeschichte,* vol. 1, *Gestalt und Wirklichkeit* (Vienna-Leipzig: Wilhelm Braunmüller, 1918); *Der Untergang des Abendlandes: Umrisse einer Morphologie der Weltgeschichte* (Munich: C. H. Beck, 1980) (contains, in revised edition, both vol. 1, *Gestalt und Wirklichkeit,* and vol. 2, *Welthistorische Perspectiven* [originally published in 1922]); *The Decline of the West,* vols. 1–2 (New York: A. A. Knopf, 1926, 1928); *Der Mensch und die Technik: Beitrag zu einer Philosophie des Lebens* (Munich: C. H. Beck, 1931) (trans. as *Man and Technics: A Contribution to a Philosophy of Life* [New York: A. A. Knopf, Inc., 1932]); *Briefe, 1913–1936* (Munich: C. H. Beck, 1963) (trans. as *Letters of Oswald Spengler, 1913–1936* [New York: A. A. Knopf, 1966]).

11. Some of the debate is summarized in Manfred Schroeter's *Der Streit um Spengler: Kritik seiner Kritiker* (Munich: C. H. Beck, 1922) and *Metaphysik des Unterganges* (Munich: Leipzig Verlag, 1949).

key to our time."[12] Indeed, in it we find in stark and extreme language precursors of today's arguments, familiar from the writings of Arnold Toynbee, Spengler's direct successor, and from the works of Theodore Roszak, Charles Reich, the last books of Lewis Mumford (who acknowledged his debt to Spengler) and the so-called New Age authors.

Spengler's key conception is that for every part of mankind, in every epoch, history has taken fundamentally the same course, obeying the same morphology. And from that inevitable course follow in each case naturally the specific forms of activity, whether social, political, literary, artistic, spiritual-religious, or indeed scientific. Each of the mighty cultures of mankind—for example, the ancient Indian, Chinese, and Arabian and the classical Greco-Roman—was not only as valid and significant as is our own Western civilization, but each is a drama with analogous structure. That is, each goes through the same seasonlike cycle, from its own nascent spring to its eventual burial in its own winter. Thus, our own inevitable destiny in the West is to go to dust according to a timetable that can be calculated from the available precedents. Our age, Spengler said, corresponds not to that of Athens in the time of Pericles, but to that of Rome under the brutal Caesars. We are very near the end of our cycle. Of great painting, music, architecture, or science there can be for us no longer any hope. Our best strategy, he says, is to be bravely resigned and try at least to get a first glimpse of the rise of the next wave, which is coming from the East to triumph over the West.

Spengler tells us how each cycle progresses, from start to finish. Following Nietzsche, Spengler declares that each beginning is characterized by what he calls the Apollinian spirit, symbolized by the sensuous, individual body which we can see in classical Greek sculpture. With it goes a worldview embracing attention to form and the organic, rather than to the mechanical or mathematical interpretation of experience that took its place later. It is the time of contemplation, not yet of investigation, of faith rather than skepticism, of high art rather than what he calls merely the "cult of science."

At some point into this cycle, however, there occurs a kind of historic change of phase of the Apollinian soul and of the culture it animates. It gives way to its opposite, a so-called Faustian one, which starts with a rather Germanic form of lonely romanticism, a yearning for the infinite, but gradually becomes more and more intellectualized, thereby changing what was a *culture* into a mere *civilization*. What then counts is the notion of causality instead of destiny; attention to cause and effect rather than what Goethe had called "living nature"; to abstractions such as infinite and empty space, rather than the palpable earth you can feel and smell. In a civilization, the primacy of soul is

---

12. H. Stuart Hughes, *Oswald Spengler: A Critical Estimate* (New York: Charles Scribner's Sons, 1952), 164–65.

replaced by intellect; concern for human needs degenerates into debates about money; mathematics pervades more and more activities; the principle of causality is forced on the understanding of phenomena; and nature is reinterpreted as a network of laws within the corpus of "scientific irreligion."

This transition from culture to civilization is supposed to have been completed in the fourth century for the world of antiquity in Europe; and Spengler proposes that the same transition began in the late nineteenth century for the cycle of our Western society. As in past cycles, the phase in which we find ourselves will not end abruptly. It will linger on for some time. Writing more than 70 years ago, Spengler declares that we have entered the last stage in world politics, too, which is the replacement of "the idea of the state's service" by the naked "will to power." As Nietzsche had predicted, ours would be the century of tyrants, of weapon-hungry Caesars engaged in a struggle for world rule—even as an entirely new culture is getting ready to take over the field.

It is of special interest to us that in Spengler's somber drama, science plays a crucial role. The Faustian element in science, Spengler informs us, is exemplified succinctly by the famous confession of Hermann von Helmholtz, who wrote that "the final aim of natural science is to discover the motions underlying all alternations, and the motive forces thereof; that is, to dissolve all natural science into mechanics." This urge is not merely an expression of the universal longing to find the One in the Many. More specifically, Spengler notes in our science, "the *seen* picture of nature [is converted] into the *imagined* picture of a single, numerically and structurally measurable order." If he were writing today, Spengler would perhaps have replaced Helmholtz's quotation with the recent one by the physicist Leon Lederman, who, encouraged by the current success of the unification program in physics, has mused that the aim of science now is to reduce all natural phenomena to one equation that will fit on a T-shirt.

Now Spengler introduces his most startling idea, one that has become familiar in new garb also. He warns that it is characteristic of the winter phase of civilization that precisely when high science is most fruitful within its own sphere, the seeds of its own undoing begin to sprout. This is true for two reasons: (1) the authority of science fails both within and beyond its disciplinary limits, and (2) an antithetical, self-destructive element arises inside the body of science itself that will eventually devour it.

The failure of science's authority outside its laboratories, he says, is in good part due to the tendency to overreach and misapply to the cosmos of history the thinking techniques that are appropriate only to the cosmos of nature. Spengler holds that the thought style of scientific analysis, namely "reason and cognition," fails in areas where one really needs the "habits of intuitive perceptions" of the sort he identifies with the Apollinian soul and the philosophy of Goethe. Even in the cosmos of nature there is an attack on the authority of science arising from within its own empire, for every conception, even in science, is at bottom "anthropomorphic," and each culture incorporates this burden in the key conceptions and tests of its own science, which thereby become culturally conditioned illusions.

For example, Spengler goes on, "to the Classical belonged the conception of form; to the Arabian, the idea of substances with visible or secret attributes; to the Faustian—ours—the ideas of force and mass." In particular, the Faustian physics of the last 300 years has been a physics of dynamics and of "methodological experiments," both of which, Spengler says, are exemplifications of the will to power that imbues the civilization phase of a people, when "Nature is not merely asked or persuaded, but forced." All our rushing after positive scientific achievements in our century only hides the fact, he thinks, that as in classical times, science is once more destined to "fall on its own sword," and so make way for the incoming world outlook, what he calls the "second religiousness." Guided by his theory of cycles, he tells us "it is possible to foresee the date when Western scientific thought shall have reached the limits of its evolution." In one of the handy chronological charts Spengler put at the end of his book, he allows us at the same time to see his millenarian roots and to find that fateful date: the year 2000.

Indeed, to Spengler's eyes, the signs of decay, disintegration, *Untergang* of science were clear already by 1918. Physics, he says—and note how familiar this too has become in recent Dionysian works about science—physics has been infected by an "annihilating doubt," as shown by "the rapidly increasing use of statistical methods, which aim only at the probability of results and forego in advance the absolute scientific exactitude that was a creed to the hopeful earlier generations." The possibility of a self-contained, self-consistent mechanics has to be given up because "the living person of the knower methodically intrudes into the inorganic form world of the known." Moreover, the ruthlessly cynical hypothesis, as he calls it, of the relativity theory strikes at the very heart of dynamics. The quantum ideas are held to be equally destructive. Spengler adds that he is alarmed at "how rapidly card houses of hypotheses are run up nowadays, every contradiction being immediately covered up by a new hurried hypothesis." So, the practice of giving up the search for exactitude and absolutes and adopting probabilism has undermined itself from the inside. Our inability, for example, to specify which atom in a sample of radioactive material will decay next points directly to the Achilles' heel of modern science. It is as if the idea of destiny instead of causality has been unwittingly reintroduced into the picture of nature.

And yet another, final cause for the self-destruction of the modern scientific world picture arises, he says, from its tendency to theory and to symbol orientation. For what is happening is that all the separate sciences are converging into one, a "fusion" characterized by the reduction to "a few grand formulas" in the winter of science. But ironically, just this path has led us now back precisely to what is the first and simplest activity in the beginning of every new culture and is always part of its primitive religious spirit: the preoccupation with numerical regularities. Number is part of the earliest religious belief and ritual; number mysticism appears in every faith in such sacred concepts as the relation of microcosm to macrocosm or in the building of prehistoric structures that served both for religious rites and for astronomy.

All these internal cancers will shortly kill science as we know it, and we shall rediscover that at bottom mankind as a whole, he says, has never wanted to analyze and prove, but has only wanted to *believe*. What he calls this orgy of two centuries of exact sciences is ending, together with the rest of what was valuable in Western civilization. Indeed, the only activities that are on the ascent during this final act are economics, politics, and technology. And as a kind of postscript, in his later book *Man and Technics* (1931), Spengler adds his opinion that advancing technology, with its mindlessly proliferating products, will also turn out to undermine the society of the West because, he predicts, there will be a failure of science and engineering education: the level of it in the "metaphysically exhausted" West will not be up to maintaining the advance there. The attraction of the scientific-technological professions is diminishing. "The Faustian thought begins to be satiated with machines . . . and it is precisely the strong and creative talents that are turning away from practical problems and sciences. . . . Every big entrepreneur has occasion to observe a falling-off in the intellectual qualities of his recruits." At the same time, the previously overexploited races, "having caught up with their instructors," have begun to surpass them and to "forge a weapon against the heart of the Faustian Civilization." One of Spengler's commentators simply summarized Spengler's prediction of 1931: "Already they can undersell the products of Western industry. Eventually they will conquer the Western nations themselves."[13]

Thus spoke the ancestor of the end-of-science movements. It is obviously rather easy to find specific faults with this work, as it is with the derivative versions that clamor for attention today. Prominent among the deficiencies is the presence of distorted versions of Hegelian and Marxian dialectics—more specifically, the frequent, basic misunderstanding about science by Spengler and his heirs. For example, the use of probability and of quantum causality is not an abandonment of all causality as such. The notion of entropy does not, as he thought, inevitably lead to the heat death of the universe. The subjectivity of the individual does not rob science of all claims to objectivity. And so on. Moreover, Spengler, who was really a nineteenth-century thinker, could not have foreseen the rapid internationalization of almost every aspect of science.

---

13. Ibid., 121.

Even if the Occident should in some deep sense eventually decay and some other culture takes its place, it is a safe bet that short of a return to total primitivism, its schools will also be teaching Euclid's geometry, Harvey's blood circulation, Newtonian dynamics, Einstein's spacetime, Norbert Wiener's cybernetics, and the Watson-Crick double helix. These wheels cannot be uninvented.

On the other hand, one must credit Spengler with the perceptive insistence that despite what he called the "irreligiousness" of science, there is a subterranean link between science and religion at their origins. That particular, unpopular aspect of Spengler's cyclicist view had some analogy in the work of a very different person. It is in fact the person I have chosen to represent now the opposite, the linearist, view of the fate of science. For this purpose, one could well have turned to the writings of other scientists, such as Johannes Kepler, Hans Christian Oersted, or Niels Bohr. But it is more appropriate to select as the linearist exemplar an essay that also appeared in 1918, within a few months of Spengler's book, written by a man of almost the same age as Spengler, and one who was then also still almost unknown outside his own circle. That essay was originally a speech given in honor of the sixtieth birthday of Max Planck, whose work Spengler had just found to be destructive to science. The name of the young speaker, whose work Spengler had also singled out as a symbol of disintegration, was Albert Einstein.

## A Linearist Theory of Science and Progress

Rising at that dark point in European history, Einstein began his short but memorable talk[14] with an image, saying, "The temple of science is a vast building with many different wings." In it, many pursue science out of the joy of flexing their intellectual muscles, and others for short-term utilitarian ends. But happily, there are also a few who do it simply because of their deep longing for knowledge itself. What led those into the temple? They have two motives for doing science. One is negative—a desire to escape one's "everyday life with its painful harshness and wretched dreariness, and from the fetters of one's own shifting desires."

But there is also a positive motive. "Man seeks to form, in whatever manner is suitable, a simplified and lucid image of the world," a world picture, a coherent view of how the cosmos of experience hangs together, "and so to overcome the world of experience, by striving to replace it to some extent by that image. That is what painters do and poets and philosophers and natural scientists, all in their own way. And into this image and its formation each individual places his or her center of gravity of the emotional life, in order to

---

14. Albert Einstein, "Motivations of Research" (but mistranslated as "Principles of Research") in *Ideas and Opinions* (New York: Crown Publishers, 1954), 224.

attain the peace and serenity which cannot be found within the confines of swirling personal experience."

The picture of the world that the physicist is building is only one among all the other possible ones. "It demands rigorous precision in the description of relationships." Therefore, the physicist must be content with studying first an idealized world, where, for example, all friction is negligible. "This allows him to portray the simplest occurrences which can be made accessible to our experience." The more complex phenomena cannot be immediately attacked with the necessary degree of logical perfection and accuracy. Therefore, at the beginning of a problem we strive for "supreme purity and clarity, but at the cost of completeness."

But such simplifying reductionism—to which the Romantic critics, from Goethe through Spengler to this day, are so opposed—is only the first, preliminary stage in this theory of scientific advance. History has taught us, Einstein continues, that once a world picture has been achieved on the basis of simplification, it turns out to be at least in principle extensible to every natural phenomenon as it actually occurs, in all its complexity and its completeness. Reductionism is only a detour on the road leading to the eternal, synthetic laws.

And now Einstein reveals the long-range agenda for science as he sees it, the destiny of science: From the general laws "it should be possible to obtain by pure deduction the description, that is to say the theory, of *every* natural process, including those of life." That program of the eventual unification of all exact knowledge of the kind to which natural science can aspire is the final aim, τέλος (telos) toward which Einstein sees science striving.

We may well note here that in the intervening years, enormous progress has been made in this direction—for example, by finding that a good deal of chemistry is just that part of atomic and molecular physics which really works; by discovering the bridge between biological and physical sciences via DNA; by finding some deep links between behavioral aspects and one's genetic endowment or biochemical imbalance; and of course by the ongoing unification of the forces of physics. In short, in modern form the old theme of finding the One in the Many has become the stuff of which Nobel Prizes are made. It is no longer entirely the dream of the much-maligned Faust, who in Goethe's drama exclaimed that either he would attain the knowledge of everything or he would have to remain a mere worm.

But to return to Einstein's talk: At this point he issues the warning that the general program for the eventual unification of all the sciences, while yielding ever deeper insights and being a powerful motivation, is likely to be one without any foreseeable end. The meandering line tracing out the advance of science is not terminating; we have an infinite task on our hands. One reason is that despite all our successes, we really lack a reliable method of guaranteed algorithm, for we have to make do with the fallible capacities of human thinking. Far from embracing the stereotype of a relentless victory march of cold rationality, which in any case exists only in some science textbooks, Einstein freely confessed here, as he was to do again and again later, and contrary to the then-reigning philosophy, that "to the [grand] elemental laws there leads no logical path, but only intuition."

That does not mean that anything goes or that science has lost its authority and is doomed to stumble blindly from one discovery to the next. While there is no logical bridge from experience to the basic principles of theory, and hence no proof of the validity of philosophical realism itself, in practice not only do we have good tests for the degree of veracity of our theories, but there is also the astonishing fact that agreement is possible within our very heterogeneous scientific community. That is a sign that "the world of experience does uniquely define the theoretical system." Even though a priori we had no right to expect any such correspondence, somehow the order we put into our theories can, and often remarkably does, turn out to correspond to the order others find in nature when they check our predictions.

Why is that possible? Why can our limited mind penetrate so often and so well behind the appearances to discern a few "eternal laws"? How can it find its way back and forth between the world of phenomena and the world of ideas? On that point, Einstein confesses freely, he has no certain answer. But that does not make him collapse in demoralized helplessness. He has a daring suggestion—that our minds are guided by "what Leibniz termed happily the 'pre-established harmony.'"

Gottfried Wilhelm Leibniz had postulated that our ability to discover the laws concerning material bodies is one aspect of the unity from which God created the two apparently separate entities of the universe, the spiritual and the material. Each of these obeys its own laws, but they can interact in sympathetic unison, somewhat in the way one stringed instrument goes into resonance and picks up the sounds made by a second one that is tuned to it. Or, to use Leibniz's own words to explain this possibility of a harmonious interaction, in which he uses an image that must have delighted Einstein: "The souls follow their laws . . . and the bodies follow theirs. . . . Nevertheless, these two beings of entirely different kind meet together and correspond to each other like two clocks perfectly regulated to the same time. It is this that I call the theory of pre-established harmony."

The argument borrowed from Leibniz is not an important part of any linearist theory of scientific progress, and today one would not make it. Scientists of our day are rightly or wrongly more likely to invoke an argument from the supposed evolutionary base of a correspondence between our ideas and our environment. They will do so less because of any proof—the considerable overlap between the workings of our minds and of the universe may indeed be entirely accidental—and more because they feel uncomfortable with the theological undertone of Einstein's metaphor, one that would have come more naturally to those who were familiar with Leibniz's discussion from their reading of the commentary on it in the writings of Immanuel Kant.

But to Einstein, just this undertone was by no means unwelcome or fortuitous. Having nearly reached the end of his essay with this image, Einstein returns briefly to the question of what motivates people to pursue science despite the lack of any guarantee of success or of a foreseeable end to the labor. It is wrong, he concludes, to trace this persistence "to extraordinary willpower or discipline." Rather, "the state of feeling which makes one capable of such achievements is akin to that of the religious worshipper, or of one who is in love. [That is,] one's daily strivings arise from no deliberate decision or program, but out of immediate necessity."

In the years that followed, Einstein continued on every occasion he could find to spell out and develop these views: Science is a program with an aim toward which one can advance, but one that has no foreseeable end. It is a mandate to produce the best objective description possible of the physical cosmos, while having to work only with one's subjective capacities and with essentially arbitrary concepts. It is an activity of persons able to combine logical rationality with intuition (contrary to the Spenglerian assumption of their incompatibility), who have the knack for acting both on hard evidence and on faith, and sometimes even on aesthetic grounds. Doing science requires analysis as well as synthesis. In short, science is the mobilization of the whole spectrum of our talents and longings, in the service of shaping more and more adequate world pictures. What to lesser minds looks like a mixture of mutually exclusive opposites between which one must make a choice, to Einstein seemed to be complementary necessities.

It is therefore not surprising that he, unlike Spengler and his followers, also saw no inherent conflict between science and religion, as Einstein hinted in this passing reference to the kinship between the scientist and the religious worshiper. In three additional short essays that also appeared in his volume *Ideas and Opinions,* he elaborated his deeply felt argument that scientific activity, the search for the evidence of rationality in the universe, is in essence a religious act. As one would expect, his description of what he called "Cosmic Religion" is not a product of sentimentality or of sectarianism; nor do religion and science, where they merge into Cosmic Religion, have much in common with the conceptions held dear by any religious establishment. Einstein's idea of God was not that of the biblical, intervening deity. Rather, his view, derived in part from Baruch Spinoza, serves as a necessary reminder that science, from its earliest beginnings to our time, has retained the signature of that single, undifferentiated totality that motivates our inherently endless human search for explanation and for transcendence.

## Coda

A few analogies can be noticed between Einstein's linearist views and those of the cyclicists such as Spengler and his followers. For example, Einstein too was opposed to the more imperialistic claims of positivism. But the essential, overriding difference between them is that for Einstein, as for most modern scientists, the notion of a foreseeable ending of science is a contradiction in terms, and there is no evidence to the contrary. For them, doing science "out of immediate necessity," with neither a determinate timetable nor guaranteed algorithms, is a compelling though turbulent activity, one well captured in a memorable analogy in Otto Neurath's essay "Antispengler":[15] "We are like sailors who on the open sea must reconstruct their ship but are never able to start afresh from the bottom. . . . They make use of some drifting timber of the old structure, to modify the skeleton and the hull of their vessel. But they cannot put the ship in dock in order to start from scratch. During their work they stay on the old structure and deal with heavy gales and thundering waves. . . . That is our fate."

This picture of science as a self-constructing enterprise against great odds was further improved by the philosopher Hilary Putnam:[16]

> My image is not of a single boat but of a "fleet" of boats. The people in each boat are trying to reconstruct their own boat without modifying it so much at any one time that the boat sinks. . . . In addition, people are passing supplies and tools from one boat to another and shouting advice and encouragement (discouragement) to each other. Finally, people sometimes decide they do not like the boat they are in and move to a different boat altogether. And sometimes a boat sinks or is abandoned. It is all a bit chaotic; but since it is a fleet, no one is ever totally out of signalling distance from all the other boats. We are not trapped in individual solipsistic hells (or need not be), but invited to engage in a truly human dialogue, one which combines collectivity with individual responsibility.

Looking back on this confrontation between two contemporaries representing in extreme form, respectively, the two most widely held, opposing theories about the eventual fate of science, it should be clear that they do not

---

15. Otto Neurath, *Empiricism and Sociology* (Dordrecht and Boston: D. Reidel Publishing Co., 1973).

16. Hilary Putnam, "Philosophers and Human Understanding," in *Scientific Explanation,* ed. A. F. Heath (Oxford: Clarendon Press, 1981), 118.

encompass all positions possible from our fin de siècle standpoint. To mention just one divergence, a small but growing group of scientists appears now to be quite comfortable with a style of work that is on neither the linearist nor the cyclicist trajectory, but opts frankly for an inherent pluralism. They disclaim any expectation for an ultimate coherence of all parts even within a given science. These might be called splitters rather than lumpers. They have an important role in the advancement of science, for that often depends on the interaction and alternation of these two traits of research—as if science moves on two feet. This point was put well, in the context of his time, by the Danish scientist Hans Christian Oersted:[17]

> One class of natural philosophers has always a tendency to combine the phenomena and to discover their analogies; another class, on the contrary, employs all its efforts in showing the disparities of things. Both tendencies are necessary for the perfection of science, the one for its progress, the other for its correctness. The philosophers of the first of these classes are guided by the sense of unity throughout nature; the philosophers of the second have their minds more directed towards the certainty of our knowledge. The one are absorbed in search of principles, and neglect often the peculiarities, and not seldom the strictness of demonstrations; the other considers the science only as the investigation of facts, but in their laudable zeal they often lose sight of the harmony of the whole, which is the character of truth. Those who look for the stamp of divinity on every thing around them, consider the opposite pursuits as ignoble and even as irreligious; while those who are engaged in the search after truth, look upon the other as unphilosophical enthusiasts, and perhaps as phantastical contemners of truth. . . . This conflict of opinions keeps science alive, and promotes it by an oscillatory progress.

A second "minority" type of divergence from the main models for the fate of science is represented by the belief of the physicist P. W. Anderson,[18] in what he calls a "hierarchical structure of science" that does not permit in principle a reduction to one set of fundamental laws from which one could then "reconstruct the universe." For example, the problems of scale and of complexity do not allow the properties of large aggregates of elementary particles to be understood merely by extrapolation of the behavior of individual particles. Rather, by a process analogous to the old conception of "emergence," in each level of complexity there can be imagined to arise entirely new properties,

---

17. Hans Christian Oersted, "Thermo-electricity," in *The Edinburgh Encyclopaedia, 1830.* Reprinted in *Naturvidenskabelige Skrifter,* by H. C. Oersted, ed. Kirstine Meyer (Copenhagen: J. Jorgensen and Co., 1920), 2:352.

18. Cf. P. W. Anderson, "More is Different," *Science* 177 (1972): 393–96.

hence each is likely to have a conceptual structure of its own and presumably also its own rate and direction of progress.

As suggested earlier, there is little hope of deciding in the abstract which of the various models of scientific progress will prevail in the long run. But on present evidence, one can predict that most active scientists will continue to take greatest exception to the cyclicist model, with its notion that science has exhausted its mandate. They will at best be bemused to hear that scientific progress is now thought in some quarters to be intellectually indefensible, an idea in crisis. Ignoring such claims, they will continue to hold that it is the particular mission and talent of scientists, as of others, to seek certifiable truths with whatever limited means come to hand; that apologies are required neither for their impulse to seek rational meaning in those signals that reach them nor for the innate tendency to seek transcendence even in science; and that their untidy mixture of motives, their unguaranteed tools, and their open-ended program will continue to motivate them as they rebuild their ships against the perils of the ocean.

# Progress: A Historical and Critical Perspective

*Bruce Mazlish*

Ours is a time when many voices are asserting the dominance of local knowledge and cultural relativism, of privileged otherness and ironic deconstruction. It is also a time when local conflict and cries for particular ethnic or religious communities fill the air; and when, vaulting over national and other boundaries, pollutants, poverty, drugs, urban degradation, and crime, to mention only a few items, seem to proliferate everywhere.

How, in such a setting (spelled out further in the Introduction), can one possibly entertain, let alone maintain, the notion of progress? In an effort to answer this question, it is well to remember that, in the middle of the nineteenth-century, the idea was already being castigated. In an 1855 essay, Baudelaire identified a "very fashionable error which I am anxious to avoid like the very devil. I refer to the idea of 'progress' . . . ." "This grotesque idea," he continued, "which has flowered on the soil of modern fatuity, has discharged each man from his duty, has delivered the soul from responsibility, has released the will from all the bonds imposed on it by the love of beauty . . . Such an infatuation is a symptom of an already too visible decadence."[1]

Yet, a century or so later, the biologist Peter Medawar could say, "to deride the hope of progress is the ultimate fatuity, the last word in poverty of spirit and meanness of mind."[2] Readers must chose which "fatuity" to embrace.

Or perhaps, more daringly, to say a pox on both your houses of extremity? I say "daringly," for the attempt, so extolled by Aristotle, to steer the proverbial middle course between the clamorous voices on either side is obviously a difficult task. It is especially so when the world appears, and is, in such

---

1. Quoted in Marshall Berman, *All That Is Solid Melts into Air* (New York: Simon and Schuster, 1982), 138. Baudelaire is also identified by Berman as the father of modernity. As such, Baudelaire was extremely ambivalent about his, and the nineteenth century's, offspring. See further my article, "The Flaneur, the Spectator, and Representation," in *The Flaneur,* ed. Keith Tester (London: Routledge, 1994).

2. Peter Medawar, "On the Effecting of All Things Possible," in *The Hope of Progress* (New York: Doubleday, 1973), quoted in the *New York Review of Books,* 16 August 1990, 13.

disarray, seeming to call for radical statements and solutions, which in any case are coming from all sides of the intellectual and political compass.[3] Nevertheless, this is the position I shall be favoring in what follows: I am proposing to be immoderate in espousing moderation during a historical and critical revisit to the idea of progress.

Whatever else, it must be clear that a major crisis in our time is the breakdown of our belief in the idea of progress. Since belief in the idea of progress is supposedly rooted in its connection to advancing *reason,* it seems a contradiction in terms to say that *faith* in the idea is eroding in our times, amounting to a major crisis. Yet, this is the case, a paradox that I hope will become clearer as we go along.

Every people or culture needs some way of ordering time in a meaningful way, of bringing temporal order out of chaos. For much of the past, for example, a cyclical conception predominated, whether among primitive societies or sophisticated Greeks. With the coming of Christianity, a linear conception prevailed in the West, with time irrevocably oriented to the before and after of the birth and death of Christ.[4] Today, however, we can no longer believe in either the classical cyclical conception or, with ease, the Christian view (though the former recurs in strange forms in odd thinkers, and the latter still determines the Western calendar). Neither view any longer suffices as an intellectual framework for modern humanity. That framework instead has been supplied in the last two or three centuries by the idea of progress, which carries forward the linear perspective but in a secular manner. However, that view too no longer appears to carry conviction in many quarters.

My task here is not to describe the progressive idea in any detail, but to signal the importance of the challenge to it today. In fact, we are in a state of

---

3. For example, the natural scientist Stephen Jay Gould seems to plump down on the side of Baudelaire when he declares, "Progress is a noxious, culturally embedded, nonoperational, intractable idea that must be replaced if we wish to understand the patterns of history" ("On Replacing the Idea of Progress with an Operational Notion of Directionality," in *Evolutionary Progress,* ed. Matthew H. Nitecki [Chicago: University of Chicago Press, 1988]), 319. Isaiah Berlin, the noted philosopher, appears to give support to this view when he asks, "Can anybody in the 20th century—certainly one of the worst centuries in human history—really believe in uninterrupted progress? Or general progress as such?" (Ramin Jahanbegloo, "Philosophy and Life: An Interview," *New York Review of Books,* May 28, 1992, 52). Not just anybody but John Maynard Smith, a noted biologist, in the same journal one issue earlier had declared that tracing the stages from "replicating RNA molecules . . . [to] animals with language . . . looks like progress, if only in the amount of information transmitted between generations . . . I do think that progress has happened . . . " (*New York Review of Books,* May 14, 1992, 35). Obviously, opinions do seem to differ, and many more quotations could be given, merely underlying the importance of the subject and the heat with which various individuals approach it.

4. Cf. Charles Norris Cochrane, *Christianity and Classical Culture* (New York: Oxford University Press, 1957).

crisis, which leaves us adrift, without a credible religious or secular meaning to the flow of events. Thus, ours is increasingly a "meaningless" world. The result is, in the words of one writer, that "The main task before us is the rethinking of the word 'progress' . . . ."[5]

To discuss the validity of the idea of progress critically, a rehearsal of some of the necessary historical stage settings is helpful in order to establish a context. Although the idea of progress has been traced back to classical antiquity and to the sixteenth century, its most significant origins must be located in the seventeenth century.[6] At that time, a number of streams began to flow together, merging into a mighty river overflowing all of Western thought. I shall identify four, briefly (for the tales have been separately told in many other places).

The first was the scientific revolution. Standing on the shoulders of their giant predecessors, such as Copernicus, Brahe, and Kepler, scientists from the seventeenth century onward thought they were constructing an edifice that would in no short time be complete.[7] Outstanding were Descartes and Newton, but behind them was an international society of empirical researchers and virtuosi. It seemed unquestionable that science was progressive.

The second stream emerged from the political revolutions of the time. Out of the religious wars of the century, with their "settlement" in the 1648 Treaty of Westphalia, a hope for a peaceful world of plenty and freedom came forth. It took shape as a secular replacement (characterized by the nation-state) of the religious sectarianism and salvationism that had led to the wars in the first place. The Puritan revolution of 1640–60 symbolized the combination of the secular and the religious aspirations in one movement, which, even though it faltered, was renewed in the revolution of 1688 that followed.

The third current was that of the millennarians. Their reading of the Bible made the advancement of humanity not merely possible, as Francis Bacon believed, but inevitable—for was it not prophesied in God's Word? Providence now took on the face of Progress. Divine inspiration would manifest itself as much in science as in religion. Overlooked by early historians of science, the religious inspiration in the scientific revolution turns out to be profound. It provides the faith in the idea of progress that reason itself might not be able to

---

5. John Lukacs, "The Short Century: It's Over," *New York Times,* February 17, 1991, 13.
6. Robert Nisbet, *History of the Idea of Progress* (New York: Basic Books, 1980), and J. B. Bury, *The Idea of Progress: An Inquiry into Its Origin and Growth* (1932; reprint, New York: Dover, 1955).
7. For the metaphor of standing on the shoulders of giants, see Robert K. Merton, *On the Shoulders of Giants: A Shandean Postscript,* Vicennial ed. (New York: Harcourt Brace Jovanovich, 1965); Piotr Sztompka, *Robert K. Merton: An Intellectual Profile* (London: Macmillan, 1986); and Matei Calinescu, *Five Faces of Modernity* (Durham, N.C.: Duke University Press, 1987).

afford.[8] John Bunyan's *Pilgrim's Progress,* an individual's path to salvation, becomes mirrored for society as the idea of secular progress.

The fourth of the streams was the battle of the ancients and moderns. There is an irony that literature, which shows little if any "advance," became a major scene, particularly in France, of the triumph of progressive modernity over classical antiquity. Yet, that is what happened.[9] Modernity, and the accompanying idea of progress, won out, first on the literary, and only then the scientific, battlefield.

It is the confluence of these streams in the seventeenth century, their feeding into one another—science, politics, religion, and literature—that made the idea of progress so irresistible. Henceforth, it was the great ocean on which smaller ships of thought might be launched. In the next few centuries, it would inundate the rest of the world, and not just the West.

There were three more waves, to continue our metaphor, in the eighteenth and nineteenth centuries that strengthened the tidal effect of the idea of progress. Again, no effort at originality is being made here; only a highlighting of the historical development.

Although Descartes had restricted scientific certainty to natural phenomena, excluding it from the moral realm (where only custom reigned), the notion took hold that human phenomena, and thus moral behavior, could also be subjected to natural laws. Inspired by Newton, thinkers such as Baron Montesquieu, Adam Smith, Jeremy Bentham, the Marquis de Condorcet, and numerous others founded the social sciences in their modern form.[10] Montesquieu, writing on the *Spirit of the Laws,* sought for a true political science; Smith, who had written on Newton in his *History of Astronomy,* wished to establish a rational science of economics; Bentham strove for a "felicific calculus"; and Condorcet, on the basis of probability theory, pursued a "social art." Thus, the Enlightenment embraced not only a scientific revolution, but a

---

8. See Ernest Tuveson, *Millennium and Utopia: a Study in the Background of the Idea of Progress* (Berkeley: University of California Press, 1949) and *Redeemer Nation: The Idea of America's Millennial Role* (Chicago: University of Chicago Press, 1968).

9. For details, see Calinescu, *Five Faces of Modernity.* Also, Paolo Rossi, *Philosophy, Technology, and the Arts in the Early Modern Era,* trans. Salvator Attanasio (New York: Harper and Row, 1970), 90–92, even though Rossi's overall emphasis is on the role of mechanics in contributing to the idea of progress.

10. As Condorcet, for example, remarked, "The author has set himself to prove that enlightenment must always increase and spread among mankind, that the progress of humanity towards happiness and civilization will follow that of enlightenment . . . " (quoted in Keith Michael Baker, *Condorcet: From Natural Philosophy to Social Mathematics* [Chicago: The University of Chicago Press, 1975], 85). Baker's book is an excellent study of the attempt at moral science by Condorcet, who is also a key figure in promoting the idea of progress.

social scientific one as well. Both gave tremendous support to the idea of progress.

In the early nineteenth century, this support became codified in the form of positivism. As is well known, Auguste Comte's work became the locus classicus of this idea. Giving scientific shape to the view that humanity has moved in its thinking from myth to religion to science, Comte set up his laws of history: fields of knowledge—that is, astronomy, physics, chemistry, and biology—moved from theological to metaphysical and then positive explanations.[11] The next field to do this would be that dealing with social phenomena, and for this new science Comte coined the term *sociology*.

While there was controversy within the social sciences—one thinks immediately of Malthus—by and large they provided a powerful underpinning to the idea of progress. The same can be said of Darwinian biology. Although in fact the theory of evolution by natural selection postulated a random development, it was read at the time as yet another scientific assurance of inevitable progress. In an uncharacteristic statement, Darwin himself gave support to this view when he said, "And as natural selection works solely by and for the good of each being, all corporeal and mental endowments will tend to progress toward perfection."[12] In any event, evolutionary theory joined positivism in *seeming* to make an invincible argument for the progressive future of humankind.

There was also, to rehearse a well-known fact, a technological counterpart to these intellectual arguments: the industrial revolution. In the short space of about 100 years—from about 1760 to 1860—humanity's material condition appeared to have improved enormously. While there were arguments during this period over the standard of living (had it gone up or down?), by the time of the Crystal Palace exhibition of 1851, the affirmative seemed conclusively to have won the day. What is more, while this development at the time was clearly a Western phenomenon, modernization theory soon came to promise its spread everywhere.

Yet, at the very moments of its greatest expansion, the idea was being shaken in its foundations. Or, to return to our earlier metaphor, the streams themselves were muddied, even polluted. Thus, the political stream was muddied by its own revolutionary nature; and the French Revolution, instead of being a glorious, untroubled expression of reason, by its excesses discredited its supposed source. As one critic has well said, "modernity begins with the historical self-

---

11. For a view that part of this shift was already occurring in classical Greece, see Henri Frankfurt et al., *Before Philosophy* (Baltimore: Penguin Books, 1946).
12. Charles Darwin, *The Origin of Species* (London: Oxford University Press, 1951), 560.

assertion of reason but ultimately places reason itself at risk."[13] Science, and positivism, pretentious in their claims to offer an unchallenged basis for morality, proved more and more unable to fulfill these claims.[14] Religion and science were increasingly thrust into adversarial positions, and the millennial source of progress thus called into question. Literature, too, became an area of conflict, with antimodernism arising within modernism itself; in fact, though the notion of an avant-garde, predicated on the idea of progress, persisted into the early twentieth century, it has been overwhelmed by the coming of postmodernism.

Ignoring almost all the shadings and colors of actual intellectual life, I have tried in a few strokes to show how the idea of progress arose in seventeenth-century Europe, seemed to become irresistible in the eighteenth and nineteenth centuries, and even appeared to move serenely into the twentieth. The underground tremblings, however, as I have suggested, were already in evidence from the beginning, and they became increasingly loud at the time of World War I and thereafter (again, reference to the Introduction is in order).

In seeking a critical reevaluation of the idea of progress, in the light of the historical context that we have sought to establish, we can proceed essentially in two ways. The first is selectively to defend the idea against those who oppose it, by refuting their criticisms. The second is to treat the idea affirmatively, with an awareness of the justified criticisms made against it. The second way seems more rewarding—and is the one I shall mainly take.

Nonetheless, as a preliminary, it seems imperative to accord some further attention to the latest critics, the postmodernists (and, blurring the lines, we can include poststructuralists under this general rubric). I shall argue that postmodernism is the current form of the criticisms of the idea of progress that have been made in every recent century. The fact is that from the beginning, the idea of progress has been in dramatic tension with opposing views: for example, in the seventeenth century, with Protestant divines, such as Luther, Melanchthon, and, in America, Cotton Mather; in the eighteenth century, with the Jesuits and their periodical, the *Journal de Trévoux;* in the early nineteenth century, with various romantics; and in the late nineteenth and early twentieth centuries, with sociologists such as Tönnies.[15]

---

13. Anthony J. Cascardi, *The Subject of Modernity* (Cambridge: Cambridge University Press, 1992), 38.

14. See, for example, Diana Postlewaite, *Making It Whole: A Victorian Circle and the Shape of Their World* (Columbus: Ohio State University Press, 1984), and Peter Allan Dale, *In Pursuit of a Scientific Culture: Science, Art and Society in the Victorian Age* (Madison: University of Wisconsin Press, 1989).

15. For an in-depth treatment of the conflict of views at the time of the French and industrial revolutions, see my book, *A New Science: The Breakdown of Connections and the Birth of Sociology* (New York: Oxford University Press, 1989; University Park: Pennsylvania State University Press, 1993). Mutatis mutandis, many of the arguments advanced against the idea of

Thus, twentieth-century challenges from thinkers ranging from Václav Havel, Aleksandr Solzhenitsyn, Christopher Lasch, Alasdair MacIntyre, Lewis Mumford, and Jacques Ellul, to name a few, to numerous anthropologists and postmodernists is hardly new, though some of the insights may be so.

Before engaging further with the postmodernist challenge, it is important to point out that there *is* one feature that is new. It is the loss of faith by those who have hitherto inclined to the idea of progress, that is, its own proponents. Ever since Copernicus displaced the idea of the earth from the center of the universe, a steady erosion of the grounding of values in religion has taken place (utterly unintended by Copernicus). The fear of hell consequently has given way to a pervasive, modern angst about an enormous, seemingly infinite, and valueless world.[16] It is this growing metaphysical anxiety, rather than the holocausts and pollutions (which otherwise might be seen simply as God's punishments) that has most fundamentally eroded the ground on which the idea of progress has stood.

It is no accident, therefore, that many of the critics of the idea of progress prize mysticism and religion in its place. Progress is equated with modernism, and philosophers such as Heidegger and his disciples dislike both the technology and the science responsible for the falling away from the earlier truths. It is interesting to note that, by and large, postmodernists as such themselves do not share this religious disposition: like Nietzsche, they accept that God is dead, and they speak out of the secular anguish that results from that loss. They are, however, as opposed as the other critics to the idea of progress.

We have remarked that the modern period more or less commenced with the battle of the ancients and the moderns. Our question must be: Is it concluding with the battle of the moderns and the postmodernists? In fact, some critics of postmodernism argue that it is a continuation of modernism, rather than a contrast to it. Typically, they advance the counterclaim "that the two basic organizing forces in modernity—capitalism and bureaucratic power—have hardly begun to dissolve."[17] Whatever our final decision in this regard, there is

---

progress by thinkers ranging from Shiller and Carlyle to Tönnies and even Weber, as treated in *A New Science,* recur in the criticisms of the idea in the later twentieth century.

16. For a splendid treatment of these issues, see Hans Blumenberg, *The Genesis of the Copernican World,* trans. Robert M. Wallace (Cambridge: MIT Press, 1987). Blumenberg's *The Legitimacy of the Modern Age,* trans. Robert M. Wallace (Cambridge: MIT Press, 1985) is also essential reading in regard to our subject. In the latter book, Blumenberg examines the claim that modernism is a secularized version of Christianity. His own view is that modernity results from a self-renewing assertion of self, seen as "an existential program, according to which man posits his existence in a historical situation and indicates to himself how he is going to deal with the reality surrounding him and what use he will make of the possibilities that are open to him" (138), and is therefore not merely a humanist rewriting of earlier religion.

17. Craig Calhoun, "Postmodernism as Pseudohistory," *Theory, Culture & Society* 10, no. 1 (February, 1993): 76. The article, in general, is an effort at a balanced treatment of its subject, seeking to give postmodernism its due while pointing out its serious flaws. An especially interest-

an irony in the belief that postmodernism is a progressive movement, supplanting modernism, when postmodernism itself no longer believes in progress.

Much of modernism can be said to be a progressive unmasking: one thinks of Feuerbach, Marx, and Freud. Postmodernism continues this tradition and can be seen as an unmasking of modernism's unmaskings. Nietzsche is perhaps the first in this sort of lifting of the masks, as when he declares, "There exists neither 'spirit,' nor reason, nor thinking, nor consciousness, nor soul, nor will, nor truth: all are fictions that are of no use . . . Knowledge works as a tool of power."[18] As one commentator sums it up, Nietzsche "conceived his enterprise . . . as an inquiry into the monumental self-deception that Western reason has succumbed to in its quest for power."

It is not a far jump from Nietzsche to the postmodernists. Thus, for example, Michel Foucault, if one can consider him a postmodernist, and Jacques Derrida seem obsessed with disclosing what they see as the hidden agenda of modernity, that is, its will to power. In this same vein of unmasking, Jean-François Lyotard writes, "I will use the term *modern* to designate any science that legitimates itself with reference to a metadiscourse of this kind making an explicit appeal to some grand narrative, such as the dialectics of Spirit, the hermeneutics of meaning, the emancipation of the rational or working subject, or the creation of wealth . . . I define *postmodernism* as incredulity toward metanarratives . . ."[19]

Progress is certainly a metanarrative. Particular aspects of that narrative as told by the Enlightenment now appear parochial and certainly need revision. For example, the eighteenth-century philosophes viewed the history of science as one of error succeeded by truth. This simplistic view has rightly given way to a highly nuanced approach, combining both internal and external analyses and an awareness of the social construction aspects of the practice of science.[20]

---

ing work on postmodernism is David Harvey, *The Condition of Postmodernity* (Oxford: Basil Blackwell, 1989). Also to be consulted is Jonathan Culler, *On Deconstruction: Theory and Criticism after Structuralism* (Ithaca, N.Y.: Cornell University Press, 1982).

18. Friedrich Nietzsche, *Beyond Good and Evil* (New York: Vintage Books, 1966), 266. The quote that follows is from Dmitri Shalin, "Modernity, Postmodernism, and Pragmatist Inquiry: An Introduction," *Symbolic Interaction* 16 (4): 307, a highly informed account. For an effort, not always successful, to bring postmodernist and sociological thought into dialogue, see Steven Seidman and David G. Wagner, eds., *Postmodernism and Social Theory* (Oxford: Basil Blackwell, 1992).

19. Jean-François Lyotard, *The Postmodern Condition: A Report on Knowledge,* trans. Geoff Bennington and Brian Massumi (Minneapolis: University of Minnesota Press, 1984), xxiv.

20. Hans Blumenberg (*Genesis of the Copernican World,* 230) illuminatingly states part of the problem: "The historiography of science has submitted, almost as a matter of course, to the criterion that it found already established by its object: It has made the present, and thus the final state of science at each present moment, into the legitimizing point on which all the efforts that preceded it converge. As a result it has become largely a process of describing what are in part

The use of science in the service of power is not new; the awareness of this use, however, has rightly been heightened, by postmodernists among others. The same can be said of Eurocentrism and a host of other time-bound aspects of the idea of progress. At a minimum, one must conclude that if the idea of progress is to be preserved as a useful grand narrative, it must rewrite itself by taking seriously the criticisms leveled at it from various quarters. Nevertheless, one can argue that postmodernism merely takes up the antimodernism in modernism and makes its points in fresh, dare one say modern, terms. Whatever our final judgment in this regard, we are still left with the question whether the idea of progress is a valid notion, which needs suitable revisions, or a basically flawed idea, which should be discarded.

Before plunging on to deal further with this critical question, a few points should be repeated and stressed.

—The first is that the idea has, in fact, been challenged from its inception (and a fuller treatment would instance Rousseau, and not just Baudelaire, along with numerous others besides the postmodernists). The present situation, therefore, is not entirely new.
—Second, the underpinnings of the idea have themselves constantly been changing; further change should hardly come as a surprise.
—Third, in revisiting the idea of progress, one is necessarily reexamining the Enlightenment project and modernity and taking positions on their values.
—Finally, if the idea of progress, in acceptably modified form, is to be rejected, the question would then arise: what is to take its place to organize time in the present (*modern* means "just now") world?

My task will not be to seek a substitute for the idea of progress (although one might try to speculate on a stable-state society). Instead, I shall try now critically to consider further three major parts comprising the idea of progress. The three parts are (1) truth, (2) the science that establishes truth, and (3) the reason that underlays the work of science. My intention is to redeem their validity. As remarked earlier, I will tend to be immoderate in my moderation.

A good starting point for the reconsideration of truth is Jürgen Habermas's view. As summarized by Anthony Giddens: "When we say something is true, we mean we can back up what we say with factual evidence and logical argument . . . Truth refers to agreement or consensus reached by such

---

interesting, in part at least charming (even if by now scarcely comprehensible) errors. And it is more difficult than it seems at first glance to extricate it again from the spell of this optics of progress."

warrants. A statement is 'true' if any disputant faced by those warrants would concede its validity. Truth is the promise of a rational consensus."[21]

Now a few things must be said taking off from this assertion. The first is that Truth is not some Platonic ideal, but a matter of rational persuasion. It would therefore be better to speak of "belief" rather than "truth"; but, as long as this point is understood, I shall continue to follow custom and use the term *truth*. The second thing to be said is that this procedure requires a "truthful" community, that is, a group of people who accept the procedures Habermas outlines to establish truth. Anyone who rejects the appeal to factual evidence and logical argument (with all the philosophical refinements necessary when using such terms) is obviously inhabiting a different universe. The third point to be made is that Habermas is describing, in its broadest outlines, the concept of scientific method (which in turn requires a "scientific community" in the aforementioned sense).

If we realize that "truth" is a matter of procedure, and not something necessarily inhering in the matter under investigation (though as a working hypothesis or assumption we *must* postulate an underlying reality that we can come "truthfully" to know, even though we can never actually reach it), then we can rescue its validity. Some statements then become true—that the earth is quasi-elliptical and revolves around the sun—and some false—that the earth is flat and is the focus around which the sun revolves. And this truth, or belief, should hold for anyone inhabiting the realm of intelligent discourse, even deconstructionists pursuing discourse analysis.

Such "truths" are cumulative. They are also provisional. They can be undone, changed, and replaced by newer or more comprehensive truths, for by the definition given, they are not eternal statements. They can be placed into systems of thought, logical structures, involving theories, that must constantly be related to factual evidence, which is itself continually being renewed and expanded. It is this that we call science. In my view, such science, existing in the minds of a community of believers, who test their beliefs according to the method outlined earlier, is a continuous paradigm, even when greatly adjusted, and not simply one of Kuhn's displacing paradigms.[22] It is consequently cumu-

---

21. Anthony Giddens, quoted in Karen Shabetai, "Facts are Stubborn Things," *Critical Inquiry* 3 (1): 110. See further Jürgen Habermas, *On the Logic of the Social Sciences,* trans. Shierry Weber Nicholsen and Jerry A. Stark (Cambridge: MIT Press, 1991). Obviously, many postmodernists set themselves in opposition to this view of truth, whether put forth in Habermasian or pragmatist guise.

22. Kuhn's *The Structure of Scientific Revolutions* (Chicago: University of Chicago Press, 1962), which has been interpreted as a manifesto for relativism (of the anthropological, not Einsteinian, mode), was, in fact, commissioned as a volume in the International Encyclopedia of Unified Sciences. The starting point for Kuhn's monograph was his observation that the social sciences were in a sorry state of disarray and uncertainty "concerning the nature of legitimate scientific problems and methods" compared to the natural sciences. His aim was to "unify" the two

lative, even if not in a simple linear fashion, and it amounts to progress in knowledge. As Georges Canguilhem suggests, scientific progress is not a matter of simple accumulation but of perpetual revision, based on historical experiences.[23]

Behind both *truth as a method or procedure* and *science as a cumulative result* lies reason. The existence and validity of reason cannot be proved by themselves—Gödel-like logic itself prevents this—and are therefore a matter of faith. But it is a faith whose attempts to "convert" others, to persuade others, is based exactly on the method, the procedure, of truth outlined earlier. In short, it is based on reason. It does not appeal to intuition as its substantiating ground, nor to revelation. It does not say "believe" because I am the authority, or because my charismatic appeal is irresistible. It simply says, judge on the basis of factual evidence and logical argument whose totality we call science: in sum, be (scientifically) reasonable.

This faith in reason, which is ineluctably connected to truth and science, as I have defined them, is the bedrock on which the idea of progress can, and must, rest. Progress in knowledge is possible, and real. The history and practice of science demonstrate this fact beyond reasonable doubt. The question then becomes: how is such knowledge related to moral existence; and how is it related to material improvement (whose achievements we have seen cast into such doubt by modern developments)?

What would moral progress look like? We can acknowledge, for example, that more knowledge of the structure of the atom is one example of mental, or scientific, progress. Would moral progress be simply greater realization of the

---

types of science.

Paradoxically, he ended up undermining the certainty and positivism of the natural sciences, rather than raising the social sciences to their level. As he stated, "Somehow, the practice of astronomy, physics, chemistry, or biology normally fails to provoke the controversies over fundamentals that today seem endemic among, say, psychologists or sociologists. Attempting to discover the role of that difference led me to recognize the role in scientific research of what I have called 'paradigms.' These I take to be universally recognized scientific achievements that *for a time* [my italics] provide model problems and solutions to a continuity of practitioners" (x).

As Kuhn himself has acknowledged subsequently, he did not intend to call into question progress in science, only the means by which it was realized. His language, however, was misleading, and when joined to Foucault's "rupture," expressed in *Les Mots et les Choses,* published four years after Kuhn's work, was taken up by those wishing to undermine natural science's claim to a superior truth. Confusion arises when the justified attack on positivism is conflated with a misunderstanding of the nature of scientific method, which, though it changes over time and in regard to particular phenomena, moves in a constant direction, as I seek to spell out in my text.

For a further, close examination of the Kuhnian controversy, see Tian Yu Cao, "The Kuhnian Revolution and the Postmodernist Turn in the History of Science," *PHYSES* 30, no. 2 (December, 1993): 1–39.

23. Georges Canguilhem, *A Vital Rationalist: Selected Writings from Georges Canguilhem,* ed. François Delaporte (New York: Zone Books, 1994), 33.

Golden Rule? A closer approximation to Kant's categorical imperative? And how would we measure these steps? To raise such questions is to suggest the difficulty of the project.

I will try to cut through the moral thickets by a series of assertions. These are all highly debatable, but I am not writing a philosophical article on morality; rather, I am concentrating on moral progress—and thus necessarily taking much for granted about morality itself.

The first assertion is that there are, at least to an observer external to a particular culture, no simple, absolute, black-and-white moral issues, but always a weighing of choices. We see Antigone having to choose between two moral "goods": obedience to the gods by burying her brother or obedience to the city law and Cleon by leaving her brother unburied. She is caught, so to speak, in a moral dilemma, and by embracing one of the choices is, in terms of the other, committing an evil. As Martha Nussbaum points out so well in her book, *The Fragility of Goodness,* Plato may have tried to make morality a matter of absolutes, but such a transcendence of real life is simply inapplicable as a matter of practice (as well as raising serious theoretical problems).

Moral values as such exist among all peoples, and there is often a surprising universality of concern: thou shalt not kill, take another's possessions, and so on. But whom thou shalt not kill and under what conditions thou shalt not take another's possessions (and who that "other" is) vary strikingly from society to society and within segments of those societies. As Max Weber, for one, repeatedly pointed out, values are vastly different and endlessly changing, and on values there can be no "scientific" agreement. They have their sources outside the scientific method and are not subject rigorously to its use of truth and reason.

If these assertions are "true" ("true believers" in absolute values, which they usually derive from a religious revelation, will assert otherwise, but, all the same, they have to live in Antigone-like terms, like the rest of us), then the conclusion seems inescapable: "accumulation" in morality is impossible. What we will have are changing choices, and changed conditions in which to make them, but no progress in moral knowledge to match the scientific. By the same token, Rousseau's moral decline, or declension, as a result of scientific progress is also ruled out of court.

Yet, convincing as such an assertion may be, the fact is that we cannot live without a moral system, no matter what it is and however different from other ones it may be. Within *our* moral system, say, Western conceptions of good and evil, we *know,* without having to prove it scientifically, that Auschwitz and the Gulag are evil. In terms of the system, we *know* that some times are more good or evil than others. Yet even stated in these terms, we suspect that there cannot be "accumulation" in morality, only better times and worse times.

Nor does the fact that we cannot establish morality in a scientific way stop us from seeking to understand the nature and roots of morality through philosophy. I have already mentioned Plato. Moral philosophy has not wanted for other thinkers since his time. More recently, Nietzsche has given a powerful thrust to our attitudes toward morality by his grounding it in power (an up-to-date version of Plato's arguments, which he placed in the mouth of Thrasymachus) and psychology. Freud has gone even further in the emphasis on the psychological bases of morality. A little earlier, Darwin seemed to support the might-makes-right position in the form of social Darwinism. In fact, a close reading of *The Descent of Man* shows Darwin's embrace of altruism as an evolutionary development, and it is on an altruistic Darwinian (*not* social Darwinian) basis that the most scientific-like explanation of morality holds out the promise of being produced.

I have touched on these matters to suggest how complicated the moral issue is. A great deal has been written on these subjects, all of which I have been bypassing. Instead, having hinted at the penumbra of speculation surrounding this topic, I want to return to my assertion that morality, unlike scientific inquiry, is not cumulative and thus not progressive; and then to suggest how, nevertheless, a certain possibility of "progress" does open up.

That possibility is that cultures, in terms of their institutions, may move in a progressive direction, even though the individuals in them are themselves not necessarily morally better. This complicated argument moves in the opposite direction from Rousseau's assertion that man is naturally good, but is made evil by social institutions. Instead, I am arguing that people are necessarily both good and evil in an Antigone-like way, but that their institutions may move in a progressive moral direction. In short, culture may become more moral (allowing for the fact that there is no absolute morality), although necessarily in terms of its own values.

Let me offer some examples. Might one not argue that the elimination of smallpox, as a result of science, is an unmitigated benefit? That the lowering of the infant mortality rate and the death of mothers during childbirth are obvious "moral" goods, as well as scientific advances? These are instances of moral progress resulting from scientific progress, and both are invested in modern culture. They are built into the society's institutions and operate independently of the moral virtue of the individual doctor or scientist.

Let us tackle other cases. There may be no ultimate way of proving that slavery is evil. In modern Western culture, however, it is so seen by most people. Slavery violates our present-day moral sense, and partly as a result now (with rare exceptions) no longer exists as an institution. Clearly, then, the abolition of slavery is "progressive."[24] In a similar way, famine with its resul-

---

24. Cf. the interesting arguments of Thomas L. Haskell, "Capitalism and the Origins of

tant starvation is admitted to be an evil. The abolition of famines by agricultural improvements is clearly a moral as well as a material advance.[25] So, too, it is generally agreed that tyranny is an evil system; movement toward a more democratic, rights-respecting political order is a moral improvement

Can one go beyond the institutional argument and contend that people's moral consciousness is also improving or being extended? Julian Jaynes, in a most provocative speculation, argues that sometime about 3,000 years ago, human consciousness itself changed, when internal voices were no longer interpreted as gods or spirits, but were recognized as generated within the mind.[26] One need not go this far to argue that consciousness itself has changed in regard to certain issues, such as war. On the assumption that the abolition of war would be a moral advance, one is struck by the way increasing numbers of people have come to consider military combat an inadmissible social action and are forming political movements to oppose it. Thus, though war, aside from world war, is in fact abundantly evident today, moral opposition to it has been growing, and we may view this as a kind of progress whose fruits will only be tasted in the future.[27]

In sum, by calling attention to changed and "better" institutions and deepened and more "enlightened" consciousness, a case can be made for the possibility of moral progress.

We must be clear, however, as to exactly what this means. There is, first, no evidence that human nature has changed. Humankind is and, as far as we can tell, always will be capable of great good and great evil. Our time witnesses terrible atrocities, just as in the past: massacres, tortures, rapes, brutal wars. What seems to be a step forward often leaves us standing still, or even moves us backward. Dr. Guillotine invented his machine to make executions more humane, but we know to what use it was put. Eugenics was put forward as a "progressive" science that would help solve social problems, and it was supported in this belief by philanthropic organizations, but we know the horrors committed in its name.

Looked at in terms of the social totality, there seems, then, little room for optimism. We see continued horrors all about us. Good intentions pave the road

---

Humanitarian Sensibility," *American Historical Review* 90, nos. 2 and 3 (April and June, 1985).

25. See Amartya Sen, *Poverty and Famines* (Oxford: Clarendon Press, 1981).

26. Julian Jaynes, *The Origin of Consciousness in the Breakdown of the Bicameral Mind* (Boston: Houghton Mifflin, 1976).

27. Perry Anderson points out that in the eighteenth century, 70 to 80 percent of the revenues of Frederick II's state was devoted to the military machine (*Lineages of the Absolutist State* [London: Humanities Press NLB, 1974], 213). Have we improved in this respect? It would appear so, but a complicated analysis of the various factors entering into this matter would have to be undertaken before we could feel secure in such a conclusion. The question is, however, suggestive.

to hell. Where we see improvement in one sector, we observe deterioration in another. On balance, it is impossible to cast up accounts, even if we were surer than we are as to what is moral and what is not, and to say whether we are better or worse off morally than our ancestors before us.

Thus, a certain realism is necessary. Disillusionment in the idea of progress arises when we indulge in too great expectations. The fact is that all social developments, say, industrialization, bring both good and evil in their train. Even when we might adjudge a development as good—for example, modernization—it will invoke a counterreaction—for example, fundamentalism—that we might judge bad (some thinkers reverse the judgments involved here).

In the light, then, of all the contrariness, contradictions, and complexities I have touched on, I would conclude with the following observations about moral progress.

—One, it is unrealistic to expect much, if any, improvement in this regard.
—Two, it is not (as Rousseau was the first to point out forcefully) a *necessary* accompaniment of progress in the "arts and sciences."
—Three, whatever progress can be hoped for will occur more in terms of institutional changes (which, incidentally, could in principle include religious developments, though I have little faith in this possibility), and perhaps consciousness, than in human nature, which seems unchangingly to rotate between good and evil (as judged by the culture itself).

In sum, we can still believe in the idea of progress if we do not expect miracles in morality; do not plunge from believing that heaven is arriving on earth to believing that hell has erupted in its place; and instead fix our eyes on the slow, tentative emergence of institutional embodiments of moral improvement. It is in these cultural developments, if anywhere, that our moral senses can "accumulate." As we know, however, even institutions are fragile structures, and can be overthrown by the forces of "evil."

Let me try to summarize where we are so far. Scientific progress is definable (though a few cranks may quibble over this), and many would accept that it has occurred. There is no gainsaying that instruments, to take some early examples, such as the telescope, microscope, thermometer, barometer, and pneumatic pump, all first employed in the seventeenth century, have expanded human sense perceptions and thus opened up worlds unknown to previous times and cultures and that observations made with such instruments have given rise to new and advanced scientific theories.

Moral progress, on the other hand, is definable only in the vaguest and most culture-bound terms, and little, if any, has occurred (though I have argued for possible moral progress in institutional form). We might add, in passing, that the same conditions hold for the notion of happiness: an Enlightenment error was to think that it could be expanded indefinitely, ignoring what Sigmund Freud was later to identify as "Civilization and Its Discontents."

Now, what of material progress, especially as science is applied in the form of technology? A case can be made as follows. The energy available to each individual has increased manyfold. Material goods are accessible in number and kind to the average person (including in underdeveloped countries) beyond, as Adam Smith put it, that available to the king of ten thousand African slaves. Life expectancy has gone up sharply for most people. The state of their health has improved; women no longer die as a routine matter during childbirth. One sign of a successful species is increase in numbers: human population has been soaring. These are all possibly signs of material progress, to which dozens of others could be added.

At this point a *but* intrudes. The mushrooming population, cited as an evidence of success, seems rapidly to be turning into a precursor of disaster. The industrial forces turning out the increased material goods are threatening irreversible pollution and causing ozone depletion, greenhouse effects, and the like. The nuclear weapons produced by the application of science in technological form loom over the very existence of the human species (if there is no future for the species, there can hardly be progress). Again, one could go on adding further examples of the way in which material change is hardly to be thought of as progressive. Indeed, as already made evident, it is these negative developments, in the domain of reality, that recently have most seriously undermined the average person's faith in progress.

Again we are faced with a dilemma. Earlier we had to deal with the question of whether scientific progress entailed moral progress, or perhaps even its reverse. Now, we have to deal with the question whether scientific progress is really producing material progress, or *its* reverse. Relating the two questions is also the further question whether material progress, or at least change, is related in a beneficial way to moral progress, or vice versa.

These are sweeping questions, again annoyingly requiring subtle and complicated answers. I will merely point here to one direction in which the argument should be pursued. It requires us to return to our emphasis on truth, science, and reason as the basis for belief in the idea of progress. For it is these elements, as I have tried to describe them, that make for the self-corrective nature of scientific knowledge, and thus the possibility of further progress. Faced with the deleterious effects, as well as the gains, of material progress, we must decide whether to repudiate science and technology or to go forward with a more "enlightened" pursuit of them. I am arguing that the very nature of reason gives us grounds for going forward with some optimism.

Our choice is between a yearning for an imagined past—the flip side of the yearning for a perfect future—and a limited but realistic belief in the progress of the species as a whole. Such progress is imperfect, halting, taking steps backward as well as forward, inconclusive, perishable—and always has been so. Human nature, as Kant and the authors of the *Federalist Papers,* Freud and the theorists of sociobiology, tell us, is "mixed," capable of both good and evil (Nietzsche's attempt to go "beyond good and evil" in this sense is misguided). Yet, with these things said, signs of progress surround this strange human species.

Some have been mentioned earlier. A fuller list is given by another scholar.[28] She instances the following.

> —that individuals should be free to adhere to the religious practices that seem right to them (although this notion is far from being universally accepted)
> —that decolonization has largely occurred
> —that slavery is now everywhere illegal (though not everywhere extinct)
> —that change in the treatment of convicted criminals, for the better, has come about (although frequent violations of the laws against brutal treatment of prisoners occur, and, this aside, the whole notion is challenged by Foucault and others; another essay would be required to enter into further discourse on this criticism)
> —that there is a growing belief and expectation that political leaders represent the led and must identify with their interests
> —that there has been improvement in the treatment of the mentally ill
> —that the enfranchisement of women is going forward
> —that there has been progress in the treatment of the truly indigent
> —that an animal rights movement has grown slowly but persistently
> —that recognition of the rights of minorities of many kinds has occurred
> —that there is wider acceptance of the obligation to make special efforts to integrate the physically handicapped into society
> —that there is a recognition that society at large must accept a basic level of responsibility for children's protection and welfare
> —that there is a growing respect for "rights," or values that are seen as

---

28. See Neva Goodwin, "Conclusion," in *As if the Future Mattered: Translating Social and Economic Theory into Human Behavior,* ed. Neva Goodwin (Ann Arbor: University of Michigan Press, 1996).

inherent in nature (though Western in origin, spreading to the rest of the world)

All these "signs" can be read in different ways and argued about in postmodernist terms. Nevertheless, they serve as pointers. They suggest that we will not be better off without our faith in the idea of progress. Indeed, we would be rudderless in the seas of time, as I remarked earlier.

We are indeed in a state of crisis—or rather, in many states of many crises—but the solutions do not reside in giving up a belief in truth, reason, science, and the possibility of moral and material improvement that have accompanied them; in that direction lie the shoals of unthinking relativism and romantic disorientation.[29]

We must cease thinking in terms of the Garden of Eden, with either the religious or secular millennial yearnings that are sown in that imaginary plot, and return to cultivating sensibly our own garden. And when we do that we must also recognize that there are many different varieties of gardens. We must trust to the power of reason, suitably reconciled to the forces of unreason (hence departing from Voltaire), to correct itself and carry us forward. To do otherwise is to act in an "unreasonable" manner that then itself becomes a self-fulfilling prophecy, undermining any, even limited, possibility of "reasonable" progress.

---

29. A sense of crisis is widespread, though it may express itself in different ways and about various concerns. For example, Tony Judt, "The End of Which European Era?," *Daedalus* 123, no. 3 (summer 1994): 1–19, especially sees us as living at the end of the European Enlightenment, declaring that "the Enlightenment *is* in crisis." Optimistically, he continues, "By this I do not mean that we are about to forget the lessons of the early modern revolutions, abandon discursive rationality and experimental thought, reject the premises of social and political modernity—though we should not too hastily dismiss the notion that there are influential thinkers in Europe who would do just that. But there is a new counter-Enlightenment in the air and its symptoms are obvious" (13–14). In his interesting article, Judt identifies especially the "crisis of the European intellectuals" (14), with their tendency to believe "that ideals are a sham, that progress is an illusion, and that short-term self-interest is the only sustainable private goal (there being no public ones . . .)" (16).

# Medicine and the Idea of Progress

*Leon Eisenberg*

During my professional lifetime, the conviction that medical research, applied in clinical practice, will lead to improvement without end in the human condition has passed from a proposition that few doubted to one that many now question. If faith has given way to skepticism, it is not because medical research did not deliver on the promissory notes issued in its name; to the contrary, it is precisely because research did pay off that medicine's rapidly growing prowess made evident the unexpected consequences of new treatment capabilities. The change in medicine's image is epitomized in two quotations, one from a philosopher of the Enlightenment some two centuries ago, the second from a savage critic of modern medicine.

Ebullient faith in medicine as an engine of human betterment has nowhere been stated with more moving optimism than in the words of the Marquis de Condorcet (1795; 1955):

> As preventive medicine improves, and food and housing become healthier, as a way of life is established that develops our physical powers by exercise without ruining them by excess, as the two most virulent causes of deterioration, misery and excessive wealth, are eliminated, the average length of human life will be increased and a better health and a strong physical constitution will be ensured. The improvement of medical practice, which will become more efficacious with the progress of reason and of the social order, will mean the end of infectious and hereditary diseases and illnesses brought on by climate, food, or working conditions. It is reasonable to hope that all other diseases may likewise disappear as their distant causes are discovered. Would it be absurd then to suppose that this perfection of the human species might be capable of indefinite progress; that the day will come when death will be due only to extraordinary accidents or to the decay of the vital forces, and that ultimately the average span between birth and decay will have no assignable value? Certainly, man will not become immortal, but will not the interval be-

tween the first breath that he draws and the time when in the natural course of events, without disease or accident, he expires, increase indefinitely?

Condorcet's belief that there are essentially no limits to medical progress has been stood on its head by Ivan Illich (1975), a contemporary critic of the "medicalization of life":

"The medical establishment has become a major threat to health" (1). "Awe-inspiring medical technology has combined with egalitarian rhetoric to create the dangerous delusion that contemporary medicine is highly effective" (19).

"The undesirable side-effects of approved, mistaken, callous or contra-indicated technical contacts with the medical system represent '*clinical iatrogenesis.*' . . . Medical practice sponsors sickness by reinforcing a morbid society that not only industrially preserves its defectives, but also exponentially breeds demand for the patient role . . . . Various symptoms of social overmedicalization, I will designate as *social iatrogenesis* . . . . When people accept health management designed on the engineering model . . . . *structural iatrogenesis* destroy[s] the potential of people to deal with their human weakness, vulnerability and uniqueness in a personal and autonomous way" (26).

"Man's consciously lived fragility, individuality and relatedness make the experience of pain, of sickness, and of death an integral part of his life. The ability to cope with this trio autonomously is fundamental to his health. As he becomes dependent on the management of his intimacy, he renounces his autonomy and his health *must* decline. The true miracle of modern medicine is diabolical. It consists not only of making individuals but whole populations survive on inhumanely low levels of personal health" (169).

I contend that it is the very progress resulting from the application of science to medical practice that has raised questions which had no meaning before physicians had the means to defer death on a mass scale. I will defend that thesis and reaffirm my continuing faith in the contribution of medicine to human welfare, once its capacities are harnessed to the goal of improving the health of populations. Having neither the skills nor the credentials of a professional historian, I will take some liberty with the concept of history in order to present what might be called a "case history": in this instance, my own.

My professional lifetime spans the interval between the end of World War II, when medicine as a source of human progress was an article of common faith, and today's agnosticism, if not atheism, about medicine. One prefatory comment may be in order. My analysis will focus primarily on changes in health and in medical care in the West because modern biomedicine has been most widely deployed among industrialized countries. However, the World Bank (1993) reports that "health conditions around the world have improved more in the past 40 years than in all previous human history. Life expectancy at birth in developing countries increased from forty to sixty-three years, and child mortality fell from 280 to 106 per 1,000." In no small part, these gains, as I shall note, have resulted from medical technology, most notably immunizations.

For my immigrant parents, a professional education for their son was a realization of their own deferred dreams; what they wanted for me was (or became) what I wanted for myself. As an adolescent, I read popular books about medicine avidly. Paul de Kruif's *Microbe Hunters* (1926) inspired fantasies of making great discoveries for the benefit of humankind, fantasies in which I strove heroically against the forces of ignorance and repression. Although in those years, I did not know the name Condorcet, let alone what the marquis wrote, the ideas I had imbibed from popular culture, though hardly so eloquent, were no less optimistic. DuPont had made the slogan "better living through better chemistry" a household phrase. I never doubted it; I do not recall any cynicism among my friends whether "better living" applied to DuPont executives and stockholders only or included the American public as well. I believed fervently that the application of science to human affairs would lead to unending progress.

On all sides, the evidence for this view was convincing. The U.S. mortality rate from tuberculosis had been 113 per 100,000 the year I was born; it had fallen to 46 by the time I graduated from high school; it was 20 when I completed my specialty training. During the 1980s, the TB death rate was to fall to less than 1 per 100,000. The control of tuberculosis is apt as the first example of medical progress because the disease had had devastating effects on my family. My maternal grandfather and a maternal uncle died of tuberculosis, the one in his forties, the other in his early twenties. My grandfather's death had been instrumental in my family's decision to immigrate to America. A half dozen of my teachers in medical school and during residency training had been obliged to change careers to psychiatry, a sedentary specialty, because of TB. Every medical student was carefully monitored for tuberculosis. A Mantoux skin test every two years was a requirement for an appointment when I joined the junior faculty at the Johns Hopkins School of Medicine.

Longevity at birth had increased from 47 years in 1900 to 63 years in 1940, the year of my high school graduation: it was to increase to more than 75 years by 1990 (Department of Health and Human Services [hereafter DHHS], National Center for Health Statistics 1994) (see table 1). The age-adjusted death rate in 1940 was only 60 percent of what it had been at the century's turn; by 1990, it was to be less than a third as high.

In 1900, the three leading causes of death were pneumonia/influenza, tuberculosis, and gastrointestinal (GI) diseases. By 1940, heart disease, cancer, and stroke led the list, as they still do (see table 2). Pneumonia had dropped to fifth and tuberculosis to seventh; GI disease no longer was in the top 10. The

**TABLE 1. U.S. Death Rates and Life Expectancies, 1900–1990**

| Year | Age-Adjusted Death Rate (per 100,000) | Life-Expectancy (Years) |
|---|---|---|
| 1900 | 1,780 | 47.3 |
| 1920 | 1,420 | 54.1 |
| 1940 | 1,080 | 62.9 |
| 1960 | 760 | 69.7 |
| 1980 | 586 | 73.7 |
| 1990 | 520 | 75.4 |

**TABLE 2. Crude Death Rates: Selected Causes, 1900–1970 (per 100,000 resident population)**

| Year | TB | Heart Disease | Cancer | Stroke |
|---|---|---|---|---|
| 1900 | 194 | 137 | 64 | 76 |
| 1920 | 113 | 159 | 83 | 81 |
| 1940 | 46 | 292 | 120 | 90 |
| 1960 | 6 | 369 | 149 | 108 |
| 1970 | 3 | 362 | 163 | 102 |

data are straightforward; the changes were enormous in magnitude; they far exceed possible errors in ascertainment or coding.

What is not immediately self-evident is the reason for these shifts. Like many Americans of the time, I took at face value the boast of the American Medical Association that the quality of medical care in the United States was unsurpassed and that the excellent health of its people resulted from "scientific" medical care. Whatever credence one wants to give the AMA claim of the superiority of U.S. medicine (in the total absence of comparative evidence), medical practice, good or bad, was in fact largely irrelevant to the changes in mortality. No new therapies for infection had been developed. The striking improvement in death rates from gastrointestinal disease resulted from public health measures: water purification, sewage treatment, milk pasteurization, and better personal hygiene, (i.e., hand washing). The decline in rates for pneumonia and influenza reflected greater host resistance and less-crowded housing, not medical treatment. Sulfonamides did not become generally available until the late 1930s; penicillin did not enter the civilian pharmacopoeia until after World War II.

Just how little medical intervention had to do with the declines in death rate during the first half of the century is evident from continuous records of tuberculosis mortality in England and Wales. Mortality fell by half between 1840 and 1880 (McKeown 1976), two years before Robert Koch identified the TB bacillus. By 1940, the mortality rate was one-sixth of its 1840 level. Mortality rates for Massachusetts fell from 400 per 100,000 in 1850 to less than 30 in 1940 (Dubos and Dubos 1952). Yet, the first effective antituberculosis drugs, streptomycin and isoniazid, were not available before the late 1940s (Medical Research Council 1948; 1952). The "rest cure" in TB sanitoria had never been demonstrated to be effective despite the faith experts had in it; sanitoria *did* serve to limit contagion by removing patients with active lung disease from the community.

McKeown (1976) has ascribed the major part of the reduction in tuberculosis mortality in England to better nutrition and less-crowded housing. Other historians of the disease have emphasized the contribution of case isolation well before Koch's discovery. English poor laws made confinement in poor houses a condition for "indoor relief," thus removing many TB patients from public intercourse; the poor law was not designed for quarantine, but that was its result. Still other authorities contend that resistance to TB increased because of the selective effects of mortality; that is, the most vulnerable died at an early age and left fewer offspring than did individuals with more effective disease resistance mechanisms (Tomes 1989; Wilson 1990).

Whatever the mix of factors that account for the gains registered prior to the midcentury, once antituberculosis chemotherapy was introduced on a wide scale, not only were most patients cured, but they were rapidly made noninfectious and no longer needed to be isolated. The decline in mortality accelerated; chemotherapy became the main agent of control. Nonetheless, the role of social factors remained powerful even when the goal of full control of tuberculosis seemed attainable; disease rates continued to be highest among poor and minority populations (Glassroth, Robins, and Snider 1980).

What explains the increase in mortality rates from heart disease, cancer, and stroke? At least four factors are implicated. First, the increase is a function of greater longevity as the infectious diseases that afflicted the young were controlled; more people in the United States live into the age of risk for heart disease, cancer, and stroke. Mortality rates for the three disease categories triple during each successive 10-year span from age 20 to age 80; death from heart disease is 880 times more likely, from stroke 770 times more likely, and from cancer 260 times more likely at age 80 than it is at age 20 (DHHS, National Center for Health Statistics 1991). A second factor is the spectacular increase in cigarette smoking during this century; by 1940, enough Americans had been smoking for long enough to accelerate mortality from lung and other cancers, heart disease, and chronic obstructive pulmonary disease. Third, changes in lifestyle in the United States resulted in an increase in animal fat consumption and a more sedentary life, both risk factors for heart disease.

Fourth, toxic industrial chemicals contributed to the increasing cancer rate (Landrigan 1992).

The intellectual foundations for the scientific revolution in medicine were laid down in the second half of the nineteenth century, but therapeutic applications did not reach the bedside until the mid-1940s (L. Eisenberg 1988). The profession I entered cloaked itself in the apparel of science, but its practices differed little from those of the empirics a half century earlier; basic science had taught doctors a great deal about the pathogenesis of disease, but little about its treatment. Indeed, the dazzling discoveries of the specific bacterial and viral causes of infectious diseases blinded physicians to the importance of host factors in determining disease outcome, an intellectual scotoma that continues to impair the scientific vision of today's physicians and researchers (L. Eisenberg 1988). Only 5 to 15 percent of individuals who contract a primary TB infection manifest clinical symptoms. Infection with the TB bacillus is a necessary, but not a sufficient, condition for illness (Glassroth, Robins, and Snider 1980).

It was my good fortune to begin my medical education just as science reached the clinic. The gains in the therapeutic capabilities of medicine during my lifetime have been simply extraordinary. Let me cite a few examples.

Throughout my childhood and adolescence, summers were a time of anguish for my parents. They lived in dread that my sisters or I might be stricken during an epidemic of infantile paralysis—polio. That fear was so deeply imbedded in all parents that the success of the Salk vaccine trial was headline news in every city and town. Even the tragic error in the Cutter Laboratory (an incompletely neutralized vaccine escaped detection and caused paralytic polio) did not sour the public; such trust is unimaginable in today's climate. Immunization against poliomyelitis, introduced in 1956, reduced cases from an average of 40,000 a year during the early 1950s to 300 a year in the 1960s, 20 a year in the 1970s, and fewer than 10 a year in the 1980s (Centers for Disease Control 1991). The last reported case in all the Americas of paralytic polio caused by wild virus occurred in August 1991 in Peru (Centers for Disease Control 1994).

Since the introduction of the measles vaccine, case incidence has fallen from hundreds of thousands to the low thousands per annum, with a corresponding decline in deaths from 500 to 1 or 2. Much the same is true for rubella (german measles) and pertussis. The cost-benefit ratio from immunization exceeds 17 to 1 (Gruenberg 1986). UNICEF estimates that three million deaths from vaccine-preventable diseases are now avoided each year in developing countries; with wider coverage, an additional 1.7 million could be averted (Grant 1993). As stated in a recent Institute of Medicine (1991) report on vaccines: "Next to clean water, no single intervention has had so profound an effect on reducing mortality from childhood diseases as has the widespread introduction of vaccines." It is unconscionable that, during recent years, the incidence of rubeola and rubella in the United States has risen sharply because we have failed to ensure delivery of the vaccine to poor children (Guyer et al. 1994).

In 1967, when the World Health Organization initiated its campaign to eradicate smallpox, there were each year 15 to 20 million cases in the Third World, with a death rate of almost 10 percent (Breman and Arita 1980). Within ten years, the disease had been eliminated; the last case was reported from Somalia in 1977. The cowpox (vaccinia) vaccine dates back to the nineteenth century, but its effective use in the developing world was possible only after: (*a*) the development of a heat-stable vaccine; (*b*) a new strategy: identification of cases and vaccination of susceptible contacts rather than the unrealistic goal of universal vaccination; and (*c*) a joint effort by the United States and the U.S.S.R. in committing financial and technical support to the WHO campaign.

In therapeutics, the availability of the birth control pill and of safe surgical abortion has given women the means to control their own fertility. Antibiotics have permitted an extraordinary degree of control over infections. Total hip replacement has restored mobility to hundreds of thousands of osteoarthritic patients with crippling disease. Some cancers, hypertension, and many types of heart disease and endocrine disorders can be relieved by medical and surgical treatments. What has been the net impact?

To return to the diseases with which this account began, by 1970, mortality rates from pneumonia/influenza had been reduced to one-sixth and from tuberculosis and from GI disease to one-hundredth of the rates at the turn of the century. The age-adjusted death rate from all causes combined had decreased to 40 percent of the earlier value (table 1) despite the two- to threefold increase in mortality from heart disease and cancer. What has happened since 1970? Table 3 presents the data. The current rate for heart disease is 80 percent and that for stroke 57 percent of what each had been in 1970. Between 1980 and 1991, the age-adjusted death rate for heart disease declined 27 percent and for stroke 34 percent (DHHS, National Center for Health Statistics 1994). However, as more people in the United States survive to old age, the incidence of cancer is increasing faster than any mortality offset achieved by earlier detection and better treatment.

That decline in heart disease and stroke mortality is not worldwide. Although the pattern for Canada is much the same as that for the United States, that for western Europe is less benign. Moreover, rates in Hungary, Bulgaria, and Czechoslovakia are not only much higher than those in the United States, but also continue to climb (Uemura and Pisa 1988). These eastern European countries are characterized by high smoking rates, high blood cholesterol levels resulting from high animal fat consumption (principally pork), little commitment to exercise programs, and demoralized medical care systems.

**TABLE 3. Crude Death Rates: Selected Causes, 1970–1990 (per 100,000 resident population)**

| Year | Heart Disease | Cancer | Stroke |
|---|---|---|---|
| 1970 | 362 | 163 | 102 |
| 1980 | 336 | 184 | 75 |
| 1990 | 290 | 203 | 58 |

Medical and surgical treatments for hypertension and coronary artery disease in the United States have had a significant impact on the death rate. Goldman and Cook (1984) estimate that some 40 percent of the mortality reduction is attributable to medical interventions; they assign improved health behavior the remainder of the credit. The most recent data from the Framingham Longitudinal Study (W. P. Castelli, personal communication, 1991) indicate that the prevalence of heart disease has remained very much the same over the past 20 years, despite the decrease in mortality. The Framingham investigators attribute two-thirds of the mortality reduction to better medical care. Whatever the precise proportion, medical care has had a major impact on disease outcomes in the second half of this century.

One way of summarizing the net health outcome is by examining secular changes in the percentage of the American population surviving into postretirement years. As shown by table 4, those age 65 and older have increased from 12 million to 31 million in the last 40 years; that is, from 8 percent to 12 percent of the total population. Even more notable is the increase in those age 85 and older: from fewer than 600,000 to more than 3 million; that is, from 0.4 percent of the population to 1.2 percent. This increase in the "old-old" reflects a new phenomenon in public health: proportionately greater gains in longevity for the old than the young. During the first half of this century, life expectancy at birth increased by 44 percent; that at age 65 increased by 17 percent. In the second half of the century, life expectancy at birth increased by only 10 percent, whereas that at age 65 increased by 24 percent (DHHS, National Center for Health Statistics 1994). Projections into the next century suggest that by the year 2050, when the total U.S. population will reach 390 million, 11 million (or 2.8 percent) will be age 85 or over; 750,000 of them age 100 or beyond (U.S. Bureau of the Census 1989)!

Should we, especially the "we" who have reached or have passed age 65, not regard this as a reason for breaking out the champagne? As one who is in that cohort, I am not quite ready to celebrate. Of Americans age 65 and older, one in three suffer limitation of activity; one in 10 experience major handicap (DHHS, National Center for Health Statistics 1994). More than one in five of those age 85 and older are confined to nursing homes; a like number of equally handicapped elders are entirely dependent for their care upon family members.

**TABLE 4. Increase in Elders in the U.S. Population**

| | 65 and Older | | 85 and Older | |
|---|---|---|---|---|
| Year | Number (thousands) | % of Total Population | Number (thousands) | % of Total Population |
| 1950 | 12,195 | 8.09 | 577 | 0.4 |
| 1960 | 16,559 | 9.23 | 929 | 0.5 |
| 1970 | 20,065 | 9.87 | 1,511 | 0.7 |
| 1980 | 25,547 | 11.28 | 2,240 | 1.0 |
| 1990 | 31,078 | 12.50 | 3,021 | 1.2 |

At least one in five of individuals age 85 and older suffer from Alzheimer's dementia (Jorm 1990). Even Condorcet recognized that there is a biological upper limit to human life expectancy; whether that age is at 85± or 110± is a topic of active dispute. More important is whether the ability to extend life by the 25-year difference between those theoretical estimates will be accompanied by decreased morbidity (Baringa 1991); that is, will there be more healthy years or more years impaired by chronic illness?

Medical technology has succeeded so devilishly well that it is no longer a matter of using it to maintain life, but of interrupting its use to permit death. At the turn of the century, the distinguished physician Sir William Osler characterized bronchopneumonia as "the old man's friend"; it provided a merciful end for patients suffering from chronic incapacitating disease. There wasn't much Osler or any other physician of his day could do to delay death. Today, in contrast, physicians not only can, but do, intervene, to intercept what would have been a "terminal" bronchopneumonia, best left to take its course in patients with metastatic cancer. The American Hospital Association estimates that three out of four deaths in U.S. hospitals each day have to be "timed" or "negotiated" (Malcolm 1991).

People in the United States are ambivalent about what medicine has wrought. In a recent poll, two-thirds of respondents expressed confidence that science would find a way to extend the average life span beyond 90 years; indeed, most expressed a wish to live to 100! Yet, four out of five reported greater fear of living out their lives in a nursing home than of sudden death. Given how recently the discussion of euthanasia has become legitimate, it is remarkable that 43 percent of voters responding to a referendum in the state of Washington approved its legalization. This sea change in public opinion led Congress to pass the Patient Self-Determination Act. Hospitals are *required* to tell patients they have a right to decide to forgo or discontinue life-prolonging medical treatment and to set out "advance directives" about care when they can no longer speak for themselves (Knox 1991).

Doubts about the wisdom of the mindless extension of life were slow to appear in the medical literature. *Medline,* the computerized citation system, lists only one article under the rubric "quality of life" before 1971. Since then, citations have increased steadily; they totalled 835 by mid-1991. The profession has only begun to appreciate that patients assess the quality of their lives by criteria that may differ markedly from those of their doctors (Eisenberg 1975; Slevin et al. 1988).

A second source of disenchantment with medical "progress" has been the wild increase in the costs of care. In 1940, national health expenditures were $4 billion; by 1970, they had risen to $74 billion; by 1991, they reached $750 billion; in 50 years, they tripled their share of the gross national product—to 13 percent (DHHS, National Center for Health Statistics 1994)—and still counting (the estimate for 1994 is $1 *trillion*). Even though U.S. per capita health expenditures exceed those of Canada by 41 percent, Germany by 87 percent, and the United Kingdom by 170 percent, U.S. infant mortality is *higher* and life expectancy is *lower* than rates in *each* of those countries; 37 million Americans are without any health insurance at all, and a like number are underinsured (Rice 1991).

Concerns about mindless prolongation of life and about escalating costs all too readily become conflated. The conjunction too easily suggests cost savings by sanctioning euthanasia. It is no coincidence that the new legitimacy of euthanasia in public debate arises at the very time when arguments are put forward that the United States "cannot afford" the costs of care. Prolonging human misery by cardiopulmonary assist is wrong on moral grounds; that it is also costly should be a secondary objection. It is one thing to assert that the patient has a constitutional right to forgo resuscitation when life quality is low; it is quite another to have the state decide whose life is worth preserving (particularly if that decision is exercised for recipients of public welfare funds but not for patients in the private sector).

A third problem with the advances in medicine is that there are gross inequities in the way health care is distributed. Black infant mortality is twice that for whites; black male life expectancy is a full 12 years less and female six years less than that for whites (DHHS, National Center for Health Statistics 1994). Agreed, these discrepancies reflect massive social disadvantage as well as medical disadvantage, but it is also true that blacks have less access to health care when it matters (Blendon et al. 1989). Blacks have higher rates of hypertension but get less treatment for it (Cornoni-Huntley, LaCroix, and Havlik 1989). End-stage renal disease is more common in blacks; yet fewer blacks receive kidney transplants (Kasiske et al. 1991). There is a substantial racial disparity in corrective surgery for black patients hospitalized for heart disease (Wenneker and Epstein 1989). Blacks are more likely to have glaucoma (Sommer et al. 1991) but are less likely to receive treatment for it (Javitt et al. 1991). And blacks continue to be underrepresented in the medical profession (Eisenberg 1990b).

Noises of dissatisfaction are heard on all sides. Malpractice suits increase; doctors respond with defensive medicine. Patients complain about waiting times, excessive charges, and imperfect outcomes; doctors complain about being buried under endless red tape, about having clinical decisions countermanded by profit-seeking insurance companies, and about incomes that no longer grow as fast as they did.

To add to the disillusionment, Condorcet's vision of "the end of . . . diseases" is fast receding. The human immunodeficiency virus, a new pathogen, has infected more than twelve million people worldwide, about a million of them in the United States (Mann, Tarantola, and Netter 1992); neither a curative drug or a protective vaccine has yet been found. HIV infection has become the leading cause of death among African-American males 25 to 44 years of age (DHHS, National Center for Health Statistics 1994). The incidence of tuberculosis infection, which had been decreasing steadily (one of my "success" stories), rose from a low of 22,000 in 1985 to a peak of 27,000 in 1992 as the bacillus found fertile soil in the weakened defenses of AIDS patients, homeless persons, and substance abusers; multiple drug-resistant (MDR) strains of the bacillus are spreading (U.S. Centers for Disease Control 1990; Bloch et al. 1994). Homelessness and drug addiction are associated with failure to follow through on antituberculosis medication schedules, incomplete treatment facilitates the development of MDR strains. To make matters worse, the usual methods to diagnose tuberculosis (skin tests and chest X rays) often fail in HIV-infected patients (Graham et al. 1992; Huebner, Villarino, and Snider 1992). The very immunodeficiency that makes such individuals vulnerable to TB interferes with the immune response on which the skin test is based; the other lung infections to which the patient is subject obscure the interpretation of chest films.

Hospital-based outbreaks have appeared, in which drug-resistant strains of tubercle bacilli in HIV-infected patients have been transmitted to other patients and to health care workers, totaling more than 200 known cases by the summer of 1992 (Fischl et al. 1992b; Pearson et al. 1992). La Quinta High School in Westminster, California, has suffered a disastrous epidemic of MDR tuberculosis; 376 of its 1,274 pupils have tested positive for TB. The epidemic was traced back to an initiating case in a 16-year-old female student whose symptoms of cough and fever were not correctly diagnosed or treated for some eight months while she continued to attend classes. The risk to her classmates was multiplied by the poor air exchange rate in the high school building, resulting from a defective ventilation system (Anonymous 1994). Whereas it had been assumed in recent years that reactivation of latent tuberculosis was the principal mechanism behind new clinical presentations, studies in San Francisco (Small et al. 1994) and New York (Alland et al. 1994) have shown that a third or more of new cases now arise from recent transmission.

Social conditions remain major determinants of risk for tuberculosis

(Packard 1989). As in 1900, so in 1992: the variables of poverty and ethnicity account for major differences in risk status. Farmer et al. (1991) have demonstrated that responsiveness to drug treatment in impoverished Haitian patients with tuberculosis is markedly enhanced when patients are given food supplements as well as careful drug supervision. Poor compliance because of "superstition" and HIV infection had too readily been accepted as the reason for the failure of conventional treatment regimes. To the contrary, when accessible medical services (including community outreach) were combined with money to buy food for TB patients who were severely malnourished, mirabile dictu, the patients recovered.

Do the appearance of AIDS, the resurgence of TB, the mindless prolongation of life, rising costs, and the persisting social class differences in health cause me to abandon my faith in medical science as an engine for progress? Not in the least. Having been aware that no Garden of Eden lies ahead, I am not disenchanted by the failure to attain it. As Rene Dubos (1959), himself a major contributor to the antibiotic revolution, said thirty-five years ago:

> Belief in a golden age has provided mankind with solace in times of despair and with elan during the expansive periods of history. Dreamers imagine the golden age in the remote past, in a paradise lost, free from toil and from grief. Optimists put their faith in the future and believe that mankind, Prometheus-like, will master the arts of life through power and knowledge. Thus, the golden age means different things to different men. But the very belief in its existence implies the conviction that perfect health and happiness are birthrights of men. Yet, in reality, complete freedom from disease and from struggle is almost incompatible with the process of living . . .
>
> The very process of living is a continual interplay between the individual and his environment, often taking the form of a struggle resulting in injury or disease. The more creative the individual the less he can hope to avoid danger, for the stuff of creation is made up of responses to the forces that impinge on his body and soul. Complete and lasting freedom from disease is but a dream remembered from imaginings of a Garden of Eden designed for the welfare of man.

The extent and distribution of disease in human populations is a function of where people live and how they live; that is, of the characteristics of the environment they inhabit, the way they interact with that environment and with each other, as well as the organization and quality of the health care they receive. Medicine is an important, but not the sole or the principal, determinant of health (Eisenberg 1990a). It is increasingly clear that eating, drinking, and smoking patterns have decisive effects on health status. Despite the evidence of the morbidity associated with obesity (diabetes, hypertension, heart disease, stroke, and osteoarthritis, among others), there is not only a disquieting rate of obesity (greater than 30 percent) in the United States, but the rate has been increasing during the last decade (Kuczmarski et al. 1994). Some 25 percent of Americans over age 18 continue to smoke cigarettes (DHHS, National Center for Health Statistics 1994). Nine percent of Americans report that they have three or more alcohol-containing drinks per day. These behaviors are not uniformly distributed in the population; they cluster among those with less education, lower income, and minority status (Flegal et al. 1988a, 1988b; Kumanyika, Wilson, and Guilford-Davenport 1993; DHHS, National Center for Health Statistics 1994).

Thus, health status continues to be extraordinarily responsive to socioeconomic factors. In the United States, as in the United Kingdom, social class differences in health, like differences in economic status, have widened rather than narrowed in recent decades (Feldman et al. 1989; Wilkinson 1992). The great pathologist Rudolph Virchow in 1848 recognized the inverse relationship between disease rates and social class. As cited in Rosen (1947), Virchow noted that as industrialization accelerated, "the proletariat in ever increasing degree became the victim of diseases and epidemics, its children either died prematurely or developed into cripples." He advocated the use of medical statistics as a social weapon: "We will weigh life for life and see where the bodies lie thicker, among the workers or among the privileged."

The organization and deployment of medical resources must be governed for human purposes. Consider: in Boston, there is no apparent racial discrimination in admissions to Neonatal Intensive Care Units (NICUs). Low-birth-weight black infants have as ready access to NICUs as low-birth-weight white infants. High-tech equipment is used without stint. Yet, neonatal mortality remains much higher among black infants in Boston. Why? The answer is straightforward: many more low-birth-weight black infants are born for every 1,000 live births. That, in turn, is a function of maternal nutrition, exposure to infection, smoking, life stress, and the adequacy of prenatal care. We have yet to assure that all mothers receive that care; instead, perversely, we build more NICUs to treat pathological pregnancy outcomes *after* the fact (Eisenberg 1990a). The impact of medicine on the health of the population depends not only upon its biological capabilities at a given moment, but also on the extent to which it incorporates a public health (populationwide preventive) orientation and on who has access to it; that is, the way its delivery system is organized and paid for.

Neither Condorcet with his unbounded optimism about the advance of knowledge (today condemned as the arrogance of science) nor Illich with his polemic against medical nemesis (and his preoccupation with the redemptive value of human suffering) provides a defensible vision of what twenty-first-century medicine can contribute to human welfare. What has been missing is an analysis that weighs benefits against costs, not only immediate, but also long-term; one that is an ecological perspective on human health in relation to population size and the carrying capacity of local as well as global environments (Eisenberg and Sartorius 1988). The issues are posed sharply with the words of Eugene Odum (1969), winner of the 1987 Crawfoord Prize of the Royal Swedish Academy for Scientific Research on the Ecosystem:

> Until recently, mankind has more or less taken for granted the gas-exchange, water-purification, nutrient-cycling, and other protective functions of self-maintaining ecosystems, chiefly because neither his numbers nor his environmental manipulations have been great enough to affect regional and global balances. Now, of course, it is painfully evident that such balances are being affected, often detrimentally. The "one problem, one solution approach" is no longer adequate and must be replaced by some form of ecosystem analysis that considers man as a part of, not apart from, the environment.

Medical examples of the folly of the "one problem, one solution" approach are legion (Chivian et al. 1992). Overprescription and inappropriate prescription of antibiotics fosters the development of organisms resistant to those antibiotics; initial victories in the fight against infection are followed by successive defeats for each new drug (Jacoby and Archer 1991). Widespread use of the fetal monitor before its signals could be interpreted unambiguously has resulted in a surge in avoidable Caesarian sections (and accompanying morbidity)—without benefit to fetal survival in low-risk pregnancies (Ewigman et al. 1993; Berkowitz 1993). Hemodialysis for end stage renal disease is a powerful technology that makes it possible to keep patients alive until kidney transplantation (which leads to a far better quality of life) can be undertaken. So persuasive were the arguments for making this treatment universally available that in 1972 Congress authorized full funding from Medicare, the first (and last) time such an action has been undertaken in the United States (Rettig 1991). Initial cost estimates were in the range of $100 to $200 million per year; they now exceed $3 billion. This dramatic escalation is not because the procedure itself has become more expensive—to the contrary, per unit costs in constant dollars are down—it resulted from applying dialysis more and more widely with less and less effectiveness.

Even the introduction of a drug highly effective in preventing parasitic infestation in cattle can have a disastrous impact on the ecological balance. Pastoral tribes had long subsisted by exploiting domestic livestock grazing over extensive areas in Africa where rainfall is insufficient for growing crops. The traditional pattern of energy utilization by nomadic peoples had been in remarkable balance with the environment they inhabit (Coughenour et al. 1985). In the Sahel Desert margin, the introduction of chemoprophylaxis against nagana (animal trypanosomiasis) led to a sizable growth of the numbers of cattle, numbers that had been kept in check by mortality from nagana. Moreover, as farmers in the new African nations began to cultivate land previously used by nomads, many of the governments would no longer allow pastoralists to cross their borders. International aid agencies for "humanitarian" reasons provided funds to bore deep water holes, around which the nomadic peoples began to settle. These simultaneous developments led to serious overgrazing in areas that had been barely able to support the small herds of the past (Sinclair and Fryxel 1985). The overgrazing itself increased the reflectivity of the earth to incident sunlight, reducing rainfall by half. The result was a worsened drought and severe human starvation (Ormerod 1976).

The threat of new or previously unrecognized diseases arising is no indictment of modern medicine; to the contrary, it is an argument for creating an early warning system composed of the most advanced scientific methods we can muster. Given the speed and the capacity of modern transport, "there is nowhere in the world from which we are remote and no one from whom we are disconnected" (Lederberg, Shope, and Oaks 1992). As the Institute of Medicine Committee that Lederberg chaired pointed out, the threat from microbes has existed for centuries, will continue, and may even intensify. What the United States needs is the capacity to recognize and respond to disease epidemics rapidly, whether they are due to the resurgence of known microorganisms after environmental change or to new bacteria or viruses establishing themselves as infectious agents for the first time.

The technical virtuosity of modern medicine is prodigious. Decisions about when and how to apply that virtuosity require moral as well as scientific wisdom. My conviction that there is a universal right to health care is not a "medical" but a political judgment. When medical means are used unjustly or unwisely, the fault lies not with the means but with their application.

As the fiftieth year since my graduation from medical school approaches, I continue to believe with undiminished faith in medicine's potential to contribute to human welfare when it is employed with intelligence and compassion. My wife, dean of student affairs first at the Massachusetts Institute of Technology and then at Harvard Medical School, wrote an essay under the title: "It Is Still a Privilege to Be a Doctor" (C. Eisenberg 1986). It epitomizes our common commitment. She points out:

> just how lucky we are to have a profession in which we do well for ourselves by doing well for others . . . [T]he satisfaction of being able to relieve pain and restore function, the intellectual challenge of solving clinical problems, and the variety of human issues we confront in daily

clinical practice will remain the essence of doctoring, whatever changes in the organizational and economic structure of medicine . . .

As physicians, we have a moral imperative to sustain the highest aspirations of the students we teach . . . [M]edical education does not exist to provide doctors with an opportunity to earn a living but to improve the health of the public. Let us enlist our students in the campaign for equity and quality in medical care.

REFERENCES

Alland, D., G. E. Kalkut, A. R. Moss, R. A. McAdam, J. A. Hahn, W. Bosworth, E. Drucker, and B. R. Bloom. 1994. Transmission of tuberculosis in New York City. *New England Journal of Medicine* 330:1710–16.

Anonymous. 1994. California school becomes notorious for epidemic of TB. *New York Times,* 18 July.

Barinaga, M. 1991. How long is the human life span? *Science* 254:936–38.

Berkowitz, R. L. 1993. Should every pregnant female undergo ultrasonography? *New England Journal of Medicine* 329:874–75.

Blendon, R. J., L. H. Aiken, H. E. Freeman, and C. R. Corey. 1989. Access to medical care for black and white Americans: A matter of continuing concern. *Journal of the American Medical Association* 261:278–81.

Bloch, A. B., G. M. Cauthen, I. M. Onorato, K. G. Dansbury, G. D. Kelly, C. R. Dwer, and D. E. Snyder Jr. 1994. Nationwide survey of drug-resistant tuberculosis in the United States. *Journal of the American Medical Association* 271:665–71.

Breman, J. G., and I. Arita. 1980. The confirmation and maintenance of smallpox eradication. *New England Journal of Medicine* 303:1263–73.

Castelli, W. P. 1991. Personal communication.

Centers for Disease Control. 1990. Up-date: Tuberculosis Elimination—United States. *Morbidity and Mortality Weekly Report* 39:153–56.

Centers for Disease Control. 1991. Summary of Notifiable Diseases, United States, 1990. *Morbidity and Mortality Weekly Report* 39 (#53).

Centers for Disease Control. 1993. Recommendations of the International Task Force for Disease Eradication. *Morbidity and Mortality Weekly Report* 42(#RR-16).

Centers for Disease Control. 1994. Progress Toward the Global Eradication of Poliomyelitis, 1988–1993. *Morbidity and Mortality Weekly Report* 43:499–503.

Chivian, E., M. McCally, H. Hu. 1993. *Critical condition: Human health and the environment,* Cambridge: MIT Press.

Condorcet, A.-N. de. 1795. *Sketch for a historical picture of the progress of the human mind.* Trans. J. Barraclough. London: Weidenfeld and Nicholson, 1955.

Cornoni-Huntley, J., A. Z. LaCroix, and R. J. Havlik. 1989. Race and sex differentials in the impact of hypertension in the U.S. *Archives of Internal Medicine* 149:780–88.

Coughenour, M. B., J. E. Ellis, D. P. Swift, D. L. Coppock, K. Galvin, J. T. McCabe, and

T. C. Hart. 1985. Energy extraction and use in a nomadic pastoral ecosystem. *Science* 230:619–24.
de Kruif, P. 1926. *Microbe Hunters.* San Diego: Harcourt, Brace, Jovanovich.
Dubos, R. 1959. *Mirage of health: Utopias, progress and biological change.* New York: Harper and Brothers.
Dubos, R., and J. Dubos. 1952. *The White Plague.* Boston: Little Brown.
Eisenberg, C. 1986. It is still a privilege to be a doctor. *New England Journal of Medicine* 314:1113–14.
Eisenberg, L. 1975. The ethics of intervention: acting amidst ambiguity. *Journal of Child Psychology and Psychiatry* 16:93–104.
Eisenberg, L. 1988. Science in medicine: Too much or too little and too limited in scope? *American Journal of Medicine* 84:483–91.
Eisenberg, L. 1990a. From circumstance to mechanism in pediatrics during the Hopkins Century. *Pediatrics* 85:42–49.
Eisenberg, L. 1990b. The early years of affirmative action. *Harvard Medical Alumni Bulletin* 64:13–17.
Eisenberg, L., and N. Sartorius. 1988. Human ecology in the repertoire of health development. *World Health Forum* 9:564–68.
Ewigman, B. G., J. P. Crane, F. D. Frigoletto, M. L. LeFevre, R. P. Bain, D. McNellis. 1993. Effect of pre-natal ultrasound screening on perinatal outcome. *New England Journal of Medicine* 329:821–27.
Farmer, P., S. Robin, S. L. Ramilus, and J. Y. Kim. 1991. Tuberculosis, poverty and "compliance": Lessons from rural Haiti. *Seminars in Respiratory Infections* 6:254–60.
Feldman, J. J., D. M. Makuc, J. C. Kleinman, and J. Coroni-Huntley. 1989. National trends in educational differences in mortality. *American Journal of Epidemiology* 129:919–33
Fischl, M. A., G. L. Daikos, R. B. Uttamchandani, R. B. Poblete, J. N. Moreno, and R. R. Reyes. 1992. Clinical presentation and outcome of patients with HIV infection and tuberculosis caused by multiple-drug-resistant bacilli. *Annals of Internal Medicine* 117:184–90.
Fischl, M. A., R. B. Uttamchandani, G. L. Daikos, R. B. Poblete, J. N. Moreno, and R. R. Reyes. 1992. An outbreak of tuberculosis caused by multiple-drug-resistant tubercle bacilli among patients with HIV infection. *Annals of Internal Medicine* 117:177–83.
Flegal, K. M., W. R. Harlan, and J. R. Landis. 1988a. Secular trends in body mass index and skinfold thickness with socioeconomic factors in young adult women. *American Journal of Clinical Nutrition* 48:535–43.
Flegal, K. M., W. R. Harlan, and J. R. Landis. 1988b. Secular trends in body mass index and skinfold thickness with socioeconomic factors in young adult men. *American Journal of Clinical Nutrition* 48:544–51.
Glassroth, J., A. G. Robins, and D. E. Snider. 1980. Tuberculosis in the 1980s. *New England Journal of Medicine* 302:1441–50.
Goldman, L., and E. F. Cook. 1984. The decline in ischaemic heart disease mortality rates: An analysis of the comparative effects of medical interventions and changes in lifestyle. *Annals of Internal Medicine* 101:825–36.

Graham, N. M. H., K. E. Nelson, L. Solomon, M. Bonds, R. T. Rizzo, J. Scavotto, J. Astemborski, and D. Vlahovd. 1992. Prevalence of tuberculin positivity and skin test anergy in HIV-1 seropositive and seronegative intravenous drug users. *Journal of the American Medical Association* 267: 369–73.

Grant, J. P. 1993. *The State of the World's Children 1993*. London: Oxford University Press. Published for the United Nations Children's Fund.

Gruenberg, E. M., ed. 1986. *Vaccinating against Brain Syndromes: The Campaign against Measles and Rubella*. New York: Oxford University Press.

Guyer, B., N. Hughart, E. Holt, A. Ross, B. Stanton, V. Keane, N. Bonner, D. M. Dwyer, and J. S. Cwi. 1994. Immunization coverage and its relation to preventive health care visits among inner city children in Baltimore. *Pediatrics* 94:53–58.

Huebner, R. E., M. E. Villarino, and D. E. Snider. 1992. Tuberculin skin testing and the HIV epidemic. *Journal of the American Medical Association* 257:409–10.

Illich, I. 1975. *Medical nemesis: The expropriation of health*. London: Calder and Boyars.

Institute of Medicine. 1991. *Adverse effects of pertussis and rubella vaccines*. Washington, D.C.: National Academy Press.

Jacoby, G. A., and G. L. Archer. 1991. New mechanisms of bacterial resistance to antimicrobial agents. *New England Journal of Medicine* 324:601–12.

Javitt, J. C., A. M. McBean, G. A. Nicholson, J. D. Bobish, J. L. Warren, and H. Krakauer. 1991. Undertreatment of glaucoma among black Americans. *New England Journal of Medicine* 325:1418–22.

Jorm, A. F. 1990. *The epidemiology of Alzheimer's disease and related disorders*. London: Chapman and Hall.

Kasiske, B. L., J. F. Neylan, R. R. Riggio, G. M. Danovitch, L. Kahana, S. R. Alexander, and M. G. White. 1991. The effect of race on access and outcome in transplantation. *New England Journal of Medicine* 324:302–307.

Knox, R. A. 1991. U.S. law challenges patients to make plans for death. *Boston Globe*, 1 December.

Kuczmarski, R. J., K. M. Flegal, S. M. Campbell, and C. L. Johnson. 1994. Increasing prevalence of overweight in U.S. adults. *Journal of the American Medical Association* 272:205–11.

Kumanyika, S. K., J. F. Wilson, and M. Guilford-Davenport. 1993. Weight-related attitudes and behavior of black women. *Journal of the American Diet Association* 93:416–22.

Landrigan, P J. 1992. Environmental disease—a preventable epidemic. *American Journal of Public Health* 82:941–43.

Lederberg, J., R. E. Shope, and S. C. Oaks, eds. 1992. *Emerging infections: Microbial threats to health in the United States*. Washington, D. C.: National Academy Press.

Malcolm, A. H. 1991. Decisions of life, death, and transition between. *New York Times*, 29 November, sec. B, p. 6.

Mann, J., D. J. M. Tarantola, and T. W. Netter. 1992. *AIDS in the world: A global report*. Cambridge: Harvard University Press.

McKeown, T. 1976. *The role of medicine: Dream, miracle or nemesis?* London: Nuffield Provincial Hospital Trust.

Medical Research Council Streptomycin in Tuberculosis Trials Committee. 1948. Streptomycin treatment for pulmonary tuberculosis. *British Medical Journal* 2:769–82.

Medical Research Council Tuberculosis Chemotherapy Trials Committee. 1952. The treatment of pulmonary tuberculosis with isoniazid. *British Medical Journal* 2:735–46.

Department of Health and Human Services. National Center for Health Statistics. 1994. *Health, United States, 1993.* DHHS Pub. No. (PHS) 94-1232. Hyattsville, Md.: Public Health Service.

Odum, E. P. 1969. The strategy of ecosystem development. *Science* 164:262–70.

Ormerod, W. E. 1976. Ecological effects of control of African trypanosomiasis. *Science* 191:815–21.

Packard, R. M. 1989. *White plague, black labor: Tuberculosis and the political economy of health and disease in South Africa.* Berkeley: University of California Press.

Pearson, M. L., J. A. Jereb, T. R. Frieden, J. T. Crawford, B. J. Davis, S. W. Dooley, and W. R. Jarvis. 1992. Nosocomial transmission of multiple-drug-resistant *Mycobacterium tuberculosis. Annals of Internal Medicine* 177:191–96.

Rettig, R. A. 1991. Origins of the medicare kidney disease entitlement: The social security amendments of 1972 In *Biomedical Politics,* edited by K. E. Hanna. Washington, D.C.: National Academy Press.

Rice, D. P. 1991. Ethics and equity in U.S. health care: The data. *International Journal of Health Services* 21:637–51.

Rosen, G. 1947. What is social medicine? A genetic analysis of the concept. *Bulletin of the History of Medicine* 21:674–733.

Sinclair, A. R. E., and J. M. Fryxel. 1985. The Sahel of Africa: Ecology of a disaster. *Canadian Journal of Zoology* 63:987–94.

Slevin, M. L., H. Plant, D. Lynch, J. Drinkwater, and W. M. Gregory. 1988. Who should measure quality of life, the doctor or the patient? *British Journal of Cancer* 57:109–12.

Small, P. A., P. C. Hopewell, S. P. Singh, A. Paz, J. Parsonnet, D. C. Ruston, G. F. Schecter, C. L. Daley, and G. K. Schoolnik. 1994. The epidemiology of tuberculosis in San Francisco. *New England Journal of Medicine* 330:1703–9.

Sommer, A., J. M. Tielsch, J. Katz, A. J. Quigley, J. D. Gottsch, J. C. Javitt, J. F. Martone, R. M. Royall, K. A. Witt, S. Ezrine. 1991. Racial differences in the cause-specific prevalence of blindness in East Baltimore. *New England Journal of Medicine* 325:1412–22.

Tomes, N. J. 1989. The white plague revisited. *Bulletin of the History of Medicine* 63:467–80.

U.S. Bureau of the Census. 1976. *Historical statistics of the United States: Colonial times to 1970.* Bicentennial edition. Washington, U.S. Department of Commerce.

U.S. Bureau of the Census. 1989. *Current population reports.* Series P-25, no. 1018. Washington, U.S. Dept. of Commerce.

Uemura, K., and Z. Pisa. 1988. Trends in cardiovascular disease mortality in industrialized countries since 1950. *World Health Statistical Quarterly* 41:155–78.

Wenneker, M. B., and A. M. Epstein. 1989. Racial inequalities in the use of procedures for patients with ischemic heart disease in Massachusetts. *Journal of American Medical Association* 261:253–59.

Wilkinson, R. G. 1992. National mortality rates: The impact of inequality? *American Journal of Public Health* 82:1082–84.

Wilson, L. G. 1990. The historical decline of tuberculosis in Europe and America: Its causes and significance. *Journal of the History of Medicine and Allied Sciences* 45:366–96.

World Bank. 1993. *World development report 1993: Investing in health.* New York: Oxford University Press.

# Rousseau Redux, or Historical Reflections on the Ambivalence of Anthropology to the Idea of Progress

*George W. Stocking, Jr.*

Granting that beginnings in intellectual history are never so simple, it might still be argued that the discourse of anthropology and the cultural ideology of progress are approximately coeval. Genealogies of anthropology commonly find their apical ancestors in the same mid-eighteenth-century period when the idea of progress is said to have achieved explicit articulation. Rousseau's second essay "on the origin of human inequality" was at one and the same time a contribution to the debate on progress and, in the often quoted tenth footnote, a call for an empirically based science of humankind. The same discursive overlap may be found among the Scottish moral philosophers who are frequently claimed as forefathers of the Anglo-American anthropological tradition. Thus, the major topic headings of Lord Kames's *Sketches of the History of Man* included "the progress of men as individuals," the "progress of men in society," and "the progress of the sciences."[1]

Indeed, to say that these writers were simultaneously contributors in both discursive realms may be misleading, should it imply a clear distinction, within

---

Although a missing final section has been added to the paper originally presented to the "progress" symposium, this chapter remains an occasional piece, covering a very wide-ranging topic in a rather limited space. Many issues are either untouched or oversimplified—or, alternatively, referred to in such a condensed way as to remain obscure to a reader not already somewhat familiar with the particular topic. Similarly, the relevant literature is extensive, and for the most part I have limited documentation to works specifically quoted or mentioned. As a (frankly egocentric) starting point for those interested in pursuing any topic further, I have cited a number of my own works and mention here also the variously thematic volumes of essays I have edited in the series *History of Anthropology* (Madison, Wis., 1983, 1984, 1985, 1986, 1988, 1989, 1992).

1. Kames, as quoted in Stocking, "Scotland as a Model of Mankind: Lord Kames' Philosophical View of Civilization," in *Toward a Science of Man: Essays in the History of Anthropology,* ed. T. T. Thoresen (The Hague, 1975), 73. See also Roger Masters, ed., *The First and Second Discourses* (New York, 1964), 203–13.

the work of a single author, between two different bodies of textual material, written in different voices, to different audiences. The discourse that we retroactively constitute as "anthropological" could not, in the eighteenth century, be sharply marked off from that which we retrospectively reconstruct as that of "progress." To write about questions that we would now deem "anthropological" was, willy-nilly, to write about "the progress of mankind"—which, in retrospect, may be seen as a central problem of eighteenth-century anthropological discourse. It is in discussions of this problem that one finds the proximate source of what came to be called the "comparative method." When Adam Ferguson suggested that it was "in the present condition" of Native Americans that we may "behold, as in a mirrour, the features of our own progenitors," he was in effect suggesting a method for the reconstruction of history (or development, or evolution) in the absence of the kind of evidence by which it is normally reconstituted—a method that has since been elaborated, debated, questioned, even abandoned, but that still today is sometimes employed, implicitly or even explicitly, in anthropological discourse.[2]

From the beginning, progress as cultural ideology and as anthropological concept was implicated in various ways with a number of other ideas. There were, by long tradition, ideas about the dynamics of history: notions of degeneration from the biblical Garden of Eden or some less specifically Judeo-Christian golden age; ideas about the contrastive pattern and movement of sacred and secular history; conceptions of the repetitive cyclical movement of time and cultural process. There were ideas about human nature and its cultural differentiation, whether by movement in space or in time; ideas about the categories of human otherness ("savagery," "barbarism"). There were ideas as well about the physical differentiation of humankind—although the elaboration of the ideas of race and of biological evolution lay still in the future. But perhaps the most closely intertwined of these mutually implicated notions were two others that were articulated at roughly the same mid-eighteenth-century moment: the idea of Europe and the idea of civilization. From that time forward the three notions were linked, sometimes in a single phrase, sometimes in unstated equation, with each other and with the idea of progress, so that any one of the three might imply the other two. Posed as problem rather than as assertion, this conceptual triad—"the progress of European civilization"— was one of the foundational issues of anthropological discourse.[3]

As the ambiguity of Rousseau's "supposed primitivism" suggests, and as the preoccupation of Kames and other Scottish progressivists with the pseudo-

---

2. Ferguson, as quoted in Ronald L. Meek, *Social Science and the Ignoble Savage* (Cambridge, 1976), 151.

3. For further argument and relevant sources, see "The Idea of Civilization before the Crystal Palace (1750–1850)," chap. 1 in Stocking, *Victorian Anthropology* (New York, 1987), 9–45.

Ossianic epics confirms, the progress of European civilization was from the beginning a focus of profound attitudinal ambivalence. There was a widespread sense of loss as well as gain (the martial virtues versus the habits of industry), of a progress of corruption paralleling that of knowledge—and there was a long tradition of "soft" as well as "hard" primitivism, realized in the eighteenth-century vision of the "noble savage" and of "nature's simple plan." There were always doubters and critics, at times and in places more numerous and articulate, whose voices, sometimes admonitory, sometimes yearning, for the next two centuries chanted a romantic counterpoint to the progressivist paean of European cultural self-confidence.[4]

Early progressivist thought on the processes of civilization achieved a characteristic articulation in the "Considerations on the various methods to follow in the observation of savage peoples" prepared by Joseph Degerando for the Société des Observateurs de l'Homme established in Paris in the later years of the French Revolution. There the implications of the "comparative method" were further specified. Since for whatever "mysterious reason" different human groups had not advanced at the same rate, it was possible to construct "an exact scale of the various degrees of civilization and to assign to each its characteristic properties," and thus to reconstruct "the first periods of our own history": The "philosophical traveller, sailing to the ends of the earth, is in fact travelling in time"; "every step he makes is the passage of an age"; "unknown islands that he reaches are for him the cradle of human society." There also, the link was asserted between the study of past progress and the guarantee of its future—by inspiring among "barbarous people" a "curiosity to know our ways and a desire to imitate them, . . . perhaps laying [thereby] the foundations of a new Europe."[5]

In the early nineteenth century, anthropological thought about the progress of European civilization was complicated by the reaction against the French Revolution, by the reassertion of traditional Christian views of world historical process, and, as Europeans came into increasing contact with and violently dispossessed the varieties of humankind at "the ends of the earth," by the elaboration of biologically oriented racial explanations of human cultural difference. The peoples stigmatized as savages were now less likely to be seen as representatives of the original human condition and more as products of cultural (and even physical) degeneration accompanying the migration of hu-

---

4. Among the many sources on "primitivism," the works of A. O. Lovejoy still command attention, including "The Supposed Primitivism of Rousseau's *Discourse on Inequality,*" in *Essays in the History of Ideas* (Baltimore, 1948), 14–37, and Lovejoy and George Boas, *Primitivism and Related Ideas in Antiquity* (Baltimore, 1935).

5. *The Observation of Savage Peoples,* trans. F. C. T. Moore (Berkeley, 1969), 63, 102. See also "French Anthropology in 1800," in Stocking, *Race, Culture and Evolution* (New York, 1968), 13–41.

mankind outward from Babel. In the words of the American anthropologist Henry Rowe Schoolcraft: "man was created, not a savage, a hunter, or a warrior, but a horticulturist and a raiser of grain, and a keeper of cattle—a smith, a musician—a worshipper, not of the sun, moon and stars, but of God"; "the savage condition is a declension from this high type. . . . " The progressive development of civilization in Europe was still a commonplace of anthropological assumption, but it was increasingly conceived in racial terms—most strikingly in the case of polygenetic writers, who by midcentury were arguing that the races of humankind were in fact distinct species, whose differences in cultural status were the direct reflection of their unequal capacity. Although advocates of human unity were not inclined to interpret this contrast in terms of fundamental distinctions of racial capacity, even leading monogenists, such as James Cowles Prichard, drew the contrast between "the splendid cities of Europe" and the "solitary dens of the Bushman, where the lean and hungry savage crouches in silence, like a beast of prey."[6]

As that passage suggests, by the time of the 1851 Crystal Palace exhibition, first of the great international celebrations of the progress of European civilization, there was already in place an image of savage bestiality as its antithesis—whether as degenerative offshoot, absolute racial alternative, or developmental starting point. The Crystal Palace helped stimulate a more systematic speculation about human progress, including notably the work of Henry Maine, in which the contrast was sharply drawn between the "progressive" societies of Europe and the "stationary" societies of Asia. But the terms of anthropological discussion were to be dramatically altered after 1858, when the archeological revolution opened up an immense abyss of time beneath the progress of European civilization and the Darwinian revolution gave a very different significance to the metaphor of savage bestiality.[7]

Since the ideological aspect of evolutionary debate seems in retrospect only too striking, it is perhaps worth noting that the issue of human progress presented itself to the generation of "classical evolutionists" also as a problem of data, method, and theory. What seemed to be required of those who would claim the sociocultural realm for positive science was to fill the vast expanse of prehistory with sequences of development that would explain the emergence of human culture by purely naturalistic means. That social evolutionism had this character of a collective scientific project is evidenced in a letter that John

---

6. Schoolcraft, *History of the Indian Tribes of the United States* (Philadelphia, 1857), 27; Prichard, as quoted in Stocking, "From Chronology to Ethnology: James Cowles Prichard and British Anthropology, 1800–1850," introduction to Prichard, *Researches into the Physical History of Man* (Chicago, 1973), lxxxii.

7. Stocking, "The History of Civilization before the Origin of Species (1851–1858)," and "The Darwinian Revolution and the Evolution of Human Culture (1858–1871)," chaps. 4 and 5 in *Victorian Anthropology.*

McLennan—a major contributor to evolutionary schemes of the development of human marriage out of "primitive promiscuity" toward monogamy—wrote to Sir John Lubbock, the leading Darwinist prehistorian, in October, 1867.

> I have been employed for the last three days on the paper which I shd be most anxious to bring out through yr society [the Ethnological Society of London], viz: "A Tentative View of Human Progress." . . . perhaps you will be good enough to consider whether between yourself & Huxley in the south and Professor Aufrecht (an excellent philologist) & myself in Edinburgh, a tentative scheme might be adjusted which might serve for some years to come as a guide for enquiry in regard to the history of the race—at the same time that it would mark for the time the results of such enquiry as has been made. . . . I am aiming at the formation of a table with a classification of stages of progress depending on the *grouping*—the table exhibiting all the stages of progress in the Arts & Sciences, etc. that have been found concurring with each phase of the development of social organization.

The attempt to correlate sociocultural phenomena in the definition of stages, although clearly conditioned by ethnocentric preconceptions, was, in the minds of its practitioners, a stage in an empirical (and itself progressive) anthropological inquiry.[8]

The most systematically articulated such scheme was perhaps that of the American anthropologist Lewis Henry Morgan, in the first chapters of *Ancient Society, or Researches in the Lines of Human Progress From Savagery through Barbarism to Civilization*. In his own latter-day adaptation of the "four-stage" scheme of the Scottish moral philosophers, Morgan defined seven "ethnical periods" or "statuses," each characteristically marked off by a new invention and/or mode of subsistence: middle savagery by the use of fire and fish subsistence, upper barbarism by the smelting of iron, civilization by the invention of the phonetic alphabet. Although he was somewhat reluctant to place his sociocultural evolutionary schema explicitly in a Darwinian context, Morgan nevertheless saw human progress in Lamarckian terms as an interactive process of cultural and biological change: "[W]ith the production of inventions and discoveries, and with the growth of institutions, the human mind necessarily grew and expanded; and we are led to recognize a gradual enlargement of the brain itself." The "inferiority of savage man in the mental and moral scale" was "substantially demonstrated by the remains of ancient art in flint stone and bone implements, . . . by his osteological remains [and] by the

---

8. McLennan, as quoted in Stocking, "Invisible Collegial Discussion among the Social Evolutionists: J. F. McLennan on the Redefinition of Civilization and Progress," *History of Anthropology Newsletter*, 8 (2): 6.

present condition of tribes of savages in a low state of development." It was only the Aryans and Semites who had in fact ascended to the seventh (and undivided) heaven of civilization, in which the leading role "has been gradually assumed by the Aryan family alone."[9]

Although the linkage of race and progress was more strongly asserted by biologically oriented writers in the tradition we retrospectively label social Darwinist, anthropologists who dealt primarily with sociocultural evolution nevertheless took for granted a certain causal correlation of culture and color— as was implicitly suggested in the British anthropologist E. B. Tylor's comment that "on the definite basis of compared facts, ethnographers are able to set up at least a rough scale of civilization": "Few would dispute that the following races are arranged rightly in order of culture:—Australian, Tahitian, Aztec, Chinese, Italian." Positive science and ethnocentric assumption thus mutually reinforced the century-old triple equation—although with an implicit qualification for the "wogs" across the channel.[10]

Tylor was by no means a systematic denigrator of savage peoples: "[I]t may be admitted that some rude tribes lead a life to be envied by some barbarous races, and even by the outcasts of higher nations." However, defining civilization "from the ideal point of view" as the "general improvement of mankind by higher organization of the individual and of society, to the end of promoting at once man's goodness, power, and happiness," he nevertheless felt that "the general tenour of the evidence goes far to justify the view that on the whole the civilized man is not only wiser and more capable than the savage, but also better and happier, and that the barbarian stands between." But if he was a scion of the middle-class reforming groups that in his lifetime had helped reshape English economic life and politics, Tylor was by no means totally uncritical of the civilization that European progress had produced, nor naively optimistic about its future. In the peroration of *Primitive Culture,* he worried that the oft-closed gates of inquiry might close again, and defended anthropology as a "reformer's science," dedicated to the furtherance of progress by rooting out "survivals" of savage or barbarous culture.[11]

Granting that the classical evolutionists did not think of human progress in simple "unilinear" terms, and acknowledging the recent literature on degeneration or "the dark side of progress" in the later nineteenth century, it may nevertheless be said that this evolutionary and racial vision of human progress provided the dominant paradigm for the preacademic generation of

---

9. Morgan, *Ancient Society* [1877], ed. E. B. Leacock (Cleveland, 1963), 36, 41, 39. See also Thomas Trautman, *Lewis Henry Morgan and the Invention of Kinship* (Berkeley, 1987).
10. Tylor, *Primitive Culture,* 2 vols. (London, 1871), 1:24. See also Stocking, "Victorian Cultural Ideology and the Image of Savagery," chap. 6 in *Victorian Anthropology.*
11. Tylor, *Primitive Culture,* 1:28; 2:410.

anthropological writers who are usually thought of today as the proximate lineal ancestors of modern sociocultural anthropology in the Anglo-American tradition. In both countries, the fin de siècle and early-twentieth-century years witnessed a reaction against progressivist evolutionism. In Britain, the life of nineteenth-century evolutionary progressivism was prolonged in the work of Tylor's disciple James Frazer, who managed to sustain a certain confidence in the progress from magic through religion to science even in the face of his anxiety about the persistence of superstition in the "volcano underneath" the class-riven civilization of pre–World War England. It was in the United States, in the work of the Jewish-German immigrant anthropologist Franz Boas, that the critique was first and more systematically developed, especially in its relation to evolutionary assumptions about racial differences and the "mind of primitive man."[12]

Predisposed to skepticism of a unitary "civilization" both his own cultural marginality and his ties to the German romantic tradition, Boas nevertheless shared many of the values of evolutionary progressivism, and in the beginning acknowledged a certain cultural presumption in favor of its racialist implications. It was no wonder, he suggested in the opening lines of his first antievolutionist salvo in 1894, that "civilized man," who had "conquered the forces of nature and compelled them to serve him," should pity people who "hear with trembling the roar of the wild animals and see the products of their toils destroyed by them," and conclude that "the white race represents a higher type than all others." To get behind a "contrast" that presented itself so obviously "to the observer" was the work of a critique Boas elaborated over the next 17 years and drew together in *The Mind of Primitive Man*. Calling fundamentally into question the prevailing ethnocentric equation of presumed racial capacity and cultural achievement in a single evolutionary framework, Boas's critique provided the basis for the modern pluralistic and relativistic conception of culture. It is worth noting, however, that just as the perorations of Tylor and Morgan left a space for cultural doubt, so did Boas's last lines leave a space for the idea of progress:

> [T]he data of anthropology teach us a greater tolerance of forms of civilization different from our own, and that we should learn to look upon foreign races with greater sympathy, and with the conviction, that, as all races have contributed in the past to cultural progress in one way or

---

12. Daniel Pick, *Faces of Degeneration: A European Disorder, c. 1848–c. 1918* (Cambridge, 1989); Stocking, *After Tylor: British Social Anthropology, 1888–1951* (Madison, Wis., 1995); *Race, Culture, and Evolution: Essays in the History of Anthropology* (New York, 1968), 133–234.

another, so they will be capable of advancing the interests of mankind, if we are only willing to give them a fair opportunity.[13]

Despite the disillusioning impact of World War I, a residual faith in progress was still evident in Boas's popular anthropological writings of the 1920s. Insisting on the difficulty of defining a standard in the face of "conflict of ideals" in modern life, Boas was nevertheless willing to "recognize progress in a definite direction in the development of invention and knowledge." Although he denied that there was any "evolution of moral ideas," he nevertheless argued that there was "progress in ethical conduct, based on the recognition of larger groups which participate in the rights enjoyed by members of the closed society, and on an increasing social control." And "while it was still more difficult to discern universally valid progress in social organization," he nevertheless felt that "in the sense of loss of fixity of status the freedom of the individual has been increasing." Translated into positive science, human fellowship, and individual freedom, these were still central values of nineteenth-century liberal progressivism—which Tylor and Morgan would surely have found congenial.[14]

That compatibility notwithstanding, it is nevertheless the case that anthropology had undergone profound changes in the period between the 1890s and the 1920s, changes which even in England amounted to the "revolution in social anthropology" that Bronislaw Malinowski had called for in 1916. There were of course differences in pace and in outcome: in England, the critique of race and the separation of biological and cultural discourse were not such central issues; in the United States, it was cultural psychology rather than functionalist sociology that emerged as the dominant anthropological viewpoint. But in both countries, anthropology was being academicized, ethnographicized, dehistoricized, and specialized. In the eyes of other professionals, anthropologists (of the subspecies that came to be called social or cultural) were people with academic training who carried out ethnographic fieldwork among non-European peoples in order to document and to understand their cultural or social modes in "the ethnographic present," rather than reconstructing their development in time (whether conceived in evolutionary or shorter-range historical terms). This orientation implied, as a methodological precondition, a relativistic stance toward the cultural values and modes of

---

13. Boas, "Human Faculty," in Stocking, ed., *The Shaping of American Anthropology, 1883–1911: A Franz Boas Reader* (New York, 1974), 221–22; Boas, *The Mind of Primitive Man* (New York, 1911), 278.

14. Boas, *Anthropology and Modern Life* (New York, 1962 [1928]), 217, 227, 231; cf. Stocking, "Anthropology as *Kulturkampf:* Science and Politics in the Career of Franz Boas," in *The Ethnographer's Magic and Other Essays in the History of Anthropology* (Madison, Wis., 1992), 92–113.

behavior of the groups being studied and, as a theoretical consequence, the backgrounding if not the exclusion of the problem of progress from the agenda of sociocultural anthropology. Evolutionary or developmental questions might be addressed in other fields that, within the Anglo-American sphere, were still included under the umbrella of a general "anthropology"—notably in archaeology and biological anthropology. But it was not until after World War II that they were again to be seriously addressed by sociocultural anthropologists.[15]

One aspect of the "revolution in anthropology" was an important shift in its motivational dynamic. Although cultural exoticism has been a continuing theme in European history and an obviously discernable motivation even among evolutionary anthropologists, it seems fair to say that a neoromantic current of "soft" primitivism ran increasingly strong within the ethnographic sensibility of the first cohorts of academic anthropologists. One has only to read the early writings of Lewis Henry Morgan, or Frank Hamilton Cushing's accounts of his initiation into the Zuni bow priesthood, to realize that evolutionary progressivists could identify strongly with those whom in other discursive contexts they stigmatized as "savages." But the primitivist impulse ran stronger among those who, questioning the verities of Victorian civilization, lived through the Great War that progress had made possible. Furthermore, the methodological redefinition of anthropology in terms of the initiatory experience of ethnographic fieldwork incorporated this impulse into the methodological, conceptual, and institutional structure of the discipline.[16]

The locus classicus of the alienated anthropological romanticism that helped motivate the ethnographic enterprise of anthropologists then (and since) was a passage on the "cultural fallacy of industrialism" by the American linguistic anthropologist Edward Sapir, the poetic confidante of Ruth Benedict and, briefly, lover of Margaret Mead:

> The telephone girl who lends her capacities, during the greater part of the living day, to the manipulation of a technical routine that has an eventually high efficiency value but that answers to no spiritual needs of her own is an appalling sacrifice to civilization. . . . The American Indian who solves the economic problem with salmon-spear and rabbit-snare operates on a relatively low level of civilization, but he represents an incomparably higher solution than our telephone girl of the questions that

---

15. Stocking, "Ideas and Institutions in American Anthropology: Thoughts Toward a History of the Interwar Years" and "Paradigmatic Traditions in the History of Anthropology," both in *The Ethnographer's Magic,* 114–77, 342–61; also, *After Tylor.*

16. Stocking, "The Ethnographic Sensibility of the 1920s and the Dualism of the Anthropological Tradition," and "Maclay, Kubary, Malinowski: Archetypes from the Dreamtime of Anthropology," both in *The Ethnographer's Magic,* 276–41, 212–75. See also Jesse Green, ed., *Zuñi: Selected Writings of Frank Hamilton Cushing* (Lincoln, 1979)

culture has to ask of economics. There is here no question of . . . any sentimentalizing regrets as to the passing of the 'natural man.' The Indian's salmon-spearing is a culturally higher type of activity than that of the telephone girl or mill hand . . . because it works in naturally with all the rest of the Indian's activities instead of standing out as a desert patch of merely economic effort in the whole of life. A genuine culture cannot be defined as a sum of abstractly desirable ends, as a mechanism. It must be looked upon as a sturdy plant growth, each remotest leaf and twig of which is organically fed by the sap at the core.

Responding to the "free love" that Margaret Mead had found in Samoa after rejecting his proposal of marriage, Sapir was by the end of the 1920s writing essays on "the discipline of sex." But it was his own earlier response to "the cultural fallacy of industrialism"—and perhaps also Mead's restatement of the long tradition of Polynesian exoticism—that archetypified the dominant motivational dynamic of the modern ethnographic enterprise.[17]

And yet, just as one can find exoticism among evolutionary anthropologists, so can one find evolutionary traces among the ethnographic anthropologists—especially, perhaps, when they were speaking to a larger public. Responding to the urging of her publisher, Mead recast her report on her Samoan research as a "A Psychological Study of Primitive Youth for Western Civilization," justifying the anthropological project in the residually evolutionary terms of the ethnographic "laboratory": "In this choice of primitive peoples like the Eskimo, the Australian, the South Sea islander, or the Pueblo Indian, the anthropologist is guided by the knowledge that the analysis of a simpler civilisation is more possible of attainment." Civilization was no longer exclusively European; but the simplicity of the primitive was a long way from the civilization of Europe.[18]

A similar ambivalent ambiguity was manifest in what came to be regarded as the classic statement of cultural relativism—which, needless to say, is centrally at issue in any consideration of the idea of progress in anthropology, insofar as any measure or judgment of progress implies some universally valid standards (Tylor's wisdom, goodness, happiness; Boas's knowledge, fellowship, freedom). Benedict's *Patterns of Culture* opens with an attack on the uniqueness of Western civilization and an insistence on the "great arc" of cultural possibilities from which each culture selects different segments to

---

17. Sapir, quoted in Stocking, "Ethnographic Sensibility of the 1920s," in *The Ethnographer's Magic,* 288–89.

18. Mead, *Coming of Age in Samoa: A Psychological Study of Primitive Youth for Western Civilization* (New York, 1961 [1928]), 7.

exploit. But Benedict (who liked her cultures "scandalous") was nevertheless preoccupied with the psychopathology of particular traditions, especially her own, and was still able to speak of "civilization" as setting "higher and possibly more worth-while goals," the most important of which would be the tolerance of individual and cultural variability. In that sense, cultural relativity may be said to have implied its own standard for the evaluation of progress, and for its continuing possibility. In the aftermath of World War II, however, the issues of cultural relativism and human progress were to present themselves with a greatly heightened salience.[19]

In contrast to the First World War, which encouraged anthropologists to call into question the verities of a "botched civilization," the Second led them to search for hope amid the ashes of Hiroshima and the Holocaust. Already before the war began, some anthropologists had become involved in applying their "science" to the social issues of the Depression years; during the war, a majority of professional anthropologists were involved in war-related activity. The progressivist spirit was clearly evident in a symposium volume on *The Science of Man in the World Crisis* dedicated, early in 1945, "to all who have applied the techniques of science to the solving of human problems." Some months later, after the "immense leap in the preposterous acceleration of man's technology" embodied in the atomic bomb had created a threat "greater than all other threats, to man's existence," Robert Redfield was able to speak not only of "the new world, with its fear," but in the same phrase of "the hope that grows large out of the very bigness of the fear."[20]

On the whole, it was the hope more than the fear that conditioned anthropological interest in matters relating to human progress in the decade or so after the war. Several anthropologists who in the 1920s had helped to define the neoromantic primitivism of the "ethnographic present" had by now turned to problems of social change within a progressivist context. The tone might be elegaic: thus Redfield, returning to a Mayan folk community he had studied in the early 1930s, wrote of the "Village that Chose Progress" as having now "no choice but to go forward with technology, with a declining religious faith and moral conviction, into a dangerous world." Or the tone might be inspirational: thus Mead, revisiting an early field site (construed now not as a laboratory of cultural determinism, but of social change), wrote of the Manus people, witnesses of thousands of American troops who "knocked down mountains" to make airstrips with "their marvellous 'engines,'" as skipping "over thousands

---

19. Benedict, *Patterns of Culture* (Boston, 1934), 24, 277; see also Elvin Hatch, *Culture and Morality: The Relativity of Values in Anthropology* (New York, 1983).
20. Ralph Linton, ed. *The Science of Man in the World Crisis* (New York, 1945), v; Redfield, quoted in Stocking, *Anthropology at Chicago: Tradition, Discipline, Department* (Chicago, 1979), 30. See also Stocking, "Ideas and Institutions."

of years of history" to move "from darkest savagery to the twentieth century" in just 25 years.[21]

As Mead's example suggests, the more obvious indicia of progressivist discourse were perhaps more likely—as indeed they had been since the 1920s—to appear in works oriented toward audiences outside the discipline of anthropology. An unsystematic examination of textbooks in the postwar period suggests that "progress" was not normally a category in media of disciplinary enculturation. One notable exception was the *Anthropology* of A. L. Kroeber, Boas's first student and by now the doyen of American anthropologists, who in the first edition of 1923 had suggested ironically that "we like to call the process 'Progress'" which is "crushing the breath out of ancient and exotic cultures." The revised edition of 1948, although treating "the idea of progress" as a Western cultural category, nevertheless included a neo-Freudian attempt to define "at least a partial standard" by which "the progress of civilization" might be evaluated: "In summary, the quantitative expansion of the content of total human culture; the atrophy of magic based on psychopathology; the decline of infantile obsession with the outstanding physiological events of human life; and the persistent tendency of technology and science to grow accumulatively—these are the ways in which progress may legitimately be considered as a property or an attribute of culture."[22]

The problem of finding any universal standpoint of cultural evaluation was central to the discussion of cultural relativism, which achieved its classic formulation in another textbook of the postwar period: *Man and His Works*. There Melville Herskovits argued that "with the possible exception of technological aspects of life, the proposition that one way of thought or action is better than another is exceedingly difficult [Herskovits clearly felt, impossible] to establish on the grounds of any universally acceptable criteria."[23]

Most anthropologists would have agreed with Herskovits that cultural relativism, as a methodological presumption, was a necessary condition of ethnographic inquiry. But in the aftermath of the Holocaust, some found more than a bit disturbing the suggestion that all evaluations were "*relative* to the cultural background out of which they arise." In an inventory-review of *Culture: Concepts and Definitions* in 1952, Kroeber and Clyde Kluckhohn insisted that "to say that certain aspects of Naziism were morally wrong" [or, in a pathetic, professionally self-protective footnote "at very least, integratively

---

21. Redfield, *A Village that Chose Progress: Chan Kom Revisited* (Chicago, 1950), 178; Mead, *New Lives for Old: Cultural Transformation—Manus, 1928–1953* (New York, 1956), 168, 8.

22. Kroeber, *Anthropology* (New York, 1923), 292; *Anthropology: Race, Language, Culture, Psychology, Prehistory* (New York, 1948), 304.

23. Herskovits, *Man and His Works: The Science of Cultural Anthropology* (New York, 1949), 70. See also James Fernandez, "Tolerance in a Repugnant World and Other Dilemmas in the Cultural Relativism of Melville J. Herskovits," *Ethos* 18 (1990): 140–64.

and historically destructive"] was not "parochial arrogance"; it was, rather, an assertion that was, "or can be" based upon "cross-cultural evidence as to the universalities in human needs, potentialities and fulfilments." Kluckhohn, particularly, devoted several essays in the 1950s to the consideration of "Ethical Relativism—Sic et Non"; and the Harvard study he directed on "Values in Five Cultures" may be regarded as an attempt to approach the problem empirically. So also, from a slightly different standpoint, Redfield's comparative study of civilizations project at the University of Chicago may be regarded as an attempt to turn anthropology toward a consideration of what might be the universal or differentiating features of the idea of "civilization"—in the context of a threat to its very continuance.[24]

During the same period, Leslie White, leader of an emerging "neo-evolutionary" movement, was defending the Victorian progressivists against misinterpretation by Boasian antievolutionists and attacking what to him seemed a systematic (if inconsistent) Boasian antiprogressivism. White argued that "progress in culture change is something that can be defined in objective terms and measured by an objective standard, or standards, and that therefore, cultures can be evaluated and graded in terms of 'higher,' 'more advanced' etc."[25]

Aside from explicit neoevolutionary approaches in the work of students of Leslie White or Julian Steward (proponent of a more flexible, ecologically oriented "multilinear" evolutionism), the 1950s were the period in which anthropologists, encouraged by American overseas policy and supported by major foundation grants, turned to problems of "development" and "modernization." The early Indonesian research of Clifford Geertz was undertaken in this context. As late as 1963, in discussing the "quest for modernity" in the "new nations" of Asia and Africa, Geertz discussed "the integrative revolution" in terms of "primordial attachments" of "blood, speech, custom and so on" which in the early stages of "political modernization" tended to be "quickened" rather than reduced to "civil order."[26]

That same year, Eric Wolf, attempting to characterize the recent development of the discipline for a conference on recent humanistic scholarship, suggested that anthropology in the postwar period had witnessed "the repres-

---

24. Herskovits, *Man and His Works,* 63; A. L. Kroeber and Clyde Kluckhohn, *Culture: A Review of Concepts and Definitions* (Cambridge, 1952), 178; Kluckhohn, "Ethical Relativity, Sic et Non," in *Culture and Behavior,* ed. R. Kluckhohn (New York, 1962), 265–85; Redfield, in *Human Nature and Society: The Pages of Robert Redfield,* vol. 1, ed. M. P. Redfield, (Chicago, 1962), I, 364–414.
25. Leslie White, "Evolutionary Stages, Progress, and the Evaluation of Cultures" [1947], in *Leslie A. White: Ethnological Essays,* ed. B. Dillingham and R. R. Carneiro (Albuquerque, 1987), 59.
26. Geertz, "Primordial Sentiments and Civil Politics in the New States," in Geertz, ed., *Old Societies and New States: The Quest for Modernity in Asia and Africa* (New York, 1963), 109.

sion of the romantic motif," a shift from unlimited cultural flexibility to the enduring features of human nature, an interest in the development of civilization as opposed to the "cultures of primitives," and a shift from "cultural relativity" toward the problem of cultural universals and the application of anthropological knowledge to the problems of society. Wolf saw the process as emergence of a "new American evolutionism" in which problems "long abandoned" were being "revived with new approaches and new techniques." Three decades farther on, however, it is clear that Wolf's picture of contemporary anthropology, however apt in characterizing the developments of the postwar decade, was somewhat less than prescient as prognostication. Within several years after his book was published, the discipline was entering what some at the time and since have called "the crisis of anthropology."[27]

The end of traditional colonialism (marked by the independence of two dozen African "new nations" in the first four years of the 1960s); the overseas involvements of the United States in the cold war against international communism (marked by the exposure of the South American counterinsurgency Project Camelot in 1965); the American descent into the morass of postcolonial warfare in Southeast Asia (marked by the rise of the anti–Vietnam War movement); the countercultural and political resistance of young people in advanced capitalist countries (marked by the urban conflicts of 1968 and after)—all these "external" historical forces were reflected within the discipline in anxious and sometimes angry discussion of the method, the ethics, the theory, the politics, and the future of anthropological research. The long-implicit definition of anthropology as the study of "savage," "primitive," or "preliterate" peoples doomed to disappearance by the worldwide "progress" of European "civilization" seemed ever more problematic, as such groups (now more difficult of access for political rather than geographical reasons) were increasingly transformed by, implicated in, and conscious of their place in the processes of the larger world. And much the same could be said of anthropology itself. By 1970 "the end of anthropology" seemed to some a real possibility; to others, what was called for was its radical "reinvention."[28]

---

27. Wolf, *Anthropology* (Englewood Cliffs, N.J., 1964), 15, 22–23, 31, 51; Stocking, "Anthropology in Crisis? A View from Between the Generations," in E. Hoebel, R. Currier, and S. Kaiser, eds., *Crisis in Anthropology: View from Spring Hill, 1980* (New York, 1982), 407–22.

28. Henri Grimal, *Decolonization: The British, French, Dutch and Belgian Empires, 1919–1963*, trans. S. De Vos (Boulder, Col., 1978); Talal Asad, ed., *Anthropology and the Colonial Encounter* (London, 1973); I. L. Horowitz, *The Rise and Fall of Project Camelot* (Cambridge, Mass., 1967); Eric Wakin, ed., *Anthropology Goes to War: Professional Ethics and Counterinsurgency in Thailand* (Madison, Wis., 1992); C. Fluehr-Lobban, ed., *Ethics and the Profession of Anthropology: Dialogue for a New Era* (Philadelphia, 1991); G. Huizer and B. Mannheim, eds., *The Politics of Anthropology: From Colonialism and Sexism Toward a View from Below* (The Hague, 1979); P. Worsley, "The End of Anthropology," *Western Canadian Journal of Anthropology* 1 (1970): 1–9.

Although at the time the volume *Reinventing Anthropology* received mixed reviews by anthropologists in professional and other journals, in retrospect many of the issues it raised foreshadowed developments of the next quarter century: the impact of various currents of Marxist thought and the concern with issues of power and domination; the study of resistance movements and the impact of world ecological crisis; the refocusing of anthropology on various minority groups (and other social and political issues) in contemporary Euro-American societies; the continued critical reflection on the ethnographic process and on the history of the discipline itself, with emphasis on their implication in the ideologies and practices of European domination. With the notable exception of the feminist issues just then pushing to the foreground of anthropological concern (which had their own somewhat ambiguous implications for the anthropological perspective on the idea of "progress"), these topics suggest a more prescient perspective on the future of the discipline than Wolf's overview a mere eight years earlier.[29]

Wolf, however, was a contributor to the *Reinventing* volume, and in 1982 his own *Europe and the People without History* was an important landmark in the growing anthropological interest in the reintegration of "so-called primitives" into the world historical processes of European expansion. The following year, an influential critical theoretical work, *Time and the Other,* attacked the "persistent and problematic tendency to place the referent(s) of anthropology in a Time other than the present of the producer of anthropological dicourse." In this context, it was not only the equation of contemporary peoples with prior evolutionary stages that was called into question, but also the attempt in any given case to reconstruct an ostensibly pristine precontact cultural form, or the associated methodological fiction of the "ethnographic present." The same reintegrative historicizing trend has been manifest in arguments that cultural features or particular groups previously presumed representative of prior evolutionary phases (e.g., the !Kung Bushmen as archetypal hunter-gatherers) were in fact the product of long-term histories of interaction with European or other culturally dominant societies—a tendency that might be called "neodegenerationist," with the qualification that such peoples are no longer seen as having fallen from a higher cultural state, but rather as "victims" of (so-called) "progress."[30]

Aside from resurgent doubts, heightened by ecological concern, about the "progress of European civilization," recent decades have been marked by

---

29. Dell Hymes, ed., *Reinventing Anthropology* (New York, 1972); Edmund Leach, "Anthropology Upside Down," *New York Review of Books,* April 4, 1974, 33–35.

30. Eric Wolf, *Europe and the People Without History* (Berkeley, 1982), 4; Johannes Fabian, *Time and the Other: How Anthropology Makes its Object* (New York, 1983), 31; Robert J. Gordon, *The Bushman Myth: The Making of a Namibian Underclass* (Boulder, Col., 1992); John Bodley, *Victims of Progress* (Menlo Park, Calif., 1982).

powerfully influential critiques of what has long been thought to be its underlying dynamic: the pursuit of scientific knowledge. Doubts about the cultural consequences of scientific progress, or assertions of the legitimacy of alternative modes of knowing the world, were nothing new: witness, in anthropology, Sapir's "Culture: Genuine and Spurious," or Boas's defense of cosmographic against natural scientific method in "The Study of Geography." But Thomas Kuhn's *Structure of Scientific Revolutions,* along with subsequent developments in the sociology of science and poststructuralist critiques of the discourses of modernity, made problematic the very notion of scientific progress itself, and of the exemption of scientific knowledge from the relativity of cultural determinism. In anthropology—which had experienced a stronger reaction against the "positivism" of 1950s than some other social science disciplines—a resurgent relativism called into question the categories (kinship), the methods (fieldwork), the products (ethnographies), and the purposes (disinterested knowledge) of anthropological inquiry.[31]

It would be a mistake, however, to assume that the late-twentieth-century critique of the "Enlightenment project" had purged anthropology entirely of progressivist or evolutionary assumption. Despite the widespread critical response to "sociobiology" in the 1970s and 1980s, evolutionary issues still have a place on the anthropological agenda, as witnessed by the recent founding of a journal devoted to and titled *Evolutionary Anthropology,* and the cultural artifacts or practices of present (or recently) existing populations are still sometimes used to elucidate temporally distant phenomena. More generally, there are signs (although perhaps to some extent age-linked) of a reaction against what some have called "science bashing." It might even be argued, in a manner analogous to some criticisms of relativism, that the various critiques of anthropology imply a belief in the possible progress of anthropological knowledge. Reflecting the continuing transformation of the world outside, the traditional subject matter of anthropological inquiry occupies an ever smaller place in the program of the American Anthropological Association's annual meetings—where a recent session on "The Global in the Local: Transnational Fast Food Industries in East Asia" consisted of papers on the impact of McDonald's in five different East Asian countries. But if "premodern" (like "primitive" before it) seems now Eurocentric, and "modernity" an early-

---

31. Edward Sapir, "Culture, Genuine and Spurious" [1924], in David Mandelbaum, ed., *Selected Writings of Edward Sapir in Language, Culture and Personality* (Berkeley, 1963), 308–31; Boas, "The Study of Geography" [1885], in *Race, Language and Culture* (New York, 1943), 639–47; Thomas Kuhn, *The Structure of Scientific Revolutions* (Chicago, 1962); D. M. Schneider, *A Critique of the Study of Kinship* (Ann Arbor, 1984); Roger Sanjek, ed., *Fieldnotes: The Makings of Anthropology* (Ithaca, 1990); George Marcus and James Clifford, eds., *Writing Culture: The Politics and Poetics of Ethnography* (Berkeley, 1984); Clifford Geertz, "Anti-Anti-Relativism," *American Anthropologist* 86 (1984): 263–78.

twentieth-century ideology rather than the achievement of cultural progress, the idea of the "postmodern" is by no means unproblematic. The studied indeterminacy of its prefix does not entirely obscure occasional echos of a yearning that A. O. Lovejoy might have called "soft primitivist"; so also the implicit teleology of the oft-associated notion of "late capitalism" hints at the possible resumption of the "progress of [hu]mankind." And the continuing critique of racism, classism, and sexism suggests that, although relativism may affirm the legitimacy (and the possibility) of alternative cultural forms, universal human values are still powerful motivators of cultural critique and of aspiration (if not movement) toward goals that even Rousseau (averting his glance from postcolonial or postcommunist ethnic strife and signs of impending global disaster) might regard as progressive.[32]

---

32. See, among others, Robert Borovsky, ed. *Assessing Cultural Anthropology* (New York, 1994), and F. V. Harrison, ed., *Decolonizing Anthropology: Moving Further Toward an Anthropology for Liberation* (Washington, D.C., 1991); Micaela di Leonardo, ed., *Gender at the Crossroads of Knowledge: Feminist Anthropology in the Postmodern Era* (Berkeley, 1991); Stocking, "Postscriptive Prospective Reflections," in *The Ethnographer's Magic,* 362–74.

# The Economic View of Progress

*Robert Heilbroner*

Is there progress in the economic view of things?

Of course the answer depends on what we mean by "progress." But we are not to be let off the hook so easily, for the answer also depends on what we mean by "economics." The second question adds an unexpected complexity to the first, for whatever it is we mean by progress takes on radically different aspects depending on whatever it is we mean by economics.

Everyone intuitively grasps both the clarifying and the perplexing aspects of probing the first answer—namely, the economic meaning of "progress." The clarifying aspect is that progress, in the economic view, is usually taken to mean an increased ability to provide for the material well-being of humanity: it is the process by which poor societies become richer ones. There is a prima facie reasonableness to this view of things, with which I am not going to argue, although perplexity arises when we begin to consider the questions that inevitably arise from this approach—namely, do we measure, or even define, "material well-being"? Anthropologist Marshall Sahlins has shown that primitive economics can be considered as societies of "affluence."[1] Many commentators have pointed out that existential impoverishment, not to mention pockets of physical misery, can be found in the richest industrial nations. Moralists tell us that man does not live by bread alone. These perplexities are real and must be confronted by anyone who attempts to assess the record of material advance. I mention them now only because, despite its associated problems, the improvement of the human material condition remains an insistent focus for anyone who confronts the idea of progress from any perspective, especially that of economics.

That now clears the decks for examining the relation of this commonsensical and inescapable idea of progress to our conception of economics. Here is where clarifications dwindle and perplexities multiply, for the discipline of economics is today construed in many different ways, each of which con-

---

I wish to thank David Gordon, Edward Nell, and Will Milberg for valuable criticisms.
1. Marshall Sahlins, *Stone Age Economics* (New York: Aldine, 1972).

stitutes a prescription for the lenses through which we view the world. Moreover, each of these construals leads to a different conception of progress. This is a difficulty that has some parallels in other disciplines—there is more than one conception of what we consider to be "history" or "religion" or even "science," and each conception similarly affects the idea of progress as perceived from the vantage point of that discipline.[2] But in the case of economics, the polarity of views is so sharp and the perspectives so extraordinarily at variance with one another that defining the character of the discipline assumes a disproportionate importance. Accordingly, that is where I shall begin.

Here we immediately encounter the difficulty to which I have already referred. It is that contemporary economics comes in many forms. To this difficulty I shall apply a Procrustean remedy. It will be to ignore all its variants, save two.

The first variant will be the regnant mainstream view called neoclassical economics. The term *neoclassical* was originally popularized by Paul Samuelson, who used it to describe a constructive compromise between the "microeconomic" (or individual-centered) approach to economics, given magisterial status by the great Victorian economist Alfred Marshall, and the quite different "macroeconomic" (or aggregative) approach that was John Maynard Keynes's equally influential contribution of the 1930s—alas, in many ways incompatible with that of Marshall.

The term *neoclassical* has since lost that flavor of economics as a rather pragmatic and worldly study. It is now used to refer to a conception of economics as a highly formal system that describes the outcome, in terms of prices and quantities of goods and services, of the interaction of individual "agents" (firms or individuals), each conceived as a bundle of fixed preferences and capabilities and motivated by a drive to maximize "utilities" (satisfactions) through "rational" (means-ends–related) behavior. All the rest—the social and technological structure, the institutional framework, the historical setting—is, as they say, "given."[3]

It must be apparent that the conception of progress that emerges from such a highly formalistic view of economics will differ from that of the older, "worldly" neoclassicism or its equally down-to-earth predecessors, Marshallian or Keynesian economics. We will come to some consideration of that in due course. But I think we can already anticipate some of the aspects of the new neoclassicism that will have relevancy to the idea of progress, both within

---

2. As Paul Feyerabend has brilliantly demonstrated, even astronomy, the most "objective" of inquiries, can be conceived in radically different ways, including that of astrology. See his *Against Method* (London: Verso, 1975), 100n., 208n.

3. See the entries for "Axiomatic theories" by Patrick Suppes, "Economic theory and the hypothesis of rationality" by Kenneth Arrow, and "Neoclassical" by Tony Aspromourgos in *The New Palgrave: A Dictionary of Economics* (New York: Stockton Press, 1987).

the field of economics and out in the world to which it presumably applies. The first such aspect must be evident. The axiomatic core imparts a lawlike basis to action—a "choice theoretic" derived from rational utility maximizing—that enables us to discern resemblances between the deep structure of economics and that of natural science.[4] To no small degree, this science-related aspect of neoclassicism has earned for it the flattery of imitation by other disciplines that have envied its axiomatic style of exposition and borrowed its penchant for functional relationships. Of even greater significance, neoclassical economics has acquired a powerful position within social inquiry because economics, so formulated, acquires a universalistic scope. I will let the distinguished economist Jack Hirshleifer speak to the latter question:

> [I]t is ultimately impossible to carve off a distinct territory for economics, bordering on, but separated from other social disciplines. Economics penetrates them all, and is reciprocally penetrated by them. *There is only one social science.* What gives economics its imperialist invasive power is that our analytical categories—scarcity, cost, preferences, opportunities, etc.—are truly universal in application. . . . Thus economics really does constitute the universal grammar of social science."[5]

In the Hirshleifer formulation, the universal applicability of economics is shared with the imperatives of "sociobiology" to yield a "master pattern" of social theory. In the words of the author, "certain ultimate principles like scarcity and opportunity cost, and the universal bioeconomic processes of competition and selection, will always remain valid for analyzing and predicting the course of human behavior and social organization." As we shall see, I am less than convinced by the conceptual premise of Hirshleifer's pronunciamento, but there is no denying the success of its "imperialist" appeal: for example, Gary Becker, winner of the 1992 Nobel Prize in economics, writes in *The Economic Approach to Human Behavior,* "I have come to the position that the economic approach is a comprehensive one that is applicable to all human behavior."[6]

One further aspect of neoclassical economics warrants mention. By the methodological criteria proposed by the late Imre Lakatos, much used in the social sciences, neoclassical economics is a highly "progressive" scientific

---

4. See the fine overview by Clive Beed, "Philosophy of Science and Contemporary Economics," *Journal of Post-Keynesian Economics* 13, no. 4 (summer, 1991) 459–94.

5. Jack Hirshleifer, "The Expanding Domain of Economics," *American Economic Review* (December, 1985): 53; emphasis in the original.

6. Hirshleifer, "Expanding Domain," 66; Gary Becker, *The Economic Approach to Human Behavior* (Chicago: University of Chicago Press, 1976), 8.

research program.[7] The progressive character is established because the hard core of "choice theoretics" illumines problems that have proven impenetrable from other perspectives. Under the X-ray examination of this approach, marriage and divorce, parent-child relationships, governmental decisions, voting, sports, foraging habits, and Stone Age changes in habitat and occupation all reveal individual agents rationally maximizing their utilities exactly as they do in the marketplace and the production site, the conventional loci of economic analysis. An early—and still stunning—example of this illuminating capability is the systematic application of the idea of utility to the phenomenon of price, a relationship that had largely eluded economic clarification until its formulation by the pre-Marshallian founders of "marginalism"—individual-choice–centered analysis—William Stanley Jevons, Francis Edgeworth, Leon Walras, and others in the 1870s.

The discovery—perhaps more accurately, the assumption—of a common mind-set buried deep within a vast range of behavior has indeed conferred on economics some of the universalism of which Hirshleifer speaks. This remarkable extension of scope must, however, be accompanied by a recognition of its limitations. The generalization of economics as a universal science requires a level of abstraction that presents grave problems for its operational use, insofar as the key terms *rational, utility,* and *maximizing* raise great obstacles when translated into real-world application. Indeed, the analytical framework becomes a tautology—valuable, as are all tautologies, in giving an orientation to analysis, but of no use in empirical work. In addition, the formal basis of neoclassical analysis makes it exceedingly difficult to handle the labile and ambiguous situations of real-life economic encounters. Neoclassical analysis starts from initial "agents," typically a group of buyers and sellers, whose presumably invariant preferences and endowments allow us to determine by logical deduction the price that will clear that market. Such an exercise cannot represent the constantly altering prices that emerge as buyers and sellers interact in real marketplaces; above all one considers the highly destabilizing effects of ever-changing expectations.

Thus, against the stunning elucidation of the role of utility maximization in determining price must be set the equally stunning necessity for Leon Walras, the father of this analysis, to resort to the description of the market as a series of tentative bids and offers elicited by an "auctioneer" who tests various prices until the marketers finally arrive at one that balances supply and demand. Hence, from the viewpoint of evaluating progress within the discipline of economics, the remarkable increase in the applicability of the fundamental

---

7. See "Falsification and the Methodology of Scientific Research Programmes," in *Criticism and the Growth of Knowledge,* ed. Imre Lakatos and Alan Musgrave (New York: Cambridge University Press, 1970). The adjective *progressive* is featured in Lakatos's explication.

posits of neoclassical analysis is offset by the disconcerting fact that the gains from this "progress" are elusive, perhaps even nonexistent.[8]

The reader will recall, however, that there is a second variant of economics. This now requires that I perform my previously announced Procrustean task of reducing a wide variety of non-neoclassical formulations—variously described as Keynesian, institutional, and (for all its recent travails) Marxian economics—to a single "alternative" view. Fortunately, this is not as contentious or arbitrary as it might seem, for all these alternative modes share certain characteristics that make such an amalgam meaningful.

Of these characteristics, by far the most important is the emphasis of non-neoclassical economics on the historicity of the research object it examines. This new focus emerges because all its formulations recognize the existence and dominant importance of an element that neoclassical analysis omits—namely, the presence of the regimatic social principles of capitalism as the organizing force behind the idea-system of economics itself.[9] Thus, in the sharpest possible contrast to neoclassical economics, which begins from the assumption of universalist principles, non-neoclassical economics starts from a conception of economics as inseparable from the specific social order within which it appears and to whose movements it is principally applied.

Economics, from this viewpoint, is based on "sociological" generalizations rather than on the timeless attributes of a choice theoretic. This removes many difficulties associated with the stringent premises of neoclassicism, but it also leaves the non-neoclassicals without the lawlike foundation that is one of the strongest appeals of the neoclassical approach. Heterodox economics must therefore be content with such semi-indeterminate formulations as "bounded rationality," "satisficing," or "uncertainty" (as contrasted with "risk") in place of the precise vectors that delineate rational utility maximizing. Not surprisingly, its central focus is directed to problems of configurational change, not of motivational constancy. All this gives non-neoclassical economics a markedly lower level of abstraction and a lessened (although not entirely

---

8. For an overview of the difficulties of the choice theoretic, see Amartya Sen, "Rational Fools: A Critique of the Behavioral Foundations of Economic Theory," *Philosophy and Public Affairs* 6, no. 4 (1977): 317–44; and essays by Sen. Alan Ryan and Tony Cramp in Guy Meeks, ed., *Thoughtful Economic Man* (New York: Cambridge University Press, 1991); as well as Amitai Etzioni, *The Moral Dimension: Toward a New Economics* (New York: Free Press, 1988). I should take notice here of a number of valiant efforts to escape from the narrow outlook of neoclassicism while remaining within its individualist straitjacket, especially Robert H. Frank, *Passions Within Reason* (New York: Norton, 1988); and Richard R. Nelson and Sidney G. Winter, *An Evolutionary Theory of Economic Change* (Cambridge: Belknap Press of Harvard University Press, 1982).

9. There is a general reference, but surprisingly little effort, to explicate these system-defining principles. I have attempted to do so in *The Nature and Logic of Capitalism* (New York: Norton, 1985).

absent) emphasis on methodological purity than in neoclassical thought. There is little or no emphasis on a Lakatosian approach, much less on the older positivism proposed by Karl Popper, and a somewhat hesitant reliance on "relativist," or "holistic," or "hermeneutical," approaches.[10]

One last problem remains to be examined before we turn to the central issue of real-world progress from an economic viewpoint. It is the question of how progress is initially defined within the two main branches of economics itself. We have already seen that neoclassical economics conceives it as the application of its theoretical hard core to an ever widening range of problematics. Non-neoclassical economics has a more difficult time. Lacking consensual unity, the very idea of linear or cumulative progress within the discipline largely disappears from view. In its place we see a competitive vying among various ways of construing and analyzing aspects of the real world that seem to elude the neoclassical net. The most striking example here is the introduction during the late 1930s of a new explanatory and predictive Keynesian framework that offered a different mode of conceptualizing the operation of the economy itself, along with previously unperceived functional relationships between the level of investment spending and the determination of aggregate national income.

At the time of its arrival on the scene, Keynesian economics constituted a remarkable example of "progress" within the discipline in that it opened up aspects of economic performance, especially with respect to the course of national income, that had previously been ignored or perhaps simply unrecognized. The postwar decline of Keynesianism—or, rather, the decreasing confidence in the solidity of its behavioral foundations and of its applicability in the changed milieu of the postwar world—signaled the vulnerability of an idea of progress that depended on institutional attributes of the system, a vulnerability that is avoided from an approach whose initial posits are assumed to be changeless. This does not mean that "progress" within the non-neoclassical school is impossible, but that it is much more ad hoc, transient, and undependable. This is precisely because the aim of non-neoclassical investigation is to explain trends or configurational changes as aspects of a specific social order, rather than as instantiations of a general economic problematic. As the arrangements of that order change, so does the cutting power of the conceptual elucidation. I think of the analysis of "externalities" (unintended consequences of economic activity), ecology, imperfect labor and other markets, underdevelopment, corporate strategy, financial instability, industrial policy, or the globalization of

---

10. The change in levels of abstraction is discussed in Edward J. Nell and Willi Semmler, eds., "Introduction," *Nicholas Kaldor and Mainstream Economics* (London: Macmillan, 1991). For a recent discussion of methodological trends, see Jon D. Wisman and Joseph Rozansky, "The Methodology of Institutionalism Revisited," *Journal of Economic Issues* (September, 1991).

markets as instances of such non-neoclassical investigations whose "progressive" character lies in their effort to understand their research objects as malfunctions of a specific socioeconomic order—modern capitalism—but whose conceptual durability and power are unavoidably weakened by this very historicity of intention.

This does not begin to exhaust the differences between the neoclassical and non-neoclassical economics, but it is sufficient to lay the basis for our main task—namely, to trace the idea of real-world progress from the viewpoints of the discipline. I trust it has by now become clear why we have had to take this lengthy detour before coming to the issue at hand. Hence, the reader will be prepared for two quite different appraisals of and prescriptions for progress, depending on which of the two viewpoints it expresses.

What does neoclassical theory have to say about the idea of progress in the world? Insofar as material improvement remains the central requisite for such progress, our focus narrows to the contribution of neoclassical economics to the understanding or promotion of economic growth. That contribution is as clear as the conception of progress within the discipline. It is the theoretical demonstration that a regime of competitive markets is the most effective social mechanism yet developed for the attainment of economic efficiency, and the closely allied theoretical demonstration that efficiency in the allocation of resources is the general directive that must be followed to reach the Kingdom of Wealth. Taken generally, this is a prescription that would win agreement from most neoclassical economists today. As such, it stands as the principal contribution that mainstream economics has made to real-world progress.

Once again, however, we face the problem of a gap between theoretical clarification and practical application. Ever since its development in the 1870s, neoclassical economics has been primarily interested in the allocational, not the accumulatory, aspect of real-world economic processes. Yet, ever since growth itself has been intensively analyzed, its principal motor has been identified as the process of accumulation, driven mainly by technological change, "the lever of riches."[11] Hence, we have the anomalous fact that in stressing allocation over accumulation, neoclassical economics ignores an aspect of the real world that seems to be crucial for progress, while concentrating on aspects that seem of secondary importance. For example, the famous neoclassical model of economic growth developed by Robert Solow buries technological advance within the model, where it appears not as a key independent variable,

---

11. Joel Mokyr, *The Lever of Riches: Technological Creativity and Economic Progress* (New York: Oxford University Press, 1990). For the allocational focus of neoclassical economics, see Vivian Walsh and Harvey Gram, *Classical and Neoclassical Theories of General Equilibrium* (New York: Oxford University Press, 1980), especially chaps. 5 and 8.

but as one of many elements that affect the relative productivities of labor and capital.

The non-neoclassical perspective accommodates itself more naturally to the idea of material betterment and its associated problems. This follows from the institutional orientation and the specific historical focus of non-neoclassical work, to which we have already paid heed. Here the affinity to the idea of economic growth is traceable in two related, but separate, strands. The first concerns the dynamics of capital accumulation, particularly in capitalist nations, where the non-neoclassical approach derives its central impetus from the work of Smith, Ricardo, Marx, and to some extent Mill, adding to their large-scale scenarios the insights of more recent followers in the classical tradition— Gunnar Myrdal, Nicholas Kaldor, Michal Kalecki, Piero Sraffa, and others, including Keynes himself. That which distinguishes these non-neoclassical analyses from their classical forebears, and from their neoclassical opposites, is a much greater emphasis on the dynamics of unstable or abortive growth than one finds in the classical writers—excepting only Marx. If equilibrating movements describe the immanent tendencies of capitalism that appear through neoclassical glasses, self-generated disequilibrating change is the tendency that insistently emerges through non-neoclassical lenses.

The second distinct aspect of non-neoclassical analysis follows from the first. It is the different significance attached to state intervention in the attainment of material well-being. Neoclassical analysis generally seeks to minimize state intervention into the spontaneous processes of the system, insofar as its emphasis on self-equilibrating forces reduces the need for and lowers confidence in the usefulness of interventory measures. In sharp contrast, the non-neoclassical approach offers state policy as the only method of forestalling failures it considered endemic to the accumulation process.[12]

I do not know of any "objective" way of choosing between these two general perspectives. There are lengthy traditions of economic optimism, for which a faith in the buoyant course of a self-steering market system seems a good proxy, and of economic pessimism, with its anticipations of crisis, stagnation, or dysfunctions of other kinds. The works of Adam Smith and Karl Marx are often taken as expressions of these contrasting views, and there are immense literatures pointing out the cogency and the errors of each. Perhaps all that can be ventured with respect to this transcendent question is that the history of capitalism seems to offer limited support to both views. There is ample evidence that it is an unstable and contradiction-ridden social order, if for no other reason than its dependence on an unpredictable and transformative

---

12. For a recent example, see Alice Amsden, Jacek Kochanowicz, and Lance Taylor, *The Market Meets Its Match: Restructuring the Economics of Eastern Europe* (Cambridge: Harvard University Press, 1994).

technology in a setting of antagonistic class relations. At the same time, this instability has not yet fatally undermined the historical vitality of the capitalist order, whether because of or in spite of increasing attempts to use public measures to assure socially acceptable levels of economic performance.

With regard to our own prospects, both neoclassical and non-neoclassical visions therefore support the probability of sufficient growth to sustain, if not to improve, material conditions within the capitalist "center," during the troubled period of technological and international adjustment through which we are passing. A longer view yields less sanguine expectations insofar as it widens the screen to include ecological and political trends that fall outside the normal reach of economic inquiry. I should add that in the past, non-neoclassical thought has also been hopeful with respect to the prospects for noncapitalist economic progress, viewing the possibilities of planning—centralized or decentralized—as also capable of yielding sustained economic growth.

Following the collapse of the East European and Soviet economies, this rather uncritical approach has given way to a much more cautious appraisal. Ironically, perhaps the most important legacy of "socialism" (Soviet style) has been the reinforcement of a profound skepticism with regard to the workability of noncapitalist economic systems in general. The prospects for capitalism are accordingly enhanced by virtue of the elimination, at least for the near-term future, of an alternative mode of socioeconomic organization. Wishful prognostications aside, I fear there is little more that an economist can venture as to the outlook for material progress over the few generations that constitute our imaginable future.[13]

There remains the question of progress interpreted not only as an improvement in human material well-being but also in its cultural, even spiritual, aspects. At its boldest, this search for a redemptive socioeconomic drama has found its expression in Marx's vision of a long upward progression from primitive communism through feudalism into the period of capitalist history, the antepenultimate stage of "history," to be followed by socialism and then full communism. Hardly less audacious is Adam Smith's view of the same process. His conception is also tied to the accumulation of capital, which, as in the Marxian schema, becomes the necessary condition for a sequence of social stages from "rude" beginnings into what Smith calls commercial society. Thereafter, however, a crucial difference separates the two prognoses. Smith's sequence does not follow an uninterrupted upward gradient into some postcommercial society, but instead reaches a period of maximum possible

---

13. For a similarly guarded assessment, see Eric Hobsbawm, *The Age of Extremes* (New York: Pantheon, 1995).

wealth under "capitalism" (a term that Smith never used), followed thereafter by a descent into social misery.[14]

I suspect that neither scenario is to be taken seriously any longer. The Marxian vision is increasingly derided as a utopia, and the Smithian prognosis hinges on a complete absence of any recognition of technological change. In much the same fashion, the long-term economic and social prognoses of other economists are today easily faulted on analytical or sociological grounds. No one any longer holds Ricardo's expectations of an imminent end to economic expansion brought about by running up against the barriers of land fertility. One does not hear echoes of Mill's version of the same fate, tempered by a belief that a stationary state, once reached, would become a mobilizing ground for an associationist socialism. Keynes's half-whimsical, half-earnest belief that capitalism would saturate its markets by the time of his grandchildren (of whom he had none) is taken as a mere fantasy. Schumpeter's drama of "creative destruction," impelling capitalism forward in a series of technologically fueled bursts, remains a hope rather than a firm expectation, and his belief that even a "successful" capitalism would opt to become a managerial socialism is viewed as no more than another naive embrace of planning.[15]

Thus, bold speculations about economic progress are out of favor these days. There is little consideration of progress as a process of social evolution, not just economic enlargement. I suspect, however, that we have not heard the last of grander "Marxian" or "Smithian" approaches to the problem. From the viewpoint of progress, at least, the most durable contribution of these greatest of the worldly philosophers was not to foretell the trajectory of human evolution. Rather, it was to point out, from different but mutually supporting perspectives, the ultimate inadequacy of accumulation itself as a measure of social betterment. This is a theme strongly emphasized by Marx in his depiction of accumulation as a contradiction-laden process that serves initially both as a source of well-being for the capitalist class and as a cause of alienation and "immiseration" for the working class. It is not until the stage of socialism that one can speak of "progress," without a recognition of its ambiguous and ironical meanings; and socialism itself, as we catch glimpses of it in *The German Ideology,* is celebrated not as a society of material abundance but as one in which we are free to "hunt in the morning, fish in the afternoon . . . , criticize after dinner . . . , without ever becoming hunter, fisherman . . . , or critic."[16]

---

14. See R. Heilbroner, "The Paradox of Progress," in Andrew S. Skinner and Thomas Wilson, eds., *Essays on Adam Smith* (Oxford: Clarendon Press, 1975).

15. See R. Heilbroner, "Analysis and Vision in the History of Modern Economic Thought," *Journal of Economic Literature* (September, 1990).

16. Karl Marx and Friedrich Engels, *The German Ideology* (New York: New York International, 1947), 22.

Smith, too, regards the accumulation of wealth in an ambivalent manner. It is seen as a good insofar as its "vulgar" appeals lead an uncomprehending humankind along a path that achieves not only material comforts, but also liberty and virtue. It is suspect to the degree that the pursuit of wealth becomes an end in itself or an instrument for the debasement of the working class: "A man whose whole life is spent in performing a few simple operations . . . has no occasion to exert his understanding . . . He naturally loses, therefore, the habit of such exertion, and generally becomes as ignorant and stupid as it is possible for a human creature to become . . ."[17]

Thus, in the view of these presumably most antagonistic thinkers, the accumulation of wealth is perceived as a necessary but not sufficient condition for the attainment of progress—necessary because the amassing of material wealth is still needed if humankind is to escape the miseries of which we catch television glimpses in Africa or Latin America or encounter in the flesh on the way to the office; insufficient not only because the dynamics of its accumulation deform the relationship of humans to one another, but also because its very possession easily generates deformations of the human character. I believe that such considerations are likely to assert themselves with increasing urgency as capitalism moves into a future big with problems of both material provisioning and political and social justice. As to what socioeconomic organization may then become the vehicle of progress, I cannot pretend to know, other than to suggest that it will be to Smith and Marx the moralists, not the economists, that we will look for guidance.

---

17. Adam Smith, *The Wealth of Nations* (New York: Modern Library, 1937), 734. See also Robert Prasch, "The Ethics of Growth in Adam Smith's 'Wealth of Nations'," *History of Political Economy* 23, no. 2 (summer 1991): 337–51.

# A Political Assessment of Progress

*Alan Ryan*

This is an ambivalent essay. As a political liberal and a loyal disciple of John Stuart Mill, I subscribe to his idea of "man as a progressive being," that is, a creature whose life is an experiment, and who sees social and political institutions as experiments in human association. This is a vision to which the concept of progress is indispensable, as Mill's famous essay *On Liberty* suggests. I am temperamentally averse to the conservative or "realist" approach to politics; it is not enough to concentrate on avoiding disaster and keeping original sin under control. Certainly we must do at least that, but any argument for doing that much must be an argument for doing more *when we can*. As Mill observed in *Representative Government,* the then conventional division of political parties into parties of movement and parties of order was fundamentally erroneous; we must not go backward, but avoiding decline is only a necessary condition of forward movement.

But I was taught political theory by John Plamenatz, who not only argued explicitly that the nineteenth-century belief in progress had no intellectual basis, but who in person gave the impression that only a very crude, English, utilitarian intelligence would find room for the idea in the first place. Pascal and Rousseau were the tutelary deities who presided over our conversations, and it seemed that anyone who questioned the vanity of earthly wishes was crass. I also learned much from Isaiah Berlin, whose emphasis on the incommensurability of different human goods and different social attachments at any rate implies that it is a rash person who says that human history is a record of unequivocal progress. As I understood Berlin, we might talk of progress in some areas and some respects—British sanitation had surely improved since 1800—but large "all-in" judgments—that the United States in 1995 is superior to Athens in 395 B.C., say—were inherently dubious. I am also a child of the Second World War; nobody whose first conscious encounter with newspapers was that of a five-year-old seeing the photographs of the Belsen concentration camp taken by the liberating forces can feel quite at ease with the concept of progress.

I therefore intend to focus this chapter quite narrowly on the subject suggested by its title, that is, on *political* progress. My strategy is simple, even crude; to the extent that we can identify some tasks or functions that all political orders have performed or must perform, we can talk of our having made progress or having failed to do so. Some rough balance of improvement and retrogression can be struck. To the degree that no such commonality in our understanding of success and failure can be assumed, the concept of progress has no place. I say this ceteris paribus; we may in addition be justified in thinking that some changes of mind about what politics is about and what counts as success and failure are themselves forms of progress. There, too, however, something must remain constant to provide the yardstick against which we measure progress, some permanent interests, hankerings, and strivings. The discussion that follows takes the course that these remarks suggest. I suggest grounds for doubt about the very concept of political progress, then offer some tentative ideas about how to define the common tasks of all political systems, spend most of the chapter contrasting the progress-minded, nonparticipatory and thoroughly instrumental politics of Hobbes with the antiquity-centered politics of Rousseau, and end with an account of the chastened liberalism of some nineteenth-century writers. It is they who best serve my own purpose—that of suggesting that we may transcend the argument between Hobbes and Rousseau and celebrate our success in opening the political sphere to persons formerly shut out of it, though we ought not celebrate very much more.

This is not a simple assertion of the fact of political progress; indeed, it is just because it is so obvious that in many respects there has been no political progress over the past two centuries that we must consider the wider question of what areas of human existence display progress and in what that progress consists. Moreover, I take it to be uncontroversial that the *political* catastrophes of the twentieth century—the Holocaust, Stalinism, colonialism, and the human rights disasters that plague postcolonial societies, together with the combination of pride and folly that has led to two world wars and a host of lesser conflicts—are what most severely try a faith in progress, and that this warrants my strategy.

This is uncontroversial, but it bears some analysis. It is often said that conservatives who believe in original sin cannot believe in progress. But Immanuel Kant, who coined the famous phrase "no straight thing can be made out of such crooked timber as man is made of," certainly did believe in political progress, and in general a belief in original sin does not forbid a belief in *political* progress. Our individual natures may remain permanently flawed, but our social arrangements can and must be improved. If the human raw material gets no better over time, our ability to develop its virtues and control its vices certainly ought to. The cruelties and follies of individuals might be deplored as the inevitable outcroppings of original sin, or the nastiness of the occasional bad apple in the barrel without subverting a belief in progress, so long as those cruelties and follies were swiftly checked and punished. The vices of governments are another matter.

Governments do not suffer from original sin; although governments are staffed by individuals, officially sanctioned evil cannot be shrugged off by appeal to the "bad apple" syndrome. The scale and the *organized* character of the atrocities perpetrated by governments lend them a nastiness that individual acts do not possess. The minute scrutiny of individual acts of cruelty may lead one to think ill of human nature, but without destroying the hope that the whole race may do much to overcome the effects of its natural handicaps and failings. The case of governments is different. The crux is that governments are artificial entities; their legitimacy rests on the fact that we set them up to do good rather than evil. Humanity was not created for a purpose, does not have to prove its legitimacy, and cannot lose it in the same way.

The evil that governments do is compounded by the good they fail to do. Governments are established to promote the welfare of all those whose lives they can lawfully affect; what they leave undone is a failure, if less glaring a failure than when they turn to evil. Even where the object of our despair is not political in the sense that it is the direct object of action by governments and their agents—for instance, the failure to provide humanly interesting work to the great bulk of the populations of affluent societies or the failure to ensure even modest economic security to the inhabitants of much of Africa, South Asia, and Latin America—the not-very-remote cause of that failure is political. The arrangements for recruiting leaders, legislating, administering, and sustaining public confidence in the moral legitimacy and organizational competence of the state order are one way and another defective.

To make these mildly dogmatic remarks about *the* purpose of government being to secure the general welfare raises a familiar philosophical issue, and it leads us to the first task I should perform. One reason for skepticism about the whole idea of progress occurs to all of us on five minutes' reflection. To talk of progress is to talk of increasing success in attaining a goal that remains constant over time. Absent that goal, the concept has no purchase. Within a given mode of art, more deft renderings of perspective counted for progress during the period when verisimilitude was a main aim of painters. But this was so only when all painters were aiming at the same goal. As between a successful rendering of perspective by a painter aiming at such a rendering and the absence of perspective in Byzantine art, it is hard and perhaps nonsensical to talk of progress. I do not mean to suggest that it is quite impossible to say more than this. Purposes also can display a form of progress. We may wish to say that Renaissance painting marked a forward movement in painting by comparison with Byzantine art; to do so, however, we must think of a common project in which all art, or all Western art, shares and in which common project the later style marks an upward movement.

Progress within and between artistic styles is by no means the only context in which such conceptual unsettling occurs. Science is often thought to be at the opposite pole to art, just because it seems obvious that science is progressive. But this thought has been undermined in recent years. The effect of the work of T. S. Kuhn was briefly (and unintentionally but nonetheless thoroughly) to dent the common assumption that science was essentially a progressive activity; *The Structure of Scientific Revolutions* seemed at first glance to say that only *within* a paradigm—a constellation of worldviews, acceptance of experimental techniques, modes of education and socialization into the scientific community—could progress be assessed. Standards for success and failure were given in the community of mutually recognized scientists, and their say-so was decisive. *Across* paradigms, however, no such common system of assessment held. As the imagery of "revolutions" suggests, the standards of legitimacy changed as the regime changed; what counted as a good explanation at $t_1$ was not what counted as a good explanation at $t_2$, and what counted as a "puzzle" before was no longer a puzzle afterwards. The idea that science was a record of progress was threatened.

Kuhn later came to see how many traps he had laid for himself, and how many unintended concessions he had offered to antirationalists of assorted stripes, and did a good deal to patch up the situation. He later argued that one simply could not imagine the history of science running backward; given two theories, any historian of science could tell you which came later. That suggested that some sort of progress was surely being made. Years earlier, John Dewey had offered a way out of Kuhn's impasse by suggesting that the metaphor of growth underlay our confidence that there was not just change in scientific understanding, but progress. A move forward in science is a move that allows further growth, and a dead end is precisely a *dead* end. Nor should we expect to say exactly what constitutes growth except tentatively and in the course of the activity itself. In my crude terms, *something* is common to the scientific enterprise across paradigm shifts, even if that something is not generally articulated by people intent on something more immediate. The contrast between situations where we think some kind of progress is at stake and where we think it is not is often but vulgarly marked by talk of "a matter of taste." When we declare a matter a matter of taste, we declare that we are abstaining from ranking ideas, activities, and institutions as more and less successful. This is vulgar, since we can and do talk about people learning to refine and improve their taste as much as any other perceptual and evaluative skill they possess. Still, it is a useful vulgarity. It raises the right question for my purposes.

That question is the extent to which politics is a matter of taste rather than a matter where humanity faces inescapable tasks that can be performed better or worse and where progress is constituted by moving from worse to better. It is disquieting that it should be so easy to reply that it is a bit of both, but that is surely the answer. When we doubt whether politics today represents progress over the politics of classical Athens, it is because we so largely see Athenian society as an alternative cultural possibility rather than as a failed attempt to do what we have chosen to do. Between such different cultures we might think there is no choosing. Some people would certainly have good reasons for preferring to live in one rather than the other; women, potential slaves, and anyone who valued everyday comfort would have good reason to prefer twentieth-century Boston to fifth-century B.C. Athens. Robust, argumentative, energetic types who liked living adventurously would have reason to choose the opposite. Trading the interests of the first against the enthusiasms of the latter is impossible. Even if lots of people would have been better off in twentieth-century Boston than fifth-century B.C. Athens, it is impossible to say that we practice a better politics or sustain a better culture. The twenty-first century will follow us in thinking classical Greece a more engrossing culture than our own, and anyone who thinks that Athenian politics is engrossing because it is a manifestation of that glorious cultural epoch will hardly be able to resist the conclusion that we have not made what he or she would count as progress in this sphere. We have made progress in innumerable fields that the Athenians themselves would admit as fields in which the idea of progress was thoroughly at home—the elimination of assorted diseases, the mastery of pain and the ability to perform surgical procedures that would have killed the patient before antibiotics and anesthetics, and the overcoming of famine and hunger in the developed world would be obvious examples—but the Athenians might say we do not know the pleasures of their civic life. We would point in vain to the constitutional protections embodied in the Bill of Rights, to the extension of suffrage and the abolition of slavery.

Not all of politics can be a matter of taste, however. Indeed, once we consider those areas that cannot be a matter of taste, we may find that the areas we first see as "matters of taste" diminish a good deal. Even if we do not, we shall certainly find ourselves fighting on the boundaries between the two realms. Suppose, however, that we avoid that fight by adopting a conception of politics something like Dewey's—that politics is a form of intelligent action directed to facilitating associated living. We shall then find the notion of political progress gaining some content. The mastery of human life by intelligent social action seems on the face of it to be a goal we might more nearly or less nearly attain, and thus to be something to which the concept of progress is applicable. It does not follow that as soon as we take that view, we are forced to decide that there has been much progress. Dewey himself was more equivocal on that score than hearsay accounts of his views suggest. We might believe that humankind has been quicker to set itself insoluble problems than to devise intelligent ways of meeting them, and thus I have to say that humankind *might* have made political progress, but had in fact made none. Or we might discover that the mastery of social life was not a stable enough goal to sustain an analysis in terms of progress, a difficulty that one might think affects both Marxism and Dewey's pragmatism. Not merely might problems accumulate faster than solutions, the nature of the goal itself might change faster than we could adapt.

It is not always a question of the goal retreating faster than our technique can match. The mastery of human life by intelligent social action is something to which much more than administrative technique, communications technology, and similar factors are relevant. One such factor is the amenability of human beings to the social control they impose on themselves. If the record of history were that they became steadily more recalcitrant, a record that might in principle be one of progression would be one of increasing chaos; we might not know whether to say we had made no *political* progress or to say that it was not so much our politics as human nature that was to blame, but we certainly would want to talk of retrogression. Alternatively, humankind might become more amenable, but in the fashion of Huxley's *Brave New World*. Then we should have to say that this was not an advance after all, because the "problem" now solved was not the problem we began with—roughly, we had hoped to achieve a social order that allowed individual liberty and spontaneity the maximum scope and had gotten a social order that had simply extirpated what we had hoped to channel, but not to renounce.

Since the concept of progress is a modern one, I will make the argument concrete by appealing to a writer who was self-consciously at odds with his classical forebears and who combined a belief in the possibility of progress with a satisfyingly grim view of the difficulty of achieving it. Hobbes is commonly thought of as a writer who is only concerned to fend off evils, and many readers suppose that his wonderful description of the "naturall condition of men" as "poore, solitary, nasty, brutish, and short" must logically issue in a vision of politics as wholly concerned to fend off the war of all against all. This is infinitely far from the truth. The object of government is "commodious living," and Hobbes's conception of the commodiousness that this entails is suggested by the list he gives of the evils of the state of nature; fear of sudden and violent death is "worst of all," but they include the absence of arts and sciences, the ignorance of the face of the earth and the heavens that a savage society must suffer, and the absence of the life of friendship and intellectual companionship that Hobbes himself so much enjoyed. What we want the state to promote is not just bodily security, but all the goods of associated living.

To say that Hobbes believed in *political* progress is to lay oneself open to any number of assaults. It seems clear that Hobbes thought the people of his own day were peculiarly prone to several sorts of folly—religious enthusiasm, an undue attachment to the political ideals of the Greeks and Romans, a superstitious reverence for the common law, and much else besides. To speak of any sort of progress against this background might seem strange. Add to that Hobbes's desire to permanently bolt in place a stable political order, and surely we have to place him in the same rank as Plato, who also wanted to keep the renovated republic out of change's way. All this must be admitted. Still, it is not decisive. Hobbes thought we must get right once and for all a proper understanding of the nature of the state, authority and legitimacy; all else was prudence and had to be adjusted to the times and their needs. I imagine that in a different political climate than that of the Restoration, Hobbes would have acknowledged that institutions could be improved along with everything else. I have argued elsewhere that Hobbes's political theory is extraordinarily individualistic. This individualism went very deep; Hobbes thought that all people needed from government was protection from the violence and economic exploitation of others and the provision of legal and similar services to help them achieve a "commodious living" by their own efforts. People did not need their soul saving by the state, nor did they need help in framing a conception of the good life. Humankind did not get into trouble harmlessly going about the business of earning a living. Merchants might not be admirable—they drove down the wages of the poor, and they had supported the parliamentary forces in the civil war—but the business of providing a commodious living could be carried on without much risk of social and political upheaval once humankind was secured against the risks of sudden and violent death. Hobbes shared Bacon's belief that the advancement of learning was the route to human happiness; one of the blessings of political peace was the shelter it offered to science, and Hobbes was sufficiently practical-minded to be aware that one of the blessings of science was its payoff in terms of earthly comfort as well as its "higher" payoff in terms of the elevation of our intellects above those of the brutes.

This frame of mind amounts to a belief in progress. The prime motor was intellectual change and its great benefit the way it spilled over into psychological and religious attitudes. Thus, if we understand the nature of sovereignty, we see that what we need from government is shelter from harm rather than a shelter from unorthodoxy; when we do this, we make it possible for governments to practice toleration by way of benign neglect—leaving each person to follow Paul or Caiaphas as he or she thinks best. When people cease to think that they have a *right* to take part in government, governments will more easily be able to seek out the advice and assistance they need, unflustered by the fear that the next step will be insurrection. When people have plenty of outlets for their intellectual curiosity and their need for friendship and an active social life, they will be less apt to swallow the nonsense of religious fanatics and so become more amenable to government, more able to look after most of their lives for themselves, less likely to invade their neighbors for ideological reasons or for gain—in short, more able to sustain both political progress and general social progress.

This is a minimalist model of political progress, in the sense that it looks less to progress in political arrangements than to political arrangements as a shelter for economic, intellectual, and moral progress. It is certainly a model of social progress, not a model of once-and-for-all attainment of a moderate but adequate human good, let alone a Platonic blueprint for a timeless and stationary perfection. Hobbes takes it for granted that the restless human mind will continue as in the past to run all over the universe, guessing and speculating about the first and subsidiary causes of things. Given peace and stability, these speculations can be turned away from anxiety and neurotic fears and toward their proper task, the improving of the human estate. And since there is no summum bonum, no repose short of death, we may cheerfully look to "continually prospering" and expanding our horizons of what to count as prosperity as we do so. As all his contemporaries complained so long and so loudly, Hobbes was utterly unwilling to look backward, to test his own views by the authority of past writers, and to constrain what people might now discover by the sacred scriptures of the past. He was a forward-looking writer. All commentators observe the discrepancy between Hobbes's emphasis on fear as the political motive to rely on and the boldness (not to say bravado) he displayed in his own intellectual activity. There is, however, no contradiction in this, though there is an agreeable rhetorical tension. The fear Hobbes wished his readers to remember is only a fear of sudden and violent death, and of those things that might be its precursors—robbery, riot, dissension over questions of legitimacy; he had no anxieties about the effects of the search for truth. Indeed, he was entirely convinced that the search for truth, honestly undertaken, was a great prop to peace, though less convinced that it would always be honestly undertaken rather than studied for the interests of those who undertook it.

It is otiose to show the same temper in other seventeenth- and eighteenth-century writers. Certainly, they cautiously balanced hopes for improvement in our earthly lot against their conviction that our ultimate good was to be found in the next world rather than this and their conviction that original sin, however it might be explained, was a striking feature of human nature to be reckoned with in any project for the advancement of human welfare. No student of Locke needs to be reminded of the way Locke's rhetoric in his *Two Treatises of Government* vacillates between suggesting that human beings might govern themselves quite satisfactorily in the absence of parliaments, monarchs, judges, and all the usual apparatus, merely by attending to the law of nature, and suggesting that people are for the most part no nice observers of the law and will behave badly unless restrained by something stronger than conscience and the amateur enforcement system of the law of nature. More interesting, perhaps, is the tension between the acceptance of the Stoic thought that humankind had left a golden age in which wants were few, passions moderate, gold and silver unknown, greed, envy, and selfishness therefore unknown, too, and a much more modern cheerfulness about the benefits as well as the problems of life in commercial society.

Mandeville satirized the gloomy virtue of the Roman Republic and its latter-day admirers in his *Fable of the Bees,* and Burke poked fun at Bolingbroke in his *Vindication of Natural Society,* but there was almost always an uneasy undercurrent to the defense of the modern world. I say "almost" because I find it hard to discern such an undercurrent in Hume, a Tory in politics who was perfectly at ease looking forward rather than backward, toward a society in which the brisk march of the spirits had abolished superstition, in which a moderate Anglicanism would give the lower classes an appropriate confidence in their society and its acceptability to the supreme management of the universe, but the "friar, the stake and the gibbet" of Roman Catholicism was as unknown as the wild enthusiasm of the Protestant sectaries. Hume had his political anxieties, to be sure; order was never guaranteed, there was always some risk of revolt from below or an overstepping of the bounds by the forces of Parliament, and he did not flinch from saying that if the British political system could not maintain its delicate balance between absolute monarchy and popular republic, he would rather see it fall toward Louis XV than Oliver Cromwell. It would not do to overstate Hume's liberalism, nor to make him a friend of the twentieth century's conception of human rights, with all that that entails about popular participation in electoral politics and governmental accountability to a democratic electorate. But, he did not share Ferguson's sympathy for the wild and obsolete races of the world—the Scythians and the Tartars as well as the Spartans and the eighteenth-century Highlanders. He had little sense of the incommensurability of different societies, different political arrangements, different gods, and different ways of life, and he was less anxious than we about the impossibility of drawing an unequivocal balance sheet of the gains and losses of urbanity.

I think that Hume was guilty of some failure of imagination because I have always been moved by the writer who is above all responsible for our sense that every silver lining has a cloud, namely Rousseau. Rousseau's first discourse on the arts and sciences was a not unconventional diatribe against modern vice and might have been written by a much lesser thinker than he. One can see in his replies to his critics, however, that once committed to the misanthropic cause, he was determined to make it his own and to lavish upon it all his rhetorical and analytical resources. His *Discourse on the Origins of Inequality* did what his earlier essay did not try to do, in the process becoming so long that the judges at Dijon refused to read it. The second discourse laid out a sketch of human history in which every gain to human intelligence, ingenuity, and sensibility was bought at an appalling price. The human beings with whom the *Discourse* commences are, Rousseau says, hardly more than intelligent great apes—orangutans—but in that hardly lies all the difference. They can learn from experience and pass the experience to their offspring. An animal is the same at six months and at the end of its life; the species is the same at the end of a millennium as at the beginning. Not so us. We change dramatically through our extended childhood and adolescence; and even in adult life our tastes and interests are exceedingly changeable. As for the species, there is hardly anything in common between Louis XV and the leader of a band of aboriginals beyond their barest physical qualities.

Human beings constituted with nothing but what nature gives them, in the true state of nature, are harmless to themselves and each other. Nature prompts them to avoid what is harmful and seek what does them good. They eat and drink simply, sleep soundly, and have no anxieties. Indeed, they cannot have the anxieties we have; being without language and reason, they are without a sense of time and so cannot consider their own mortality. Like other animals, they may feel intense fear and perhaps intense pain, but they will not remember them once they are over and will not find their lives dominated by apprehension. In particular, they cannot fear their own extinction. Moreover, they cannot feel the kinds of misery we feel—the nagging sense of inferiority to others, that we are sexually unattractive, that we are not sought out by others to make friends. These harmless creatures share our basic impulses; they need food, drink, sexual pleasure, and shelter. These impulses do not set them at odds with one another, nor do they provide the basis of society. The first family groups would have consisted of mothers and their infants; inarticulate copulation followed only at such a long interval by its consequences could hardly hold a family together, and women would have had no need of men for protection in a world with so few dangers. What keeps the peace is the two emotions of *amour de soi* and *pitié*. These are not what we would call "self-love" and "pity," because they are too uncomplicated and have no moral overtones; they are more nearly a disposition to flee what damages ourselves and an uneasiness at the suffering of another creature of the same species. They are enough to make the Rousseauian state of nature quite other than the Hobbesian state. There might be occasional squabbles over food, drink, sex, whatever took our fancy, and it might be that these would occasionally get out of hand; fundamentally, our condition would be peaceful because we would lack the imaginative resources to get into trouble.

The invention of language, followed by the creation of simple societies, followed by the invention of property, followed—or accompanied by—the discovery of agriculture is the sequence by which human beings are civilized and ruined. Language allows us to reason, to compare ourselves with others, to consider our lives as a whole. We become capable of morality at the same time that we become less ready to accept its dictates. Whereas we once had simple wants adapted to our needs, we now consider that we have rights; we begin to assess ourselves, to inquire how well we are doing. Now we can envy others, think poorly of ourselves, suffer all the slights of social failure.

Rousseau's essay is directly relevant to political progress in the sense that it sets out to show how the simplest, savage condition yields gradually to an increasingly settled state, and then with the first person who thinks of enclosing a piece of ground and saying "this is mine" to a society where property in the land needs government to sustain it. Although Engels admired the *Discourse* and thought it a precursor of historical materialism, the essence of Rousseau's diagnosis is psychological rather than economic; the tension between rich and poor is a tension of esteem rather than merely of access to commodities. Material inequalities are of interest because of the fantastical social conflicts that can be erected on the basis of economic disparities; and it is the former rather than the latter that cause the miseries that assail us in civilized society. The true heir of Rousseau in this particular is not Engels but Freud. Rousseau's conception of what has happened in history is therefore multiply at odds with Hobbes's optimistic picture.

This is not simply a matter of their differing assessments of the state of nature—"nasty, brutish and short" in Hobbes, tranquil, timeless, mindless, balanced, and well adjusted in Rousseau (and especially in Rousseau as understood by Durkheim)—and the obvious covert implication that almost any social and political order is an improvement over Hobbes's state of nature, while only savage society and austere republics score highly with Rousseau. It is, rather, that where Hobbes saw progress, Rousseau saw degeneration: Hobbes's citizenry were to concentrate hard on what they *really* needed from their governments, namely security against private ill will and an efficient civil law system, and with that taken care of, they were to get on with life as they saw fit. For Rousseau this was a hopeless aspiration. We do not know what we want, at any rate not once we are civilized and therefore chronically on the verge of incoherence. We need the moral reassurance that a compact and coherent social and moral order provides, less the reassurance that we shall get what we want than reassurance that what we want is what we *ought* to want. To achieve this, the politics of a privatized society such as Hobbes admires will not do at all; citizen engagement is part and parcel of the process of turning ourselves outward to stabilize our inward selves. To become richer but more anxious, to live longer but more boringly, to live under benign but uninteresting governments is no sort of progress.

How this strikes one is partly a matter of temperament. While it is not true that we are born Hobbesians or Rousseauians in quite the way that Gilbert and Sullivan's *Iolanthe* claimed that "every little boy and girl that's born into this world alive / is either a little Liberal or else a little Conservative," there is something to be said for the thought that only those of us who spend our lives trying to do justice to as many political theoretical perspectives as possible can remain neutral between them: the "sanguino-choleric" types will side with Hobbes and laugh off Rousseau's deep misery, while the Rousseauians will think that the Hobbesians are too coarse-grained and too vulgar to feel the sentiments that Rousseau depicts. Though an appeal to the spleen and stomach is not merely not an argument but a positive assault upon the whole idea of conducting an argument on the ends of life in the first place, we might in this case allow temperament a small say in its own defense. The familiar observation that different people will see the glass as half-full or half-empty has in the past twenty-five years mattered to political philosophers. Innumerable critics have pointed out, for instance, that John Rawls's *A Theory of Justice* is vulnerable to the charge that its view of politics is absurdly defensive. Needless fear underlies and therefore undermines its analysis of political liberty. The concentration on the fate of the least-advantaged member of society that underlies its analysis of distributive justice reflects an excessive aversion to risk. Since we can know nothing of the psyches of those who contract behind the "veil of ignorance," they being figments of our theoretical imagination, the question is whether it is reasonable to think of them as driven by fear of disaster rather than hope of gain. Many critics have complained that it is not. Cheerier contractors might have opted for something more democratic and less restrictively constitutionalist, more of an economic free-for-all, where the winners got really fat prizes.

Some view about the degree of optimism with which it is reasonable to face life appears to be a rather important, though underdiscussed, ingredient in most political theorizing, and one might reasonably debate the question whether Hobbes was not too frightened of violence and insufficiently frightened of alienation or anomie, while Rousseau was too frightened of psychological distress, too unappreciative of the pleasures of the modern world, too quick to deny that we had gained at least as much as we had lost in living in "commercial society" rather than the virtuous republic of his imagining. This response does not settle the question whether we have made political progress where a particular stress falls on the word *political*. It is a reply that opens the door to the thought that *politics* is a systematically equivocal term and that we might well think that we have two noncomparable dimensions of assessment at stake. Along one, we would assess politics in terms of the opportunities it offers for political engagement, for people to experience the pleasures and hazards of citizenship, and its success in achieving "the liberty of the ancients." Along the other we would assess politics in terms of the lawfulness and orderliness of the conduct of government, its success in allowing the people at large to get on with their lives, to make a living, to worship as they choose, to attend whatever forms of education seem good to them, and its success in achieving "the liberty of the moderns." Hobbes thought that the liberty of the ancients was so much confusion, and the belief that the legitimacy of a government has something to do with its form was one source of the chaos and misery of the civil wars, the gentlemanly classes having been corrupted by their reading of the classics. Hobbes, therefore, was not in the least inclined to think that there had been loss as well as gain. Writers of a not dissimilar temper, such as Ferguson and Smith, were prepared to concede that the small, tough city-states of the ancient world had virtues that the modern world was short of, and they worried that modern people might be too self-centered, too attached to the pleasures of everyday life, to display the loyalty, public spirit, and willingness to go and fight for their country that Spartans, Athenians, and Romans had. This was partly a reflection of the fact that for many people, life in the modern world had more to offer and was not to be put at risk frivolously or merely for the sake of bella figura.

But the writer who encapsulated the thought most exactly was Benjamin Constant in his "Essai sur la liberté des anciens comparée à celle des modernes." The cleverness of Constant's essay was that it addressed the right issue—why we feel nostalgia for the politics of antiquity while being perfectly aware that we cannot recreate them in the modern world. The French Revolution had demonstrated once and for ever that you could not recreate the Roman Republic by dressing 1790s Parisians in togas. This was a great deal more delicately done than Burke's denunciations of the revolutionaries' rationalism, atheism, and antitraditionalism. Burke treated the revolutionaries as more-or-less mad, guilty of hubris and inviting the fate proper to their crime, almost unspeakably arrogant in their readiness to embark on the kind of social remodeling that God alone was entitled to engage in. Constant's cooler approach allowed him to steer a delicately drawn line between the revolutionaries and their enemies. They had not been mad, but they had been wrong. They had been wrong because their ideals were inapt to the modern world. This was not to deny the attractions of their ideals, only their viability as the basis of a life for modern people. The liberty enjoyed in the ancient city-states was real liberty, and Rousseau's account of it as a distinctively political liberty was to that extent right; but it had come at a price that nobody could seriously propose a modern society should pay. It was exclusively male; it shut out not only women, but also most of the people we would now call lower middle class; it was, if not xenophobic, at least founded on the idea that foreign residents were properly to be shut out of local politics. It demanded a degree of interest in politics that was probably not appropriate to all societies and in the ancient world at least had required the support of a substantial slave population to allow the citizenry the leisure to spend their time in the agora. Finally, it was a politics built around more-or-less continuous warfare. Politics bulked so large because it was a life-and-death business in the most literal sense. Archaic societies did not have much sense that mercy and self-restraint were qualities to be esteemed in the victor—on the whole, the thought seemed rather to be that it was sensible to spare those who might be ransomed or sold as slaves, and otherwise anything went. Constant did not pile on the agony, but suggested that one reason why the Greeks and the other ancients generally had set such a high value on fights, games, and debates was that life in the ancient world was fundamentally very boring.

This enabled him to answer Rousseau, not so much by denying Rousseau's complaints or by shrugging his shoulders at Rousseau's neuroses as by accepting that there was a radical discontinuity between one form of social and political life and the other and going on to say that *we* cannot on reflection see the change as other than progress. In what is it progress? That is a hard question, and I have deliberately made it harder by admitting at the outset that the disjunction of lifestyles, like the disjunction of aesthetic aims in artistic creation, may make it almost impossible to rank one production—or one way of life—unequivocally an improvement over the other. My reply is that there is no conclusive demonstration that we have made progress, and there is no way of persuading the recalcitrant such as the Nietzsche of *The Genealogy of Morals* that they are just wrong. What we can do is proceed forensically or dialectically, not quite saying, as Richard Rorty suggests we might, that our opponents are "mad," but certainly being willing to say that they will be isolated, and that they will find themselves sabotaged by their own views. It is, in the modern world, an implausible project to live among women while holding Rousseau's political beliefs; women believe that they are entitled to the full rights and duties of citizenship and that these include the right to pursue their own careers, to share equally in making decisions about their families, and to enjoy all the obvious corollaries of modern citizenship such as the chance to run for office, join political pressure groups, take part in union activities, and all the rest of it.

To live among them—and what goes for women goes for male manual workers, too—while still cleaving to a view of politics that shuts them out and a view of their nature that implies in the case of women their subordination within the family and in the case of women and the working class alike their isolation from the public realm generally may not be absolutely impossible; but it will be exceedingly difficult for anyone to take your views seriously and exceedingly difficult for you to engage in ordinary human relations with people who cannot but think that you are utterly eccentric and misguided. I do not mean that there can be no valuable purpose served by attempting to live like this, nor that the passion for ancient liberty cannot still contain many grains of truth. We may try to make real to ourselves the intellectual universe of the ancients by a sort of playacting. More importantly, we may get a critical purchase on the shortcomings of late-twentieth-century politics by emphasizing the contrast between what the ancients refused to extend to women, foreigners, slaves, and lower-class men, and what we have offered them. To extend the vote is not nothing, but it is not the experience of debate and decision making in the Athenian *agora;* to extend the chance to join trade unions, pressure groups, and political action committees is not nothing, but it is not the same as offering an equal chance to be selected by lot to serve on the committee that sends the young out to fight or negotiates with our neighboring state's leaders. What we have extended to previously excluded groups is not the citizenship of the ancients, and what we have given them is in some crucial ways thin stuff by comparison with what all of us have lost. Nonetheless, the believer in a sort of progress will still want to say that what we have extended to everyone is one sort of citizenship and that the fact of its extension casts doubt on the underlying premises of the old conception, that is, the belief in the natural incapacity of women as well as certain classes and races for political life as such.

The contrast between modern politics and the politics of the ancient or medieval world is not so sharp as the contrast between our and their technology, therein included such dubious technologies as the capacity to wage total war. The same must be said about the contrast between the tragedies of Sophocles and Aeschylus and the plays of anyone whomever. What is perhaps worth insisting on is that there have been genuine inventions and discoveries in the political realm, but we are so used to them that we do not notice them. Modern political representation is one such. Madison and James Mill both knew that it was something that set modern politics apart from anything before; it allowed the many to take part in politics without the dangers of mob rule and despotism that Plato and Aristotle had feared, and allowed what one might call a graduated participation in politics to all who sought it. Here was a way of combining the benefits of democracy and aristocracy without resorting to the implausibilities of the theory of the mixed constitution. Again, for all that Aristotle wrote that laws, not men, should rule, he had no real conception of what that might mean in a large and complex society, for he had no inkling of the modern understanding of law. We know, if partly because we have seen what happens when the rule of law fails as it does under totalitarian regimes and under the petty dictatorships with which the world is still, repulsively, littered. It is, however, progress to understand what protection the law can in principle offer and to have aspired to make its protection universal. In the same way, the United Nations falls far short of what we hope from it, but it still marks an extraordinary leap forward in political aspiration. It is the first attempt in human history to institutionalize the thought that a government may fail to answer to its own people but must still in some fashion answer to the opinion of humankind at large.

To acknowledge that none of this will persuade the unpersuaded is to recognize that several retorts are open to the friends of ancient liberty. One is that nothing in the modern world can compensate for the loss of whatever it was that the Athenian citizen felt for his city. I do not see what room there is for argument at this point. Some middle-aged persons lament their lost youth and remain inconsolable; talk of "growing up" and "maturity" means nothing to them. Another is that although the rule of law, constitutional government, uncorrupt and public-spirited administration, and all those other good things that early nineteenth-century progressives wished for are undeniably good things in themselves, yet their achievement is patchy, imperfect, constantly being undermined by corruption, nepotism, fanaticism, nationalist fervor, and other ills that appeal to our desire for short-term excitement or to our taste for unkindness to out-groups.

This, though, is not a conceptual or philosophical anxiety about the possibility of progress; it is a gloomy first-order judgment about the sheer intractability of the world. We may well admit that improvement is slower and more patchy than we should like without rejecting the thought that improvement is an intelligible and a proper goal. We may also refuse to be gloomy; the world may well be in a terrible state and susceptible of improvement, too. Wherever there has been a fair competition between the progressives and their opponents, the progressives have won; wherever the soil is moderately propitious, progressivism takes root. Failures and setbacks are seen to be failures and setbacks. Even such long-drawn-out attempts to avoid joining the modern world as that which the Iranian Islamic Republic has engaged in for 15 years erode as soon as normality returns. Only a regime of constant war or the threat of it enables any substantial regime to resist the slow filtering of liberal democracy into its people's consciousness. (Sufficiently small societies seem to be a law unto themselves.) Regimes that exist on a constant war footing have some obvious self-limiting features, too. No doubt all this has to be said with fingers crossed, and no doubt we have to acknowledge Marx's familiar point that humanity has sleepwalked its way to its future. But that is how political progress has thus far been made; its untidy and unplanned character may make our celebrations less exuberant, but it should not drive the very concept of progress out of our lexicon.

# Feminist Views of Progress

*Jill Ker Conway*


In western feminist speculation about the ideal shape of society, the idea of progress has taken five distinct forms. Two of these dreams of progress emerge in the transition from the early modern period to the dominant rational mode of thought associated with the Age of Reason. A third took its inspiration from the characteristically optimistic assessment of the likely outcomes of nineteenth-century technological change, which made the Victorian era so uncritically confident about the future improvement of white European society. The fourth took shape in the early twentieth century when those concerned with the advancement of women developed inflated expectations arising from scientific advances in the understanding of the human reproductive system. The fifth, emerging in the 1960s, rested upon revolutionary expectations about the possibility of remodeling hitherto accepted sex-role behaviors, behaviors seen in that heady era as part and parcel of European white male hegemony, about to be dismantled by the national revolutions of former colonial societies.

Dreams about an ideal future, when women and men would occupy equal positions in society, are the driving force of feminist thought. This source of energy has been sustained, even in the face of postmodern skepticism about linear development in history, though now in a form that asserts that increasing women's political and social authority will arrest cataclysmic environmental or military events. Thus, in their current form, feminist ideas about the future are more concerned with arresting decline than with future improvement. While postmodern skepticism is attractive for members of elites whose status is deteriorating, many women reformers, even in the late twentieth century, still hope for some form of improvement in women's position, whether by reducing the rates of violence against women in contemporary society or by bringing about a more just economic order that allows women to secure more of the product of their labor. To this extent, though they might now disavow much of the Enlightenment view of history in which the exercise of human reason was expected to result in cumulative social improvement, some feminists today still retain a belief in the possible improvement of women's social status, even while entertaining apocalyptic visions of environmental disaster for the planet.

As was characteristic of early modern mentalities, feminists in early modern society tended to look backward to an imagined golden era of the past, while strenuously advocating improvement in the present. One of the most articulate exponents of women's concerns, Christine de Pizan (1365–1430) was inspired by the dissonance between her life experience, as a widowed head of a family, consumed by genuine mourning for her lost husband, and the standard view of the female in the tradition of courtly romance, a view that characterized all women as faithless and inconstant. Christine de Pizan knew that she, as a chaste widow, was accorded none of the vaunted courtesies of the romantic tradition and that she had to fight for her own and her children's rights, without any male protector. In her writing she looked back to a golden age, during which women had possessed self-rule and had managed their own communities of learning—an echo of the myth of the Amazon kingdom, a recurring theme in feminist thought until the nineteenth century. In her "City of Ladies," women govern themselves, cultivate knowledge, and speculate about a better world where women can retreat from society to establish their own community of learning.[1] We may classify Christine De Pizan as seeking improvement in women's condition by disproving mysogynist views about them and by advocating improvements in women's education so that they could become more informed contenders for their rights to property and status. Not surprisingly, she saw Joan of Arc as her ideal of the strong woman, possessor of all the chivalric virtues, and defender of her nation.

The expectation that women could gain equality alongside men (in contrast to the medieval idea, open to few women, of securing equality through withdrawing from the world of men) emerged during the Enlightenment when the assumed universality of human reason was seen as a justification for dismantling hereditary rank and hierarchy associated with gender. The sources of Enlightenment feminism were twofold. Religious skepticism made the philosophes reject the idea that all women were inheritors of Eve's sin. The importance placed on human powers of reason led Enlightenment figures such as Condorcet (1743–94) or French Revolutionary leaders such as Olympe de Gouges (?–1793) to conclude that women's powers of reason were the same as men's and, therefore, that education and the exercise of political rights could, within a very short time, be expected to elevate women to a position of equality with men. Olympe de Gouges's *The Rights of Women* (1791) claimed full citizenship for women in legal, political, and social arenas and anticipated the arrival of a just society of equality based on reason and natural law. A strong critic of the institution of marriage, she advocated a much looser and more easily terminated contract between male and female partners, together with

---

1. Christine de Pizan, *The Book of the City of Ladies,* trans. Earl Jeffrey Richards (New York, 1982); and Charity Cannon Willard, *Christine de Pizan: Her Life and Works* (New York, 1984).

common responsibilities for the care of children. She expected these changes to remove any of the existing disabilities of women as mothers and to produce significant improvement in the lives of children.[2] Olympe de Gouges, an actress and independent figure in the Parisian demimonde, ended her life, as did so many French feminists of the Revolutionary era, on the guillotine. But her ideas were to be taken up again and again by Western feminist proponents of the belief that women and men were the same in their capacity for human reason and should therefore receive the same political rights and the same access to productive labor.

The popular response to Enlightenment skepticism and the violence of the French Revolution was a heightened acceptance of emotional religion, accompanied by an increased respect for what were seen stereotypically as the more emotional religious responses of women. These qualities became progressively more highly valued in the late eighteenth and early nineteenth centuries, until the emphasis on women's emotional religiosity became seen as a source of progress. At the extreme of religious enthusiasm, the millennial sects of the Rhine Valley and early industrial England developed a conviction either that the second coming was at hand or that it had already occurred. In either case, believers were convinced that women were freed from the sin of Eve and that the day was at hand when Christ would be "one in all his males and females."

Since reproductive life loses significance for those preparing for the end of the world, most millennial groups practiced sexual continence, thereby relieving women of the demands of child rearing. Thus, the British Mother Ann Lee became the founder of the Shaker faith in the 1770s and was accepted by her followers as the risen Christ.[3] The Shaker belief in the equality of women resulted in the development of a broad range of domestic labor-saving devices and a striking simplification of diet and dress so that women and men would each be able to devote equal amounts of time to prayer and religious celebration. Since the Shakers expected a perfected world to emerge under female leadership, their communitarian arrangements were always designed to foster the appropriate equality so that the pace of progress would not be hindered. Yet, we should see their attitudes as backward looking, in the sense that all these efforts at securing equality were in preparation for a millennium, albeit one in which human transcendence would be embodied in both female and male forms. It is chastening to reflect that all underground resistance movements, like millennial sects, appear to grant equality to women because, facing

---

2. Olympe de Gouges, *The Rights of Women* (Paris, 1791).

3. J. Tallcott, Jr., and J. Deming, Jr., *Testimonies of the Life, Character, Revelations and Doctrines of Our Ever Blessed Mother Ann Lee, and the Elders with Her* (Hancock, Mass., 1816). See also Edward Deming Andrews, *The People Called Shakers: A Search for the Perfect Society* (New York, 1963); Edward Deming Andrews and Faith Andrews, *Work and Worship among the Shakers: Their Craftsmanship and Economic Order* (New York, 1982).

total annihilation in the event of failure, reproductive life essentially ceases to claim significant social priority.

The Oneida Community, established in upper New York State in the 1840s, based its religious faith and sexual arrangements on the idea that the Second Coming had already taken place and that, as a consequence, women were freed from the sin of Eve. The community expected progress to occur through eradicating pair bonding in marriage, placing reproductive life under community control, and developing the physical strength and intellectual capacities of female as well as male members. Complex birth control arrangements allowed for what the community called group marriage, with community responsibility for the raising and rearing of all offspring so conceived. Within the framework of religious rhetoric used to legitimize these arrangements, we may see the Oneidans as early practitioners of the idea that women's progress toward equality can best be achieved through controls on fertility, collective responsibility for child care, and a psychological transformation that eradicates the idea that either sex partner has emotional property in the other. Like the Shakers, the Oneidans simplified dress and diet, with the objective of freeing women's time for study and leisure.[4] The driving force behind the Oneidans' rearrangement of sexual and reproductive life was an early technological utopianism, inspired by the belief that neither physical work nor reproductive work required the subordination of women in a world where machines could simplify agricultural work and human artifice could regulate conception. Unlike the Benthamite technocrats of early industrialization, the Oneidans saw the machine as freeing the human spirit and intellect, rather than as a model to which human beings should approximate.

Throughout the late eighteenth and early nineteenth centuries, technological change was most readily apparent to social observers through the use made of the labor of women and children in the early stages of industrialization. Thus Robert Owen's textile factory, established at New Lanark, Scotland, in the 1780s, used women and children to tend mechanical looms. It was accompanied by a model village in which women and their children had access to education and were housed in more sanitary and substantial dwellings than had been their lot in rural life. For Owen, human beings were "vital machines" with "curious mechanism" and "self-adjusting powers." What they needed to develop their full potential was a "proper main spring," a source of motion, which Owen proposed to provide through universal education.[5] He thought women and children particular sufferers because of the nature of the family and the current system of property, and he believed that modern technology, with

---

4. John Humphrey Noyes, *History of American Socialisms* (New York, 1961).

5. Robert Owen, *Thoughts on the Connection Between Universal Happiness and Practical Mechanics* (London, 1795).

its capacity to provide useful work for women and children, could be the engine of their improvement.[6] The spectacle of the massed labor of women and children accomplishing tasks in which their strength was enhanced by mechanical means convinced many social theorists—Comte (1798–1857) and St. Simon (1760–1825) in France as well as Owen (1771–1858) in England—and the founders of the Oneida community in the United States that a new era was dawning in which women, freed from the consequences of their lesser physical strength, would equal men in productivity and hence in political and social rights. These expectations were intensified by demographic change, as the opening of new territories for settlement attracted single males from Great Britain and the eastern coast of North America to new cheap land. The excess of women of marriageable age left behind fostered broad social concern for women's independence, leading to the founding of schools, and later colleges, for women. These, mostly religious in inspiration, inspired further dreams of unbounded moral progress, based upon the enhanced influence of educated women.[7]

The implications of technological change were elaborated in the second half of the nineteenth century by evolutionary thinkers, who, along with the French utopian socialists and Marx, concluded that machine production would lead to the social and political elevation of women, because machines could equalize the strength of the sexes, and the factory system offered respectable work outside the home and gave women the chance to participate, like men, in the paid labor force.

Technological change fed the most utopian thinking of late-nineteenth-century feminists, such as Patrick Geddes (1854–1932) in England[8] and Jane Addams[9] (1860–1935) in the United States. They were inspired by a vision of industrial societies as bourgeois and commercial in nature and therefore peaceloving in the interests of commerce. Unlike Thorstein Veblen or Charlotte Perkins Gilman, two contemporary evolutionary theorists of society who saw the potential for consumerism and ritual consumption in industrial plenty, Geddes and Addams believed that the imperative of technology and commerce would remove all the political disabilities inherited by women from warlike feudal society and

---

6. See Sidney Pollard and John Salt, *Robert Owen, Prophet of the Poor: Essays in Honour of the Two Hundredth Anniversary of His Birth* (London, 1971). See also J. F. C. Harrison, *Quest for the New Moral World: Robert Owen and the Owenites in Britain and America* (New York, 1969).

7. A good introduction to these trends can be found in Elizabeth K. Helsinger, *The Woman Question: Society and Literature in Britain and America, 1837–1883* (New York, 1983).

8. See Philip L. Boardman, *Patrick Geddes, Maker of the Future* (Chapel Hill, N.C., 1944); and Patrick Geddes, *The Evolution of Sex* (London, 1903).

9. See Jane Addams, *Democracy and Social Ethics* (New York, 1902), and *Newer Ideals of Peace* (New York, 1907).

would permit them to emerge as leaders in societies of balanced and peaceful consumption. This viewpoint lost all credibility during the carnage of World War I (1914–18), when social thinkers first understood modern technology as an enhancement for militarism and a new force for mass destruction.

While the nation-states of Europe were amassing the weapons with which to fight the war, developments in the biological sciences made it possible, for the first time, for researchers to begin work on understanding the inheritance of characteristics. Early in the twentieth century, research in biology began to highlight the importance of the human endocrine system, leading in the 1930s to better understanding of the cyclical nature of ovulation.[10]

Concurrent with this research, but unrelated to it, was a popular movement aimed at making available current medical knowledge on birth control techniques for the industrial working classes. The diaphragm, available to middle-class women in the late nineteenth century, increased in reliability as the technology of rubber production improved, but cost and the necessity for expert training in its use limited its availability. One of the dynamizing images of the popular birth control agitation was the idea that women, free to control their own fertility, could make child bearing and child rearing a chosen, rather than forced, occupation and that they, like men, might enjoy sex for pleasure.[11] Thus technology was presenting a practical counterpart to the millennial religious idea of freeing women from the sin of Eve, though women's new existence was to be lived in a world of arms races rather than peaceable commercial societies. Because of the new emphasis on military uses of technology, the potential for the machine to eliminate the significance of male-female differentials in physical strength was replaced by the stress on technologies of warfare and the persistence of taboos about female participation in military conflict. These led to a greater cultural stress on male-female differences even as technology presented the potential for removing the major physical differentials and for allowing the control of conception.

The popular birth control agitation was unsuccessful in the early twentieth century because of the appropriation of distribution of birth control information by the predominantly male medical profession and because of religious opposition to the widespread dissemination of birth control information.[12] This

---

10. See Paul Robinson, *The Modernization of Sex: Havelock Ellis, Alfred Kinsey, William Masters and Virginia Johnson* (New York, 1976); and Eleanor E. Maccoby and Carol N. Jacklin, *The Psychology of Sex Differences* (Stanford, Calif., 1976).

11. Linda Gordon, *Woman's Body, Woman's Right: A Social History of Birth Control in America* (New York, 1976).

12. See G. J. Barker-Benfield, *The Horrors of a Half-Known Life: Male Attitudes Toward Women and Sexuality in Nineteenth Century America* (New York, 1976); and Ruth Hubbard, Mary Sue Henifen, and Barbara Fried, eds., *Women Looking at Biology Looking at Women* (Cambridge, Mass., 1977).

opposition was expressed in legislation limiting the use of the mails for dissemination, diverting attention from women's rights to control their bodies to the legal battle for freedom of information. Success, when it came in the 1930s, came purely on the matter of freedom to use the mails, without further attention to mass distribution and education.

In the 1960s, two developments temporarily interrupted the trend toward cultural emphasis on male-female difference. The world population explosion, fueled by the capacity to sustain larger populations achieved during the early stages of the so-called "green revolution," led to the ideal of zero population growth in industrialized societies and thus changed attitudes concerning the significance of child bearing in the total span of a woman's life. Concurrently, priorities placed upon easily distributed and readily available forms of control of conception led to the development of new technologies for the manipulation of female fertility. The appropriation of birth control by the male medical profession and medical research community meant that interventions in the female endocrine system (rather than in the male) were the focus of study and that tests of the new technologies were initially carried out on female populations in third world countries. "The Pill," when first available for widespread use in the developed world, unleashed millennial expectations not unlike those of the early birth control movement. Here was a supposedly "safe" technique, usable with no expertise, controllable by women. In this context, the feminist movement of the 1970s was born, emphasizing the importance of work in women's lives and stressing their ability to compete on equal terms with men in all areas of work. The expectation that equality could be readily achieved was based upon the notion that male biases against working with women could be easily eliminated and that Western-style marriage, based upon romantic ideals of love, ideals in which "conquest" and "surrender" were central, could be easily adapted to equal partnership. These changes, so confidently expected, were thought of as simple preliminaries to an era of undreamed-of progress and freedom for women.[13]

If we ask what were the actual social consequences of these five ideologies, the answers are complex, often defying definitive evaluation.

The Enlightenment ideal of equality under the aegis of the Goddess of Reason was overthrown in the early days of the Reign of Terror, Condorcet himself being denounced to the Revolutionary Tribunal and Olympe de Gouges sentenced to the guillotine. Nonetheless, Enlightenment rationalism was blamed for the excesses of the Reign of Terror, and future efforts to elevate women's political position were based on notions of their emotional comple-

---

13. The 1960s expectation of progress can best be seen in Alix Kates Schulman, "A Marriage Agreement," *Up From Under* 1, no. 2 (fall 1970); and Ann Crittendon Scott, "The Value of Housework," *Ms. Magazine* 1, no. 1 (July, 1972).

mentarity to male reason, rather than on their similarity as rational intellects. The romantic revival succeeded in equating the female with the spontaneity and nonrationality of nature, while the low church evangelical response to the Enlightenment stressed women's natural religiosity, their piety, and their service motivations. Thus, the early-nineteenth-century curriculum for the education of women excluded classical learning, emphasized piety, and stressed decorative female arts such as drawing and music. The noted Methodist moralist and campaigner for women's education Hannah More (1745–1833) set the tone for the nineteenth-century expansion of women's education by urging that its major component be reenforcement of traditional sexual morality for women and a renewed stress on their capacity for service. The result was a rapid increase in female literacy in the early nineteenth century, but its uses were in social service rather than in participation in secular and scientific culture along with men.

The utopian communities, whether religious or secular, were enclaves of freedom for women in North America during the years from the 1780s to the 1860s. Much early American domestic labor-saving technology came from these communities, which were also the forging ground for many varieties of popular health reform involving dress and diet, all of which (with the exception of the bloomer costume) ended up in the mainstream culture by the late nineteenth century. However, given the commitment of the majority to sexual continence, these communities could only grow through adult recruitment, and their influence as models for gender relationships was modest. At the other extreme, the sexual experimenters, such as the Oneida community, throve until the general movement of settlement caught up with them, when outraged clerical attacks forced their dissolution.[14]

The actual experience of participation in the industrial work force proved disappointing for women, because they entered doing low-paid work requiring little skill and were systematically excluded from the kinds of skill training that made gains in earning possible. Thus, throughout the nineteenth century, women workers earned a half to a third of a male wage, within occupations that were segregated by sex. When the scale of industrialization spawned the large business organization at the turn of the century, the same pattern was replicated in clerical and service activities. By the late nineteenth century, most industrial economies had developed dual labor markets in which jobs with poor prospects, little skill training, and low wages were reserved for women.[15] The post–1960 wave of feminist agitation changed this pattern by outlawing

---

14. See Constance Noyes Robertson, *Oneida Community: The Breakup, 1876–1881* (Syracuse, N.Y., 1972).

15. Joan Scott and Louise Tilly, *Women, Work and Family* (New York, 1978).

discrimination at the entry level into the work force, but classifications of work within large-scale organizations have still maintained a segregated occupational pattern that limits female opportunity.[16]

However long the battle to secure access to safe birth control for the mass of women in modern industrial societies, it is nonetheless clear that women's life expectancy has been dramatically changed by developments in medicine. There is heated discussion about whether alternative female-led medical training might have produced even better results. Nonetheless, one in three pregnancies ended in the mother's death in early nineteenth-century industrial cities. By the 1880s, the advent of disinfectants and the development of obstetric surgery had radically changed female life expectancy. More dramatic changes have occurred in the twentieth century as national health schemes in Europe have made adequate health care available during pregnancy.[17] This should not obscure the hostility to women imbedded in much medical training, the practice of many kinds of needless surgery, and the conversion of pregnancy from a natural process into an "illness" requiring medical supervision. Nonetheless, life expectancy is a key indicator, and in this respect there has been almost a century of improvement for women—except in the United States, where poor women, especially African-American and Hispanic, exhibit rates of illness and disease closer to those in the underdeveloped world. However, the female is still the only member of the reproductive team subject to endocrine manipulation for purposes of birth control, although there is clearly no technical reason why a "male pill" could not be developed.

The end result of the 1970s movement to assert the importance of work in women's lives and to enable them to pursue all forms of work on equal terms with men has had mixed results. Within the large work organization in 1991, some 38 percent of U.S. managers were female, although women remained clustered in the ranks of middle management. Within the professions, women's access to training has produced dramatic changes in recruitment in the fields of law and medicine, though in medicine women tend to congregate as salaried employees of health maintenance organizations, gaining a place within an occupation experiencing declining status. Whatever their occupational field, women still carry the responsibility for 80 percent of household labor and child care, so that enlarged work opportunities have been incremental to female work patterns, rather than substitutes for work shared with a spouse.

Most recently, the taboos on female participation in military conflict appear to have been crumbling, mainly because the armed forces can tap a pool

---

16. See Martha Blaxall and Barbara Reagan, eds., *Women and the Workplace: The Implications of Occupational Segregation* (Chicago, 1980).

17. Robert D. Rutherford, *The Changing Sex Differential in Mortality* (Westport, Conn., 1975); Paul E. Zopf, *Mortality Patterns and Trends in the United States* (1992).

of highly motivated working-class women volunteers, who see military life as a vehicle for education and social mobility.[18] Progress in this respect runs against all the nineteenth-century female ideas of future improvement, since it equates women and men as equal in warlike behaviors, something nineteenth- and twentieth-century feminists have hitherto believed to be against female nature. Whether we shall see a recasting of gender categories as the United States deals with its self-designated role as international policeman, relying on a volunteer army to enforce its will, remains to be seen, though we could confidently expect female opportunities to contract were the United States to ever face a military threat requiring the reintroduction of the draft.

Here, as in many other respects, increased opportunities for women rest upon demography, more than on any other factor. So far, the more challenging task of seeking to shape the technology of warfare has not been an interest of feminists. Indeed, although feminist speculation about progress has rested for over a century upon assessments of the direction of technological change, women's interest in technological careers remains at a plateau set in the 1970s, while the most rapidly growing wing of the feminist movement has been concerned with articulating a special, sex-linked female interest in environmental protection. It is this latter interest that has, for the first time, brought about an intersection between the concerns of Western feminists and those of women in non-Western societies, where environmentalism and the critique of Western-style technology have long been important feminist issues. In this respect, the convergence of Western and non-Western feminist concerns may herald a style of feminist thought in the West less concerned with improvement and progress than with environmental balance and more critical assessments of Western technology.[19]

---

18. Cynthia Enloe, *Does Khaki Become You?: The Militarization of Women's Lives* (Boston, Mass., 1983); Kate Muir, *Arms and the Women* (London, 1992).

19. Carolyn Merchant, *Radical Ecology: The Search for a Liveable World* (London, 1992); Mary Mellor, *Breaking the Boundaries: Toward a Feminist Green Socialism* (London, 1992); Vera Norwood, *Made from the Earth: American Women and Nature* (Chapel Hill, N.C., 1993); Carol J. Adams, *Ecofeminism and the Sacred* (New York, 1993); Anita Gordon, *Its a Matter of Survival* (Cambridge, Mass., 1991); Petra Kelly, *Fighting for Hope* (London, 1994).

# The Nature of Progress: Progress and the Environment

*Richard White*

In its conventional phrasing, the relationship between nature and progress in the United States has been direct and simple. Progress equals the conquest of "nature" by "culture." It is this sense of progress that Alexis de Tocqueville captured in the 1830s.

> Europeans think a lot about the wild, open spaces of America . . . but the Americans themselves hardly give them a thought . . . The American people see themselves marching through wilderness, drying up marshes, diverting rivers, peopling the wilds and subduing nature.[1]

Surveying the history of the idea of progress in the United States in 1950, Arthur Ekirch thought "the conquest and control of the immense forces of nature" was the "underlying note" of nineteenth-century conceptions of progress. And when he wrote, the note still echoed. The anthropologist Leslie White, although recognizing the dangers that a nuclear future presented, praised culture's triumph over nature with a certainty and approbation that might now seem out of place even in a Republican campaign speech. "The evolution of culture," he wrote:

> was a fascinating story of adventure and progress; of a species lifting itself up by its cultural bootstraps from the status of a mere animal to a radically

---

1. Alexis de Tocqueville, *Democracy in America,* trans. George Lawrence, ed. J. P. Mayer and Max Lerner (New York: Harper and Row, 1966), 453, quoted in Gunther Barth, *Fleeting Moments: Nature and Culture in American History* (New York: Oxford, 1990), 123. See also Leo Marx's remarks on Crèvecoeur in Marx, *The Machine in the Garden: Technology and the Pastoral Ideal in America* (New York: Oxford, 1964), 115.

new way of life, a way destined to win mastery over most other species and to exert a powerful and extensive control over the natural habitat.[2]

But now, with nearly another half century having passed, the American story of "adventure and progress," which is the subject of this chapter, has been recast into something a bit more uncertain and ironic. The examples White intended his prose to call to mind have yielded to others. "Mastery over most other species" now conjures up images of the mass extinctions that threaten the planet rather than the desired images of humans domesticating animals. "Control over the natural habitat" is more likely to be linked with global warming or the erosion of the ozone layer than with the beginnings of agriculture. Progress has become, as in William McKibben's title, the end of nature. And the end of nature becomes, in yet another formulation, the end of progress. Christopher Lasch, who shared with the advocates of progress he criticized a quite cramped idea of nature as a set of resources, saw "the belated discovery that the earth's ecology will no longer sustain an indefinite expansion of productive forces" as dealing "the final blow to the belief in progress."[3]

In the late twentieth century this kind of ironic rereading of White, and of the larger formulation of the American relation between the natural environment and progress, is inviting. It is simple; it provides an obvious moral lesson, one sympathetic to modern environmentalism. Materials for such ironic readings are readily available through a quick, if selective, perusal of American rhetoric about the conquest of wilderness, the building of civilizations.[4]

But, historically, the definition of progress as the conquest of nature by culture is too pat. Such a formulation follows but a single strand of a much more tangled conversation. Indeed, a case for the opposite reading of the relationship between nature and progress can be made.

Today nature seems to many Americans destined to die at the hands of progress, but two centuries ago the role of victim and murderer were reversed. It was nature that threatened to dispatch progress. Malthus had, in effect, handed nature a general weapon against all humanity in the capacity of human beings to outrun their food supply. Buffon presented a natural check to progress

---

2. Arthur Ekirch, *The Idea of Progress in America, 1813–1860* (New York: Peter Smith, 1951), 267; Leslie White, *The Science of Culture: A Study of Man and Civilization* (1949; reprint, New York: Farrar, Strauss and Giroux, 1969), 390.

3. William McKibben, *The End of Nature* (New York: Random House, 1989); Christopher Lasch, *The True and Only Heaven: Progress and Its Critics* (New York: W. W. Norton, 1991), 529. Lasch, who is certainly no environmentalist, has in his long book relatively little to say about nature. It emerges as a sort of deus ex machina to counter progress when needed (see 24, 100, 169).

4. I have in mind here the kind of rhetoric summarized in Roderick Nash, *Wilderness and the American Mind,* rev. ed. (New Haven: Yale University Press, 1976), 8–43.

more particular to the Western Hemisphere: living things degenerated in the Americas.

Malthus, as Robert Young has argued, had formulated his law of population in opposition to the doctrines of unlimited progress of Godwin and Condorcet, which had put nature at the service of progress. Malthus had used his law of population to attack "the belief that man and his environment were in harmony." The tendency of population to increase geometrically while food supplies increased only arithmetically presented a formidable check to human progress. Malthus himself eventually proved vulnerable to the progressive tendencies of his culture and made hunger the spur that caused humans to emerge from barbarism and thus to progress. But Americans rejected both the original Malthus and the revised Malthus where progress came at the price of hunger, want, and suffering. They preferred a happier vision of progress that did not put hunger in the saddle.[5]

Buffon, for his part, presented a version of nature that did not block progress per se but did block American progress for the foreseeable future. Buffon argued that the problem with the New World was that it was, quite literally, new. Having more recently risen from the waters than the Old World, North America was wet, cold, and miasmal. Nature "had not had time to carry out all her plans." Species native to the Americas were smaller in size, and many American species were not distinct at all but, rather, degenerate forms of European types. Nature deteriorated in the Western Hemisphere. In the long run Buffon was optimistic about America: the climate would evolve toward European norms; species would progress and develop, but the short-term outlook was not good. Not all Buffon's disciples were even this sanguine. Cornelius de Pauw extended Buffon's arguments to humans, native and immigrant, making a case for American degeneration and inferiority.[6]

Just at the time that American republicans positioned themselves as a people of progress opposite a degenerate Europe, European versions of nature seemed to reverse the relation. In response, Americans countered malign nature by creating a progressive nature. They conceived of American nature less as an obstacle than as an ally that validated their republican experiment and supported the possibility of human progress over the foreseeable future.

Against Malthus, they erected a barrier of American exceptionalism. Special American conditions rendered Malthusian arguments irrelevant. In the

---

5. Robert M. Young, *Darwin's Metaphor: Nature's Place in Victorian Culture* (Cambridge: Cambridge University Press, 1985), 23–24, 29.

6. For Buffon and American discovery of nature, see Charlotte M. Porter, *The Eagle's Nest: Natural History and American Ideas, 1812–1842* (University: University of Alabama Press, 1986), 16–25; William Goetzmann, *New Lands, New Men: America and the Second Great Age of Discovery* (New York: Viking Penguin, 1986), 62–64.

Madisonian republic it was the "gifts of nature" that enabled the United States to fulfill its republican destiny. The country's "natural advantages," particularly its low ratio of population to land, ensured its future progress. Through Frederick Jackson Turner, this republican vision of progress based in nature found its way into academic history. So thoroughly did this rooting of progress in nature take hold that Arthur Ekirch explained the appeal of progress as an idea by essentially adopting the Madisonian position as literally true: "the successful development of a seemingly limitless expanse of land and resources" explained the idea's allure.[7]

Americans undertook a more direct refutation of Buffon. Jefferson himself urged it forward in his *Notes on the State of Virginia*. American naturalists eagerly took it up. So great was their success in refuting Buffon and defending American nature that this brand of nationalist natural history ceased to be a matter of much concern after 1815. American naturalists had replaced Buffon's degenerative nature with a progressive nature whose laws presaged a republican and even egalitarian society.[8]

Ralph Waldo Emerson gave this connection between American progress and natural progress its most influential and last cultural formulation. Nature made beauty and spirit accessible to human reason, a Kantian reason that intuitively and spontaneously grasped larger patterns.[9] Kantian reason perceived the beauty and order of nature, but Kantian understanding grasped its utility. Understanding transformed nature into the machine. Nature did not object to such manipulation; it happily consented. "Nature is thoroughly mediate. It is made to serve. It receives the dominion of man as meekly as the ass on which the Saviour rode."[10] Nature educated its students in the "doctrine of Use, namely, that a thing is good only so far as it serves."[11] The mechanical was not the antithesis of nature, but its realization in a new form. Steam was wind in the boiler of the boat, trains imitated eagles or swallows darting from town to town. What seemed ugly in isolation became beauty when reattached to "the Whole."[12]

In thinking of themselves both as children of nature and as children of the machine (masters of American know-how), Americans were Emersonians. Emerson reconciled nature with the busy, manipulative world of American

---

7. Ekirch, *Idea of Progress*, 13.
8. Porter, *Eagle's Nest*, 5, 7–8, 10, 17–24, 49–51.
9. Ralph Waldo Emerson, "The Poet," in *Selections from Ralph Waldo Emerson: An Organic Anthology*, ed. Stephen Whicher (Boston: Houghton Mifflin, 1960), 224; Emerson, "Nature," in *Selections*, ed. Whicher, 226–30; Marx, *The Machine in the Garden*, 233.
10. Emerson, "Nature," 38.
11. Ibid., 39.
12. Ibid., 25–26; Emerson, "The Poet," 229–30; Marx, *Machine in the Garden*, 233.

material progress. When humans acted on nature they did not defile it, they purified it. "Art was nature passed through the alembic of man."[13]

Emerson could simultaneously rejoice in the ability of the machine to subjugate and control nature and in the spiritual truth and inspiration nature provided. Emerson, in Leo Marx's words, found the industrial revolution "a railway journey in the direction of nature."[14] Emerson rejoiced in the "magic" of railroad iron, "its power to evoke the sleeping energies of land and water."[15] Every American, he also proclaimed, "should be educated with a view to the values of the land."[16] The "nervous, rocky West" would be transformed into a garden, and its people, "grown up in the bowers of a paradise," would transform the nation.[17]

The linkage between nature and progress became so close that even those thinkers who had doubts about either the damage done natural systems or the moral price of progress returned in the end to mere variants of the ultimate restorative connection between nature and progress. Nature as a bulwark of republican progress, for example, found its deepest expression even in a work that in many ways forms a transition to late-twentieth-century irony and pessimism: George Perkins Marsh's *Man and Nature*. Marsh's book, which stressed the ravages humans visited on nature and the price they paid for them, is now usually read as embryonic environmentalism. But Marsh never doubted that human beings were meant to subdue nature. The past disasters he detailed had resulted from oppressive government and tyranny. Europe and Asia with their despotisms formed a cautionary tale rather than the inevitable result of human domination of nature. Despotism brought environmental degradation, for "man cannot struggle against crushing oppression and the destructive forces of inorganic nature." Republican citizens, free to enjoy the fruits of their labor, would conquer nature while avoiding environmental disaster.[18]

Similarly, the conquest of nature was not only a recipe for progress, but also a corrective to the dangers of progress. Concerned with the materialism, smugness, and injustice involved in the ideology of progress itself and the irrationality, authoritarianism, and militarism of the turn-of-the-century critique of the pursuit of material progress, William James sought a corrective to

---

13. Emerson, "Nature," 31.
14. Marx, *Machine in the Garden*, 238.
15. Ralph Waldo Emerson, "The Young American," *Essays and Lectures*, (New York: Library of America, 1983), 213.
16. Ibid., 214.
17. Ibid., 216.
18. George Perkins Marsh, *Man and Nature, or Physical Geography as Modified by Human Action*, ed. David Lowenthal (1864; reprint, Cambridge: Belknap Press of Harvard University Press, 1967), 10, 11, 38.

both in a war on nature. Conquering nature, in one formulation the essence of progress, could also become the antidote for the ills of progress.[19]

Lewis Mumford, in his earlier writings, also saw nature, whose conquest was essential to progress, as an antidote to the ills of progress. Mumford described nineteenth-century industrialism, which he, following Patrick Geddes, labeled the Paleotechnic, as an "upthrust into barbarism" that was hardly progress at all. It had produced a world of steady, unremitting, repetitive, monotonous toil. Its first and defining mark of the Paleotechnic was air pollution; its by-products yielded a "befouled and disorderly environment; the end product an exhausted one."[20] The Paleotechnic had treated "the environment itself, . . . as an abstraction. Air and sunlight because of their deplorable lack of value in exchange had no reality at all." The Paleotechnic had made abstractions into realities "whereas the realities of existence were treated . . . as abstractions, as sentimental fancies, even as aberrations . . ."[21]

Electricity represented what Mumford called the Neotechnic. The Neotechnic represented true progress because it would rejoin progressive nature and progressive society.[22] Hydroelectric power would purify polluted industrial cities, and they would also purify human society. Electricity would restore workers to the countryside. The Neotechnic would work toward "ecological balance."[23]

The two versions of the relationship between nature and progress offered by American believers in progress are obviously somewhat contradictory. Nature as an obstacle whose conquest is the measure of progress and nature as essentially a progressive force in and of itself stood in opposition; but the opposition was only partial. Both identified history with progress, and both made historical progress natural.

When conceived of as the conquest of nature, progress often yielded a history that conformed to what amounted to natural laws. In talking about culture overcoming nature, for example, Leslie White reduced culture to the ability "to harness and control energy." Cultures could be quantified and measured. They conformed to laws of cultural development that were hard to distinguish from natural laws: "Other factors remaining constant, culture

---

19. William James, "The Moral Equivalent of War," in *The Writings of William James,* ed. John J. McDermott (New York: Random House, 1967), 660–71.
20. Lewis Mumford, *Technics and Civilization* (New York: Harcourt, Brace and Company, 1934), 157–67.
21. Ibid., 168–69.
22. Ibid., 109.
23. Ibid., 256–57. This was a theme Mumford would continue in *The Culture of Cities;* see Lewis Mumford, *The Culture of Cities* (1938; reprint, New York: Harcourt Brace Jovanovich, 1970), 233, 235, 249, 250, 255, 348, 379.

evolves as the amount of energy harnessed per capita per year is increased, or as the efficiency of the instrumental means of putting the energy to work is increased." In conquering nature, culture (and its expression in history) conformed to the laws of nature itself, and, in this sense, history became naturalized. In its subjugation, nature yielded a measure by which degrees of historical progress could be determined.[24]

Conceiving of nature as itself progressive naturalized history even more obviously and easily. Progressive nature yielded progressive history. When Senator William Seward spoke of the "law of progress and development impressed upon us by nature herself," he was following a logic that would find even more vigorous expressions in the popular Darwinism of the late nineteenth century when evolution as progress became the preferred understanding of evolution for the Victorians. This was a reading of his theory to which Darwin himself at least partially consented. By assimilating evolution and natural selection to the doctrine of progress, nineteenth-century social theorists removed the earlier threat Malthusian nature had posed to progress. Indeed, they gave "the doctrine of unlimited progress . . . the additional support of being guaranteed by the laws of nature."[25]

Twentieth-century American academics rarely put the matter as crudely as Seward did, but they offered similar, if more subtle, linkages. Most "scientific" historians, for example, did not adopt nomothetic positions and search for laws of progress, but they did adopt a Baconian stance that an objective study would reveal a true historical order. For the Progressive historians such an order was, obviously, progressive. And for Turner and his followers, in particular, this progress was grounded in the old Madisonian vision of American nature. Even with the decline of Progressive history, the link remained intact in more subtle metaphorical forms.[26]

---

24. White, *Science of Culture*, xxxiii–xxxxiv; 368–69. White drew sharp distinctions between human beings as biological entities and as a "vehicles for culture," but these differences blurred in his naturalization of culture and history. *Science of Culture* aims to restore evolutionary thought to anthropology, 20–21. It had considerable influence; see David Kaplan and Robert Manners, *Culture Theory* (New York: Prentice-Hall, 1972), 43–49, 97–98.

25. Seward quoted in Ekirch, *Idea of Progress*, 65, see also 124–25, 128–29; Young, *Darwin's Metaphor*, 16, 17, 23–55, 79–125. See also Stephen Jay Gould, *Wonderful Life: The Burgess Shale and the Nature of History* (New York: W. W. Norton and Company, 1989), 257–59.

26. For a summary of the idea of history as progress in American historiography, see Peter Novik, *That Noble Dream: The "Objectivity Question" and the American Historical Profession* (New York: Cambridge University Press, 1988), 105, 313, 405, 465. Belief in history as progress did not necessarily mean a belief in historical laws or nomothetic (law-generating) history, but some late-nineteenth- and early-twentieth-century historians combined the two. Even more appealed to a model of Baconian science in which Darwin's work served as a direct model (24–25, 33, 39). Although all varieties of scientific history underwent crisis and decline (137–38), progress lingered.

For much of the twentieth century, evolution has arguably been the reigning historical metaphor. And, during this time, popular evolutionary thought has been, in the broadest sense, progressive. Both those who thought of progress as rooted in nature and those who conceived of it as a conquest of nature resorted to the same evolutionary trope. Take, for example, the earlier quotation from Leslie White. In writing so easily of the "evolution of culture," White metaphorically connected the social sciences with the natural sciences; culture and history evolved, and supposedly progressed, in the same manner as nature. In yet another way, history became naturalized. And in all of these ways of naturalizing history what was surrendered was a meaningful sense of history as contingency. Accidents, of course, occurred; events changed direction; there were setbacks, but these didn't change the larger teleological and progressive march forward.

Progressive nature and naturalized history, so long the bulwarks of progress, have, however, suffered serious defections in the twentieth century. To defect from a nature that itself enabled constant growth and progress was to stress, as the Club of Rome did in 1970, *The Limits of Growth*. To defect from a naturalized history that produced human progress in the same way that nature supposedly produced more and more advanced species was either to challenge the measurements of progress or else to stress the deleterious side effects, particularly the environmental costs, that could bring progress to a disastrous halt.

Doubting the ability of nature to promote or sustain growth need not have any overt concern with environmental deterioration. Frederick Jackson Turner, for example, who had rooted his view of progress in a Madisonian and Jeffersonian nature of open space and "vacant" lands, grew more pessimistic with the end of the frontier. It was the loss of an American environment capable of "Americanizing" immigrants rather than environmental deterioration that made Turner worry about his country's future. Turner's doctrine of closed space, as James Malin phrased it, could, however, easily develop an environmental component, as it did at least briefly during the New Deal when the dust bowl became the symbol of too much pressure on fragile lands.[27]

By the late 1950s the defections had grown more numerous, and they had developed a different environmental emphasis. Turner had lamented the lack of nature left for individuals to conquer; critics now attacked unrestrained mastery over nature itself. Where Turner had feared there would be no more room for progress, the new critics inverted the term. Their use of the word *progress*

---

27. For further discussion of Turner, see Richard White, "Frederick Jackson Turner," in *Historians of the American Frontier: A Bio-Bibliographical Sourcebook,* ed. John Wunder (New York: Greenwood Press, 1988), 660–68. For Malin's attack on Turner, see James Malin, *The Grassland of North America: Prolegomena to Its History, with Addenda* (Gloucester: Peter Smith, 1967), 331–35.

became ironic. In a *New Yorker* column, "These Precious Days," E. B. White began "to assemble bulletins tracing Man's progress in making the planet uninhabitable." Bulletin number one concerned nuclear fallout, global warming, and air pollution. White's irony was simple and effective. Progress had become for Americans, in Christopher Lasch's words, "the promise of steady improvement with no foreseeable ending at all." There was no particular goal to be achieved. White acknowledged the movement, accepted the technical mastery that made it possible, and proclaimed an ultimate, horrific, unintended result.[28]

The calculations of the price of progress steadily mounted in the 1960s and 1970s, and the coin in which it was paid became largely environmental in a double sense: the natural world suffered, and human beings became alienated from nature itself. Revelations of the price progress exacted occurred locally in the *Silent Spring* of Rachel Carson and globally, as Barbara Ward warned in her *Progress for a Small Planet:*

> The means at mankind's disposal for producing the vast increase in material goods required to underpin the contentment of six billion earthlings may be so potentially destructive that the system could be handing out plumbing, cars, and breakfast foods with one hand and cancer of the lungs with the other. Industrial systems may spread while the ozone layer is depleted, technology be shared and the icecaps begin to melt. . . . It is the human race itself that must resolve the dilemmas or conceivably follow the dinosaurs.[29]

Ward, like White, recognized that *progress* was a malleable word, a concept without specific goal, and she intended as much to capture it as subvert it.

But subversion was the easier task; when environmental critics of progress have changed what was measured, progress began to add up to something other than a more abundant life for all. Partially this involved a simple reversal of older standards; partially it was the creation of new standards. The support of ever increasing human populations, once an essential mark of progress, has become a sign of danger. The elimination of undomesticated, or at least unprofitable, species and their replacement by domesticated, useful species, long a hallmark of progress, has become a crisis. Biodiversity has recently emerged as a new standard. It is, admittedly, a standard sometimes assimilated into the old logic of progress: we are, for example, losing plant species that might provide the cures for diseases. But biodiversity has also been presented as a

---

28. E. B. White, "These Precious Days," *New Yorker* 35 (May 16, 1959): 180–81; Lasch, *True and Only Heaven,* 47.

29. Barbara Ward, *Progress for a Small Planet* (New York: W. W. Norton and Company, 1979), 10.

good without utilitarian trappings. The loss of a species has become a tear in the fabric of life itself.[30]

Progress, so dependent on technological mastery, became in a dual sense a victim of its own success. Undesired as well as desired results were the fruits of technology. But in a deeper sense, technology undermined the cultural foundations of a progress that had always assumed a nature separate from human beings. This belief may have been naive and misguided, "an aberration of the Victorian Age," as J. B. Jackson contended, but it was quite powerful. William McKibben could talk about the end of nature and get serious attention because our cultural and historical conception of nature as something outside of ourselves, something that remained patterned, repetitive, and predictable no matter what we did, no longer seemed to hold. Suddenly, we touched everything. Basic chemical processes of the planet, long taken for granted, were no longer constants, but instead were vulnerable to our unintentional manipulations. The ozone layer develops holes; we change the climate. The ability to manipulate the very atmosphere or alter climate once would have stood as milestones of progress; now they were signs of a world slipping out of control. Progress seemed to have betrayed the twentieth century. We embarked in the vehicle thinking we had control and the road was straight. All that mattered was how fast we went. But as the century ends, the road curves and our only control over the vehicle, it turns out, is the accelerator. We seem in the critics' view to be able neither to stop nor to steer.[31]

In such circumstances the old polarity of history as progress has been reversed. Change has become negative. A large portion of the population now thinks we are liable to be much worse off just down the road. Change is loss. The technological progress that generated prosperity has also produced new and more dangerous pollutants. The by-products of progress—the disappearance of open spaces, the pollution of air and water, the loss of biodiversity, the dangers presented to the planet by energy sources that fuel human production—all loom nearly as large as or larger than the benefits. The impossibility of unlimited growth on a finite planet has done relatively little to promote change on a policy level, nor has it done much to erode a culture of

---

30. E. O. Wilson, ed., *BioDiversity* (Washington, D.C.: National Academy Press, 1988). For an example of utilitarian argument in this collection, see Norman Farnsworth, "Screening Plants for New Medicines," 83–97, and Hugh Iltis, "Serendipity in the Exploration of BioDiversity: What Good are Weedy Tomatoes?" 98–105. There are also arguments for biodiversity that try to avoid this kind of utilitarianism; see, for example, David Ehrenfeld, *The Arrogance of Humanism* (New York: Oxford, 1978).

31. Jackson quotation cited in Denis E. Cosgrove, *Social Formation and Symbolic Landscape* (London: Croom Helm, 1984), 35. I have borrowed this use of nature from Barbara Jeanne Fields, who used it in a very different context. See Barbara Jeanne Fields, "Slavery, Race, and Ideology in the United States," *New Left Review* 181 (May–June 1980): 106; see also McKibben, *End of Nature*.

consumption that pervades environmentalism itself, but it has instituted a deep unease as the effects of growth and technological mastery are felt in the daily life of the developed countries: in smog, in congestion, in occasional shortages of water and energy.[32]

This doubting of progress has, however, hardly been unanimous. *The Limits of Growth* and *Global 2000 Report to the President,* both documents that replaced predictions of progress with predictions of environmental decline, provoked vigorous rebuttals. Julian Simon and Herman Kahn in *The Resourceful Earth* tried to restore an image of the planet as a storehouse of resources whose exploitation knew only the limits of human ingenuity. Simon and Kahn maintained the old faith in constantly improving material life. They proclaimed that some perceived environmental problems were actually solutions and asserted that other problems just did not exist. Starting from the relatively safe assumption that "human beings are the only possible source of human progress," they argued that more human beings meant more progress since "larger population size has been a clear-cut sign of economic success and has accompanied improvements in the human lot." They dismissed predictions of a loss of 40 percent of forest cover in the least developed countries by the year 2000 as "nonsense." The only clear danger they saw was environmental pessimism, which might restrict the free market and lead to greater governmental restrictions on development.[33]

And yet in proclaiming the old faith, the defenders have turned as shrill and uneasy as their critics. In earlier environmental controversies, proponents of development believed they had only to label their opponents enemies of progress to discredit them. In the controversy over Con Edison's attempt to carve an electric generating system out of Storm King Mountain in the 1960s and 1970s, for example, Con Edison presumably thought it had delivered crushing rhetorical blows when it identified opponents as "birdwatchers, nature fakers, and militant adversaries of progress."[34]

But when in this and other controversies the critics won, the very fact of criticism, and not its merits, became the key issue. Those who questioned progress no longer were mere cranks or eccentrics; they became dangerous

---

32. Many of these issues receive consideration in Charles Birch and John B. Cobb, Jr., *The Liberation of Life: From the Cell to the Community* (Cambridge: Cambridge University Press, 1981). See, for example, chapter 8, "A Just and Sustainable World," and chapter 9, "Economic Development in Ecological Perspective," 234–95. Technological progress as the cause of pollution was a major theme of Barry Commoner, *The Closing Circle* (New York: Knopf, 1971), a theme that he still reiterates: Barry Commoner, "Why We Have Failed," in *Learning to Listen to the Land,* ed. Bill Willers (Washington, D.C.: Island Press, 1991).

33. Julian Simon and Herman Kahn, eds., *The Resourceful Earth: A Response to Global 2000* (New York: Basil Blackwell, 1984), 1–51, esp. 4, 12, 20, 26, 30.

34. Cited in Victor B. Scheffer, *The Shaping of Environmentalism in America* (Seattle: University of Washington Press, 1991), 134.

doomsayers and Cassandras who will bear the responsibility if progress ceases. Calling critics Cassandras was a doubly weird choice of metaphors, for not only was Cassandra always right, but she was also always ignored. Cassandra, so ineffectual in her original incarnation, has come into her own. For Kahn and Simon, predictions of environmental decline and proclamations of environmental pessimism (such as a lack of faith in nuclear power) now rank with nuclear war as the only forces powerful enough to derail progress. When mere predictions of disaster can derail progress, this idea that had once seemed a virtual law of nature has become fragile indeed. Only a few, such as Freeman Dyson, manage to accept something of the environmentalist critique and retain anything like the old sanguine faith in progress.[35]

Defenders of progress now seem themselves confused. They lament that at a time when life in the developed world has never been better, the faith in progress should be replaced by fear. "What are Americans afraid of," Mary Douglas and Aaron Wildavsky rhetorically ask:

> Nothing much really, except the food they eat, the water they drink, the air they breathe, the land they live on and the energy they use. In the amazingly short space of fifteen to twenty years, confidence about the physical world has turned to doubt.[36]

Judged by many of the old measures, progress should, these critics contend, be thriving. "Life expectancy continues to increase; accident rates and infant mortality are way down . . . life is growing longer not shorter, health is better not worse." Wildavsky and Douglas, Simon and Kahn admittedly pick and choose, but so too do the Cassandras. The issue sometimes seems nearly religious. Advocates of progress still have faith that science and technology

---

35. Simon and Kahn, *Resourceful Earth*, 4, 30. See also Bernard Cohen, "Statement of Dissent," in *Resourceful Earth*, ed. Simon and Kahn, 566. See also, J. L Simon, "Resources, Population, Environment: An Oversupply of False Bad News," *Science* 208:1431–37. For countercritique, see Violetta Burke Cook and Earl Cook, "Romance and Resources," in *The Cassandra Conference: Resources and the Human Predicament*, ed. Paul R. Ehrlich and John P. Holdren (College Station: Texas A&M University Press, 1988), 299–316. Dyson maintains many of the old themes in his work. For his vision of a postindustrial society, see Freeman Dyson, *Disturbing the Universe* (New York: Harper and Row, 1979), 203–204, and *Infinite in All Directions* (New York: Harper and Row, 1988), 104. For his tendency to naturalize history and his use of evolutionary metaphors, see Dyson, *Disturbing the Universe*, 221, 237; this same kind of metaphorical naturalization extends to history and culture: Dyson, *Infinite in All Directions*, 91–92. For a progressive nature, see Dyson, *Infinite in All Directions*, 117. Many of those who have criticized progress have rather happily accepted the label of Cassandra and pointed out the irony of its use (Ehrlich and Holdren, *Cassandra Conference*, ix–x, 299–316).

36. Mary Douglas and Aaron Wildavsky, *Risk and Culture: An Essay on the Selection of Technological and Environmental Dangers* (Berkeley: University of California Press, 1983), 10.

will provide the solution to whatever dangers the manipulation of nature and the exhaustion of resources present. The Cassandras have lost their faith.[37]

It is not that the environmental critics deny technical mastery; they often admit it. Indeed, some even admire it. But in the hands of an environmental writer such as John McPhee, such mastery is also gently mocked. In McPhee's *The Control of Nature,* the conventional celebrations of human mastery and ingenuity go slightly off center. Control is temporary if ingenious; elemental forces—the gravity that gives mountains their desire to be flat and that gives rivers the force to cut new channels, the molten core of the earth that causes volcanoes to erupt, render ultimate human control so much hubris.[38]

The very virulence of the defenders of progress in attacking environmentalists seems to demonstrate the threat environmentalism poses to a faith in progress, but environmentalism's own relationship to progress is somewhat more ambiguous. Its tangled pedigree, after all, includes George Perkins Marsh, Gifford Pinchot, and other progressive conservationists, and various strains of popular Darwinism and evolutionary biology. Its political alliances have historically been with liberals who have clung to their belief in progress like a lifeboat in a storm. As a mass movement, its social origins, as Samuel Hays has argued, lie in postwar consumerism, and concern with consumption has been a hallmark of capitalist progress. To be sure, a romantic strain also runs through the movement. Thoreau, Emerson, Muir, and modern deep ecologists seek, in a sense, to restore wonder as the primary human response to a nature reduced by progressive instrumentalism to a mere collection of resources.[39]

It has never been entirely clear whether environmentalists seek to use the current environmental crisis as a way to discredit the belief in progress or as a

---

37. Quoted from Douglas and Wildavsky, *Risk and Culture,* 10, 14. They attribute the acute sense of pessimism and risk to a cultural change that has led to what they call sectarianism—a devotion to human goodness, equality, and purity. Sectarians eschewing authoritarianism are border organizations; they have to keep the group together by creating common and pervasive dangers. Sectarians are thus inherently intolerant and radical in their solutions. They choose the threat technology poses to nature against all objective evidence because such threats are hidden, involuntary, and irreversible. They are a means of attacking the established order. This suits their cultural needs; their judgments are social and not scientific. Implicit in all this is the argument that there is nothing to modern pessimism about nature that a good dose of hierarchy and authoritarianism wouldn't cure. Although there are profound cultural elements involved in these debates, this is a frankly silly, simplistic, and polemical analysis, 10–14, 47–48. For a discussion of this argument, see Birch and Cobb, *Liberation of Life,* 239–64

38. John McPhee, *The Control of Nature* (New York: Farrar, Straus, Giroux, 1989).

39. This is most apparent in the deep ecologists, William Devall and George Sessions, but it pervades popular ecology. Christopher Lasch, whose own account of the relationship between critiques of progress and environmentalism can be at times problematic, nonetheless offers a cogent account of the romantic critique of progress and the defense of wonder: Lasch, *True and Only Heaven,* 231, 262–63, 277.

means of capturing and reworking the ideology of progress. Barbara Ward, for example, tried to capture the term and turn it into a movement toward a new "planetary society" whose marks would be frugality, conservation, and cooperation. But this amounted to little more than a semantic trick. By the late twentieth century, Americans knew what progress was: it was more, and then more still—more people, more things, more comforts. By pointing out that more also meant more pollution, more cancer, more extinctions, and more crowding, critics scored points. But they did not reconcile people with a future that redefined progress as search for less. *Small is Beautiful* had its day, but it was a brief one. Americans seemingly still wanted more; they now, however, recognized that they might not be able to afford it. This was not a change of values. Most people did not feel liberated; they felt deprived.[40]

Mainstream environmentalism, however, has never really demanded deprivation, at least from its supporters. It, in the best progressive tradition, often only seeks to make consumption more efficient. Environmentalism has been, and remains, a largely middle-class and metropolitan movement. And, as Samuel Hays has argued, it has represented not a rejection of consumption, but a new aspect of it. In saving the earth, middle-class environmentalists also opened it up for their own leisure activities. Wild lands no longer consumed for their ore, timber, or energy are now consumed as sources of experience: hiking, skiing, rafting, photography. It would be hard to read a magazine such as *Outside* or an REI or Eddie Bauer catalog as a rejection of consumerism and consumption. And as organized groups, environmentalists assert a privileged claim to valued resources.[41]

The same contradictions arise on a larger, less personal scale. Metropolitan environmentalists have moved forward to solve urban and suburban environmental problems, but here, too, it becomes easy to overestimate the depth of the renunciation of material progress and the acceptance of its costs. Material progress often does come at the price of serious environmental deterioration. And, although there have been some attempts to modify behavior and reduce environmental impacts, there have also been less noble attempts simply to redistribute the costs by exporting the problems elsewhere. Los Angeles has begun to pass strict air quality standards, but it can do so, in part, because it imports power from external sources such as the coal-burning plants that have fouled the skies of the Grand Canyon and strip-mined Black Mesa on the Navajo and Hopi reservations. Seattle might enforce a strict recycling policy by removing paper, metal, and some plastic, but this still leaves tons of

---

40. Ward, *Progress,* 277; E. F. Schumacher, *Small is Beautiful* (New York: Harper and Row, 1973).

41. Samuel Hays, *Beauty, Health, and Permanence: Environmental Politics in the United States, 1955–1985* (New York: Cambridge University Press, 1987), 3–5.

daily garbage, some of it toxic, that the city ships out to rural Washington and Oregon in order to avoid polluting its own water table. Progress in cleaning air or water is thus partial; it merely shifts the site of pollution.

Environmentalists do recognize the problems created by consumption and a progress defined in terms of constantly increasing per capita consumption. Environmentalists do talk about limits, but it often seems that they seek to limit the number of consumers rather than the amount of consumption. And the limits they advocate can fall more heavily on others than themselves. There are very good reasons to limit the amount of grazing, logging, and mining in the American West, for example, but the fact remains that the cost of such reduction will not by and large be borne by the metropolitan environmentalists who advocate it most strenuously.

That saving nature will come at some human cost is not the issue so much as which humans will pay the price. There has sporadically arisen in environmentalism an unpleasant undercurrent that can give the movement a tinge of nasty class and racial distinctions. This has shown up particularly clearly in questions of overpopulation. In his famous lifeboat analogy, Garrett Hardin compared rich nations to lifeboats into which drowning poor struggled to get on board. Hardin recommended letting the poor drown; rescuing them would only overcrowd and swamp the lifeboats.[42]

Hardin's example echoed the older Malthusian position with which this essay began, but the frame of reference has changed. Malthus used nature to check material progress. Hardin's argument both limited the range of such natural checks—to the undeveloped countries—and has nature, in effect, acting out of desperation to prevent total degradation. Nature was not so much master as victim, and Hardin moved Malthus from description to prescription.

Malthus's theory was originally seen as a barrier to progress, but Hardin's formulation connected with another harsher version of the morality of progress: social Darwinism and a nature red in tooth and claw. Today when the issue is overpopulation and immigration from poor to rich countries, some environmentalists can view the suffering of others as necessary for the good of the planet. Some of them, it turns out, share with the conservatives they have often otherwise opposed the inner strength to bear up well under other people's troubles.

The second interesting thing about Hardin's argument is how excessive consumption disappeared behind the issue of excessive population. The amount of consuming done by those within the lifeboat ceased to be an issue. That the occupants of the lifeboats were 300-pounders consuming many times

---

42. For the analogy and the reaction, see Scheffer, *Environmentalism in America,* 106. For the original, see Garrett Hardin, "Living on a Lifeboat," *BioScience* 24, no. 10 (1974): 561. See also Roderick Nash, *Rights of Nature* (Madison: University of Wisconsin Press, 1989), 160.

the resources of the 100-pounders struggling in the water did not apparently matter to the metaphor. Saving the environment and saving the ability to consume on a lavish scale intersected.

Hardin's position, repudiated by many other environmentalists, came close to reducing morality to carrying capacity; it retained progress, but at the price of abandoning the conventional individual rights thinking that had been a foundation of more liberal versions of progress. A second strain of environmentalism struggled to maintain the links with progress by broadening this conception of individual rights. These environmentalists commonly contend that the ultimate problem facing the planet is a moral one and that the emergence of environmentalism is itself a sign of progress toward a more inclusive and thus higher morality.[43]

The premises of much of this morality are not new. According to Roderick Nash, environmentalist morality represents an extension of American liberal reform and rights language to nature. Environmentalism and the animal rights movements thus supposedly join the American Revolution and abolitionism as movements that force radical and revolutionary extensions of natural rights, this time not to new groups of human beings, but to nature itself. Such extensions of rights supposedly constitute moral progress, and Aldo Leopold, who first formulated a "land ethic," placed his argument squarely within the evolutionary logic of progress:

> The extension of ethics to this third element in human environment (i.e. man's relation to land and to animals and plants) is . . . an evolutionary possibility and an ecological necessity . . . Individual thinkers since the days of Ezekiel and Isaiah have asserted that the despoliation of land is not only inexpedient but wrong. Society, however, has not yet affirmed their belief. I regard the present conservation movement as the embryo of such an affirmation.[44]

Not all environmentalist morality, however, fits comfortably within the liberal ethical tradition of rights and progress. Deep ecologists and more radical environmentalists devalue individual life in relation to the good of the "ecosystem" as a whole. And it is here that a definite break with the belief in

---

43. For an example of the counterposition, see Wayne Davis, "Overpopulated America," in *Learning to Listen to the Land,* ed. Bill Willers (Washington, D.C.: Island Press, 1991), 177–82, reprinted from *New Republic,* January 10, 1970.

44. Nash, *Rights of Nature* 10, 13, 34, 138, 143, 160, 199–200. For an attempt by Christopher Stone, who first argued for rights and standing for trees and other natural objects, see *Earth and Other Ethics: The Case for Moral Pluralism* (New York: Harper and Row, 1987). Quotation from Aldo Leopold, *Sand County Almanac and Sketches Here and There* (1949; reprint, New York: Oxford University Press, 1987), 203. Leopold's version of moral history is, of course, questionable.

progress seems to occur. Deep ecologists draw from a romantic tradition that was always critical of the conventional ideology of progress and lamented the disappearance of wonder from human contacts with the natural world.[45]

Things would be simple enough if deep ecologists were merely romantics or mystics, but they too claim the mantle of science. A favorite axiom of deep ecology is Barry Commoner's third law of ecology, "nature knows best." Deep ecologists tend to run Commoner's third law, James Lovelock's Gaia hypothesis of the earth as a living organism, and Aldo Leopold's land ethic together into a brew that scientists regard as metaphysics but which deep ecologists still view as scientifically validated view of nature.[46]

In terms of the relationship between progress and nature, the older, progressive nature has yielded to a balanced, harmonious, and stable nature. Just as nature had once condoned—indeed, demanded—progress, now it demanded stability and cooperation. Deep ecologists carry this analysis the farthest, but other environmentalists appeal to similar versions of nature. Barbara Ward, for example, thought nature provided the model for an interdependent, planetary society. Physical interdependence, which she considered the chief insight of the twentieth century, demanded a new order.[47]

Environmentalists of all stripes, from deep ecologists to environmental radicals to officials of mainstream environmental organizations, have invoked this supposedly natural harmonious model. For deep ecologists Bill Devall and George Sessions, wilderness exists in a "natural self organizing ecosystem state." For the anarchist and environmentalist Murray Bookchin, an ideal society " would approximate a (normal) ecosystem; it would be diversified, balanced and harmonious." Under this flood of balance and harmony, an admittedly reduced progress still survives among more moderate environmentalists swimming, as it were, with the tide. Like Ward, many environmentalists (the "shallow" ecologists, as the deep ecologists called them) retain a sense of progress that demands proper management to achieve the new goal of stability and interdependence. David Brower insists he is not "blindly against progress, but against blind progress."[48]

---

45. See, for example, Thomas Berry, *The Dream of the Earth* (San Francisco: Sierra Club Books, 1988), xiv, 1–5.

46. See, for example, Bill Devall and George Sessions, "The Development of Natural Resources and the Integrity of Nature," *Environmental Ethics* 6 (winter 1984), 304–5. For Commoner, see *Closing Circle,* 41; James Lovelock, *The Ages of Gaia: A Biography of Our Living Earth* (New York: Norton, 1988); Leopold, *Sand County Almanac.*

47. Ward, *Progress,* 277.

48. Nash, *Rights of Nature,* 164; Devall and Sessions, "Development of Natural Resources," 305; in Roderick Nash, *The Rights of Nature* (Madison, Wisc: University of Wisconsin Press, 1989); David Brower, "Foreword," in *Learning to Listen to the Land,* ed. Bill Willers (Washington, D.C.: Island Press, 1991), xiii.

Rhetorically, this turn to a stable harmonious nature has been quite successful. It has proven an effective counter to visions of nature that have amounted to little more than a set of resources to be exploited as fully and rapidly as possible. But its claims to scientific validity are weak. Intellectually, harmonious nature has been built on a scientific foundation that is now shifting underneath it.

Because *ecology* has become the name of a mass popular movement, a scientific discipline, and a term used to refer to all of nature, using the word is like referring to people by their surname alone on a block where everyone is named Smith. It can be difficult to keep the activities of one ecology separate from the others. On our block the science of ecology has received credit for many of the ideas and activities of popular ecology even when the two have gone in different directions. When environmentalists buttress their arguments with appeals to the science of ecology, they tend to appeal to a much older Clementian ecology or to the ecology of Eugene Odum where balance, order, and harmony did in a real sense reign. And this earlier version of ecology did provide a critique of doctrines of unlimited progress. But ecological thinking at least since the 1960s, the period when modern environmentalism gathered strength, has emphasized not a harmonious, balanced nature but, rather, a contingent, unstable nature.[49]

This turn to a contingent, unstable nature has, on the one hand, aided critics of progress by cutting away the last vestiges of a progress ordained by nature itself. Progressive nature had naturalized history—making progress and history the virtually identical evolutionary expressions of natural laws or the natural environment. But as nature itself became historicized, the product as much of contingent events as natural laws, the idea of evolution as purposeful or directional lost its supports. The newer evolutionary scheme in which numerous outcomes were possible, each "sensible in itself, but each utterly unpredictable at the outset," threaten, in Stephen Gould's words,

> Our most precious hope for the history of life, a hope that we would relinquish with greatest reluctance, (which) involves the concepts of progress and predictability.[50]

---

49. For a good account of these trends, see Donald Worster, "Ecology of Order and Chaos," *Environmental History Review* 14 (spring/summer 1990): 1–18. For a set of essays that developed the growing critique of such ideas, see Hugh Miller Raup, *Forests in the Here and Now* (Missoula, Mont.: Montana Forest and Conservation Experiment Station, 1981). Also see Daniel Botkin, *Discordant Harmonies: A New Ecology for the Twenty-First Century* (New York: Oxford University Press, 1990), 3–13.

50. Stephen Gould, *Wonderful Life,* 233, also 244, 257.

Unable to appeal to evolutionary thought, advocates of progress have lost their natural model and their reigning trope, and to this extent, environmentalist critics of progress have benefited from the new historicized, contingent nature. But this same kind of thinking has simultaneously eroded ecological ideas that made natural environments balanced, harmonious, and stable. Environmentalists still often write as if Frederick Clements and Eugene Odum controlled the paradigms in ecology, but a very different view now dominates.[51]

Modern scientific thinking about the environment owes more to Henry Gleason and Hugh Raup than Frederick Clements and Eugene Odum. Not only have Clementian ideas of succession and climax faded, but the whole idea of ecosystems seems hazy and imprecise. The environment has become "a veritable shimmer of populations in space and time," as ecologist Edward Goldsmith has put it. Or, as Hugh Raup wrote, "a complex, fluctuating system, wherein there is endless, essentially indeterminate change, and wherein capacity for readjustment rather than extreme vulnerability is given primary emphasis." Or, to quote a last and very recent example from Daniel Botkin:

> Whenever we seek to find constancy, we discover change. We find that nature undisturbed is not constant in form, structure, or proportion, but changes at every scale of time and space. The old idea of a static landscape, like a single musical chord sounded forever, must be abandoned for such a landscape never existed except in our imagination.

In this kind of ecology a strong emphasis on genetics and evolutionary biology has replaced studies of community as the major research trend.[52]

In this unstable, contingent nature, larger patterns may exist, but they have become less and less determinative of what actually happens. The environment becomes analogous to an orchestra made up of numerous different instruments—and there is a score for the orchestra to play, but there is no concert hall. Instead, they have to play out in a very busy street. Between the conductor being arrested for obstructing traffic, the string section getting flattened by a truck, the percussionists running for their lives, and a touring mariachi band deciding to sit in, whatever emerges from the surrounding din will probably have only a chance resemblance to what the score intended. Those ecologists who insist on studying only the score will be somewhat

---

51. Here see Worster, "Ecology of Order and Chaos," 1–18; Botkin, *Discordant Harmonies*, 3–13, 171–201; Paul Ehrlich, *The Machinery of Nature: The Living World Around Us—And How It Works* (New York: Simon and Schuster, 1986), 169, 185, 232.

52. Edward Goldsmith, "Ecological Succession Rehabilitated," *Ecologist* 15 (1985): 106; Botkin *Discordant Harmonies*, 62.

bewildered by the actual experience of the orchestra in action. And those environmentalists bent on replacing an ideology of progress with one of harmony, stability, and interdependence will probably have to look somewhere besides ecology or environmental history for a model. As a science, ecology undermines progress, but it also undermines current counterformulations of nature as stable and harmonious.

Environmentalists trust in nature the way economic conservatives trust in the market; they substitute the guiding hand of nature for the guiding hand of the market in their journey toward the future. And like conservatives, environmentalists sometimes envision the future by inventing an ideal past. Where Americans had once imagined an arcadian future to be created out of a wilderness, environmentalists fantasize about regaining an arcadian past: the golden age when nature benignly ordered the world. Indian peoples, whose own past progress destroyed, have become the symbols of this once and future world for many beneficiaries of progress disillusioned with its fruits. Modern society represents a declension from a better world, but some retain the hope that through a new, higher morality, they will "progress" back to an arcadian past.[53]

A century that began with so many willing to imagine revolutionary futures cut free from the past has seen many of those futures turn nightmarish and horrific. The immediate past offers no models for environmental relations. Socialism once seemed to offer an alternative set of economic, and thus presumably environmental, relations to an inherently exploitative capitalism, but it has in practice yielded even greater environmental problems. History has, for the moment, stolen the future, the present is dangerous and in disarray, but progress is a malleable and adaptable idea, and so it becomes in some environmentalist thinking the movement toward a mythic, arcadian past.[54]

---

53. See Marx, *Machine in the Garden,* 102–107. Antonello Gerbi, *Nature in the New World: From Christopher Columbus to Gonzalo Fernandez de Oviedo* (Pittsburgh: University of Pittsburgh Press, 1985), 256–58; Cosgrove, *Social Formation and Symbolic Landscape,* 166–69.

54. For analyses of past environmental relations, see William Cronon, *Changes in the Land: Indians, Colonists, and the Ecology of New England* (New York: Hill and Wang, 1983); Donald Worster, *Dust Bowl: The Southern Plains in the 1930s* (New York: Oxford University Press, 1989); Arthur F. McEvoy: *The Fisherman's Problem: Ecology and Law in the California Fisheries, 1850–1980* (New York: Cambridge University Press, 1986); Richard White, *Land Use, Environment and Social Change: The Shaping of Island County, Washington* (Seattle: University of Washington Press, 1980).

# Particular, Universal, and Infinite: Transcending Western Centrism and Cultural Relativism in the Third World

*Zhiyuan Cui*

The current debate on the possibility of progress in the Third World is dominated by two contrasting positions. In one view, the Third World must accept the existing Western institutions and ideas as a whole package for the sake of "progress"; in another view, the particular cultural and institutional traditions in the Third World must be preserved as they are, and any outside criticism of local traditions is neither possible nor desirable. The formal view is Western centrism, the latter cultural relativism.

I will argue in this chapter that the both views are seriously misleading. One simple example is enough to illustrate the inadequacy of both. In many of today's third world countries, women's rights are still restricted and even repressed. Are we going to accept this as culturally given? Or if we want to break the local tradition in order to improve women's social position, does it mean we must also adopt existing Western institutions as a whole? The answer to both questions is no.

This example points to the problem that lies in both views' failure to grasp the dialectical relationship between the "particular" and the "universal." In a sense, they both overcelebrate their particular traditions, though for different reasons. The Western centrists celebrate their particular tradition because they mistakenly view their particular institutions and ideas as universally valid; in contrast, the cultural relativists just celebrate their particular tradition for its own sake. What they both lack is a view of the "universal" being both embodied in and separated from the particulars.

The central theme of this chapter is that the "universal" underlying all these particular traditions is "human self-assertion." Different societies and cultures present different degrees of human self-assertion, but none of them

---

I would like to thank professors Leo Marx and Bruce Mazlish for their comments on this chapter.

will ever be able to exhaust its possible meanings. This notion of "human self-assertion" is due to Hans Blumenberg, who defines it as "an existential program according to which man posits his existence in a historical situation and indicates to himself how he is going to deal with the reality surrounding him and what use he will make of the possibilities that are open to him."[1] Though Blumenberg mainly discusses human self-assertion in the context of early modern Europe, we can easily discover its germ latent in almost all other parts of the world.

The first section of the chapter develops my understanding of human self-assertion, by exploring three philosophical concepts: particular, universal, and infinite. The second section, by drawing on some concrete historical cases, shows that Western centrists and cultural relativists both misunderstand the "infinite" nature of human self-assertion. The last section argues that the chance of possible progress in the Third World lies in institutional innovation, that is, the invention of institutions that have so far been absent in both the West and the Third World. I will put the shareholding-cooperative system (SCS) in Chinese rural industry in the perspective of the current Western debates over property rights, arguing that the Chinese SCS represents an institutional innovation with the feature of "disintegrated property."

In Hans Blumenberg's fascinating *Legitimacy of the Modern Age,* the theme of "human self-assertion" is closely related to the theme of "possible progress." He distinguishes between "possible" and "inevitable" progress. In his view, the notion of progress as an inevitable process is certainly not essential to human self-assertion; indeed, it might almost be described as its antitheses. Blumenberg argues forcefully that "possible progress" is overextended to "inevitable progress" due to the efforts of modern thinkers to "reoccupy" the positions of medieval Christian schema of creation and eschatology. As the translator of Blumenberg's book explains, "Christianity, he says, through its claim to be able to account for the overall pattern of world history in terms of the poles of creation and eschatology, had put in place a new question, one that had been unknown to the Greeks: the question of the meaning and pattern of world history as a whole. When modern thinkers abandoned the Christian 'answers,' they still felt an obligation to answer the questions that went with them—to show that modern thought was equal to any challenge."[2]

The implications of Blumenberg's distinction between "possible progress" and "inevitable progress" are profound. They amount to recharting the future of progress according to the human potential of self-assertion, rather

---

1. Hans Blumenberg, *The Legitimacy of the Modern Age* (Cambridge: MIT Press, 1991), 138.

2. Ibid., xx–xxi.

than imposing a "pattern of history" onto human self-assertion. But, given the importance of the notion of human self-assertion to Blumenberg's whole argument, why doesn't he give it a precise definition? The answer, I think, is to be found in the "infinite" nature of human self-assertion. Harry Wolfson has given an interesting interpretation of the notion of "infinite":

> In medieval discussions of infinity the term "infinite" is said to have two meanings. It may be an accident either of magnitude or of number, or it may be an essence, that is to say, a self-existent substance, immaterial like soul and intellect. As an accident of magnitude it means an unlimited distance or length, something that has no end or boundary. As an accident of number, it means something that is endlessly addible or divisible. "Finite" as the antithesis of this kind of infinite means just the opposite, a distance that is bounded and a number that is limited, or, in other words, something comparable with others of its kind and exceeded by them.
> But an essentially infinite substance means something entirely different. It means a substance whose essence is unique and so incomparable that it cannot suffer any form of limitation and hence cannot have any form of positive description, for every description necessarily implies a limitation, or as Spinoza puts it: "determination is negation." To call a substance infinite in this sense is like calling voice colorless. When voice is described as colorless it does not mean the negation of a property which we should expect it to have and which it may have, but rather the absolute exclusion of voice from the universe of color . . .[3]

Obviously, human self-assertion belongs to the second form of "infinite." This notion of infinite is in turn closely related to the notion of "universal," as Roberto Unger's following interpretation makes clear:

> The universal must exist as a particular, just as a person is inseparable from his body. There is no formal universality, no circumstance in which the universal can be abstracted from its particular form. It always exists in a concrete way. Yet no single particular incarnation of the universal exhausts its meaning or its possible modes of existence. Thus, there is no one state of a person's body that at any given time, or over the course of his life, reveals all the sides of his identity . . . In this conception, the universal and the particular are equally real though they represent different kinds of reality. The universal is neither abstract and formal, nor capable of being identified with a single concrete and substantive particu-

---

3. Harry Austryn Wolfson, *The Philosophy of Spinoza* (Cambridge: Harvard University Press, 1934), 133–34.

lar. Instead, it is an entity whose universality consists precisely in the open set of concrete and substantive determinations in which it can appear . . .[4]

Unger's characterization of the dialectical relation between universal and particular is certainly very much in the tradition of Aristotle and Hegel. For example, Aristotle believes that "form" has infinite embodiments in "matter," but that "matter" can never exhaust "form." In other words, the form cannot exist apart from matter, but it is capable of assuming different embodiments. However, I want to stress here that the relation between universal and particular also is crucial in many other cultures. Taoism in China is about the relation between "one" (universal) and "many" (particular). Because Tao is unitary and consequently cannot be more or less present in some things than in others, the equality of all things is assured; but because Tao is present in individual things, it is possible to talk of individual differences between things. The paradox of how the One can be in the Many and yet retain its unity had long-range effects on religious Taoism and on Chinese Buddhism.[5]

The parallel questioning of relationship between One (universal) and Many (particular) in Taoism indicates that this very relationship is a focus of intellectual pursuits in many cultures. In my view, it is exactly because human self-assertion—with its concepts of "infinite" and "universal"—is embodied in many different particular traditions that we can talk meaningfully about the following things: (1) learning between traditions; (2) self-transformation of the given tradition; and (3) outside criticism of a given tradition, without assuming any particular tradition as the only embodiment of the "universal."

What is wrong with Western centrism? It is its insensitivity to the diversity and tension within third world cultures. Max Weber's understanding of Confucianism in China is a case in point. In his *Religion of China,* Weber characterizes the Confucian as a gentleman politely accommodating himself to the status quo.[6] Therefore, in Weber's view, we cannot speak of Confucians as prophets, who constantly challenge the existing order. This characterization overlooks the tension between the given world and Heaven's imperative within a Confucian mind. In fact, according to Confucius, it is the imperatives of Heaven that serve as the ultimate criteria in judging human affairs. This makes

---

4. Roberto Mangabeira Unger, *Knowledge and Politics* (New York: Free Press, 1974), 143.

5. Donald J. Munro, *The Concept of Man in Early China* (Stanford, Calif.: Stanford University Press, 1969).

6. Max Weber, *The Religion of China,* trans. Hans Gerth (New York: MacMillan, 1965), 227.

at least some Confucians "prophetic," in the sense of being the voice of transcendence and transformation of the existing order.

This example illustrates the fact that Christian tradition cannot exhaust the possible forms and meanings of transcendence. Indeed, Shmuel Eisenstadt has called Confucianism "this-worldly transcendentalism."[7] To the extent that transcendentalism contributes to human self-assertion by encouraging "social iconoclasm," Weber's mistake in understanding Confucian transcendentalism shows once again the "infinite" nature of possible forms of human self-assertion.

The insensitivity of Western centrism to the diversity and tension within third world cultures also results in insensitivity to the diversity and tension within Western culture itself. This is only natural: indeed, they are the two sides of the same coin. Take Weber as an example again. When Weber defines *prophet* as "a purely individual bearer of charisma,"[8] he necessarily overlooks the very complexity of "prophecy" in the Western tradition. According to Harry Wolfson's important study on Philo, ever since Philo substituted Plato's theory of "recollection" as the highest kind of knowledge with prophecy, prophecy has performed at least four functions and assumed three forms.[9] The details of Wolfson's analysis will not concern us here. My point is simply that once we recognize the infinite nature of "the universal," we must realize that both Western and non-Western traditions are just "particulars." Western centrism's claim to the status of the universal for the particular Western tradition is a mistake, because it directly equates "finite particular" with "infinite universal."

The following statement by Cornelius Castoriadis vividly demonstrates this mistake:

> Before Greece and outside the Greco-Western tradition, societies are instituted on a principle of strict closure: our view of the world is the only meaningful one, the "others" are bizarre, inferior, perverse, evil, or unfaithful. As Hannah Arendt has said, impartiality enters this world with Homer . . . This is the meaning of the creation of historiography in Greece. It is a striking fact that historiography properly speaking has existed only during two periods of human history: in ancient Greece, and in modern Europe—that is, in the cases of the two societies where ques-

---

7. S. N. Eisenstadt, *This-Worldly Transcendentalism and the Structuring of the World: Weber's Religion of China and the Format of Chinese History and Civilization* (Jerusalem: Hebrew University of Jerusalem, 1983).

8. Max Weber, *The Sociology of Religion* (Boston: Beacon Press, 1963), 46.

9. Harry Austryn Wolfson, *Philo*, vol. 2 (Cambridge: Harvard University Press, 1947), 3–72.

tioning of existing institutions has occurred. In other societies, there is only the undisputed reign of tradition, and/or simple "recording of events" by the priests or the chroniclers of the kings.[10]

Any careful reader of Joseph Needham's *Science in Traditional China* will easily perceive how wrong Castoriadis, or Hanna Arendt, was. Interestingly, Castoriadis is the founder of the journal *Socialisme ou Barbarie*, publication of the noncommunist revolutionary group that greatly influenced the 1968 student-worker rebellion in France. This fact shows how pervasive Western centrism is!

Having criticized Western centrism, let us now turn to cultural relativism. What is wrong with cultural relativism?

Basically, cultural relativism is a pseudo-historicalism. It insists that the sole discourse we can have about our subjective experience of social life is a particularizing discourse: the attempt to explicate and elaborate the assumptions that distinguish a given culture from all others. But, as Roberto Unger sharply points out, this prohibition "imposes an arbitrary constraint upon the principle of historicity because it fails to recognize that the extent to which our contexts imprison us and reduce us to a compulsive passivity is itself one of the things up for grabs in history. This unhistorical limit upon historical variability illustrates the indefensible version of the modernist view of our relation to our contexts: the version that combines skepticism with surrender, by teaching that all we can do is to choose a social world or a tradition of discourse and to play by its rules."[11]

In *A Quiet Revolution,* an eloquent study of women's education in rural Bangladesh, Martha Chen describes her effort as a member of a government development group, the Bangladesh Rural Advancement Committee, to increase the rate of female literacy in rural areas. The project began from a conviction that literacy is an important ingredient in the development of these women toward a better life. This conviction did not derive naturally from the local traditions of the villages, where women were repressed to the extent that they were not allowed to go marketing.[12] Chen's and her group's initial effort failed, because the content of their textbook was not related to the local context and hence seemed to be irrelevant to the lives of local women. But Chen's group never abandoned the conviction that literacy is important for these

---

10. Cornelius Castoriadis, *Philosophy, Politics, Autonomy* (New York: Oxford Odéon, 1991), 82, 114.

11. Roberto Mangabeira Unger, *Passion: An Essay in Personality* (New York: Free Press, 1984), 79–80.

12. M. Chen, *A Quiet Revolution: Women in Transition in Rural Bangladesh* (Cambridge, Mass.: Schenkman Publishing Co., 1986).

village women's self-development. By trying new textbooks and exploring a local cooperative network, they finally succeeded in getting local women interested in learning how to read.[13]

This example indicates that we don't have to be the prisoner of an arbitrary, particular culture. We have the capacity to change it if we want to. The elements or germs of human self-assertion exist in every culture. Cultural relativism amounts to the denial of this human potential of infinite self-assertion. Ironically, the cultural relativists' proposition "anything goes" is just another way of uncritically celebrating particular traditions; thus, they are no different from Western centrists in this respect.

I hope that so far the inadequacy of both Western centrism and cultural relativism has been demonstrated. In a nutshell, both views downplay the infinite nature of human self-assertion. They arbitrarily limit human creativity to some particular traditions. In order to make "possible" progress in the Third World, we must transcend both Western centrism and cultural relativism. The key is to engage in institutional innovations that are new to both today's West and the Third World. Let me illustrate this point with a discussion of institutional innovation in Chinese rural industry.

Chinese economic reform since the late 1970s has been considered a successful story by many partial and impartial observers. From 1978 to 1994, real gross national product (GNP) grew at an average annual rate of 12 percent, and per capita GNP doubled in real terms. Especially, rural industry is the most dynamic sector in the whole period.

Chinese rural industry goes far beyond traditional handicraft. It belongs to all China's 40 major modern industrial sectors, except petroleum and natural gas extraction. While the average annual rate of increase in total output value of the whole country between 1980 and 1988 was 11.8 percent, the total output value of rural industry increased annually at the rate of 33.2 percent. It is rural industry rather than grain production that accounts for the increase of peasant incomes.

Two striking features are to be noticed in Chinese rural industrialization. First, it is very unusual among today's developing countries. In many of these countries, the existence of industrial urban centers gives rise to rural-urban migration that exceeds the capacity of the cities to employ new settlers. In fact, not only in today's developing countries, but also in eighteenth-century England and nineteenth-century France, industrial urban centers had "a limited capacity to transform and absorb the traditional sector, leaving the peasantry

---

13. Martha Nussbaum has used Chen's case to support her Aristotelian approach to "non-relative virtues": Martha Nussbaum, "Non-Relative Virtues: An Aristotelian Approach," in *The Quality of Life*, ed. Martha Nussbaum and Amartya Sen (Oxford: Clarendon Paperbacks, 1993).

with a peripheral role in the industrialization process."[14] The Western way of industrialization and urbanization may be unique and uncopiable for other countries. In this sense, innovation, rather than coping the existing Western institutions, is a necessary condition of progress in the Third World.

Second, and more importantly, Chinese rural industry developed a new type of ownership structure. In their effort to create a proper ownership form for rural enterprises, the Chinese "peasant-workers" and their community governments have designed an ingenious shareholding-cooperative system. After three years of experiments in three areas in Shandong, Zhejiang, and Anhui provinces, the Ministry of Agriculture issued "The Temporary Regulations for Peasant's Shareholding-Cooperative Enterprises" in February, 1990. It indicates that this form of collective ownership will become more and more important in Chinese rural enterprises. This SCS is an indigenous innovation on the part of Chinese peasantry. I conducted preliminary field research in the summer of 1993 in the Zhoucun district of Zibo (Shangdong province), where the SCS was invented in 1982 as a response to the difficulties of dismantling the collective properties of the People's Commune. The peasants found that some collective properties (other than land) are simply physically indivisible. They decided to issue shares to each "peasant-worker" on equal terms, instead of destroying the collective property (such as trucks) by selling them in pieces (which had occurred in many other regions). Soon after, they realized (or conceded) that they should not divide up all collective properties into individual shares to the current work force, because the older generation of "peasant-workers" had left the enterprises, and the local governments had made previous investments. Thus, they decided to keep some proportion of "collective shares," which would not go into individual labor shares. These collective shares are designed to be held by outside corporate bodies, such as local governmental agencies, other firms in and out of the locality, banks, and even universities and scientific research institutions. The following figure shows the flow of profits of SCS in Zhoucun District.

Clearly, the development of SCS is the joint product of two factors: (1) accumulated change in Chinese rural institutions (such as the dissolution of the commune) and (2) improvised solutions to the indivisibility of commune property. However, the significance of SCS is much broader. It challenges the conventional Western theory of consolidated property rights that goes back to William Blackstone in the eighteenth century. In essence, the SCS system is an example of a disintegrated property rights arrangement. Let me be more specific about the distinction between "consolidated" and "disintegrated" property.

---

14. Colin Haywood, "The Role of the Peasantry in French Industrialization, 1815–80," *Economic History Review* 34, no. 3 (1981): 300.

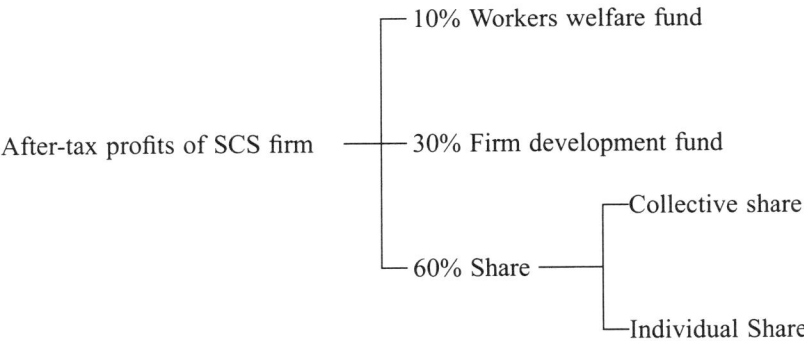

Fig. 1. Distribution of profits in the shareholding-cooperative system of Zhoucun district of Zibo, Shangdong province

Basically, the "consolidated" view of property seeks to "concentrate in a single entity, usually an individual person, the relevant rights, privileges, and powers of possessing, using, and transferring discrete assets."[15] By contrast, the "disintegrated" view conceives property as a "bundle of rights," which can be distributed among different holders, be it individuals or collectives. The current Western legal debates are between the conventional "consolidated" view and the emerging "disintegrated" view. Thomas Grey explains these two views clearly as follows:

> Most people, including most specialists in their unprofessional moments, conceive of property as things that are owned by persons. To own property is to have exclusive control of something—to be able to use it as one wishes, to sell it, give it away, leave it idle, or destroy it. Legal restraints on the free use of one's property are conceived as departures from an ideal conception of full ownership. By contrast, the theory of property rights held by the modern specialist tends both to dissolve the notion of ownership and to eliminate any necessary connection between property rights and things. Consider ownership first. The specialist fragments the robust unitary conception of ownership into a more shadowy "bundle of rights." Thus, a thing can be owned by more than one person, in which case it becomes necessary to focus on the particular limited rights each of the co-owners has with respect to the thing.[16]

---

15. Gregory Alexander, "The Dead Hand and the Law of Trusts in the Nineteenth Century," *Stanford Law Review* (May, 1985): 1189.
16. Thomas Grey, "The Disintegration of Property," *Nomos* 22 (1980): 69.

The crucial point of the "bundle of rights" view is that "what we call property is merely a collection of heterogeneous faculties. These faculties can be broken up and assigned to different entities."[17] None of the holders of these faculties has the exclusive right with regard to the whole bundle of property rights.

The implications of this "bundle of rights" view of property are far-reaching. "The substitution of a bundle-of-rights for a thing-ownership conception of property has the ultimate consequence that property ceases to be an important category in legal and political theory."[18] As Joseph Singer points out,

> phrasing the problem as "identifying the owner" is fundamentally wrong. It is simply not the right question. To assume that we can know who property owners are, and to assume that once we have identified them their rights follow as a matter of course, is to assume what needs to be decided. Property interests can be divided in various ways, including: (1) over time (current versus future interests); (2) into co-ownership (joint tenancy, tenancy in common, partnership, corporations); (3) into leases (landlord/tenant relations); (4) into trusts (trustee/beneficiary); (5) into easements and covenants; and (6) into mortgages (mortgagor/mortgagee). Who owns the property in these cases? The landlord or the tenant? The trustee or the beneficiary? The mortgagor or the mortgagee? The question is meaningless. Just as the landlord, life tenant, defeasible fee owner, trustee, and fee simple owner may be "owners" of property, so may tenants, reversioner, trust beneficiaries, holders of future interests, and owners of easements. There are even cases in which it is difficult to identify anyone as the owner. Who owns a university? The board of trustees? The graduates? The students?[19]

Though the latest development of Western legal theory endorses the disintegrated view of property, the Western practice is still dominated by the consolidated view of property. Thus, the current industrial restructuring in the West has a lot to do with the difficult introduction of disintegrated property relations to the various stakeholders of the firm.

However, when we look at Chinese rural enterprises from this perspective, we find distinctly disintegrated property rights. It is the particular form of

---

17. Roberto Mangabeira Unger, *The Critical Legal Studies Movement* (Cambridge: Harvard University Press, 1986).

18. Grey, "Disintegration of Property," 81.

19. Joseph Singer, "The Reliance Interest in Property," *Stanford Law Review* (February, 1988): 611–751.

arrangement of the bundle of property rights rather than cultural relativism or Western centrism that explains the success of Chinese rural enterprises.

The Chinese practice of the SCS suggests that the right question to ask about reform in China or anywhere else is not who the consolidated exclusive owner is, but how the bundle of property rights is being disintegrated and recombined. The lesson is very relevant for Western industrial restructuring.

Viewed as pure types, shareholding and cooperative systems are in conflict. The principle of shareholding is, as practiced by most conventional capitalist joint-stock companies, "one share, one vote." It is a system that mainly serves the outside stockholders' interest. In contrast, the principle of the cooperative system is, as advocated as early as by John Stuart Mill, "one worker, one vote," which mainly serves the interests of internal laborers. The conflict of these two principles is most vividly reflected in the so-called "degeneration problem" of workers' cooperatives in the capitalist environment: if a cooperative is successful, it becomes the target of buyout by external investors; if it does not resort to external financing in the first place, or only issues nonvoting shares to the outsiders, it becomes uncompetitive and therefore ruins itself.

In order to reconcile the conflict of interest between outside investors and inside workers, the Nobel laureate James Meade has proposed a system of "discriminating labor-capital partnerships." In this system, each firm will issue two kinds of share certificates, namely:

1. Capital share certificates which would be distributed to all the persons who were in fact receiving directly or indirectly through profit, interest, rent, etc., the capitalists' 20 per cent share of the firm's revenue . . .
2. Labor share certificates which would be distributed to all employees pro rata to their individual earnings of the remaining 80 per cent of the firm's revenue.
   All share certificates, whether capital or labor, would carry an entitlement to the same rate of dividend . . . everyone concerned in the operation of the business would now have a share in the future success or failure of the enterprise.[20]

The Chinese stockholding-cooperative system is similar to Meade's labor-capital partnership in that both systems have labor shares and capital shares;[21] however, the Chinese SCS is distinct in that capital shares themselves

---

20. James Meade, "Forms of Share Economy," in *Collective Papers of James Meade,* vol. 2 (London: Unwin Hyman, 1988), 235.

21. It is important to notice that both systems differ significantly from the Employee Stock Ownership Plan (ESOP) in the United States. ESOP promotes "worker participation in the firm's

are mainly collective, in the sense of belonging to the representatives of the community—township and village governments. Thus, the SCS in China's rural industry serves to harmonize the interests of inside workers and outside members of the same community. While Meade's system is only a theoretical proposal, the Chinese practice of the SCS will provide many useful lessons for this kind of institutional innovation forthcoming in the West.

Therefore, the SCS in China's rural industry is a good example of institutional innovation in a third world country, which turns out to be a contribution to the theoretical and institutional development in the West as well.

To summarize, the Third World has an opportunity to transcend both Western centrism and cultural relativism so that all parts of the world can bravely engage in institutional innovations that will contribute to the progressive course of human self-assertion by humankind as a whole. This kind of institutional innovation, in essence, is the core of democratic experimentalism, which promises to give a new meaning to the notion of "progress" in the twenty-first century.

---

fortunes only in so far as a part of the work's past pay has taken the form of compulsory savings rather than the receipt of freely disposable income, whereas Labor Share Certificates depend directly upon the employee's current supply of work and effort to the firm without any reference to past compulsory savings" (James Meade, *Alternative Systems of Business Organization and of Workers; Remuneration*) (London, Allen and Unwin, 1986), 117.

# "Progress": Illegitimate Child of Judeo-Christian Universalism and Western Ethnocentrism—A Third World Critique

*Ali A. Mazrui*

Never has the concept of *progress* been more influential than it has been in the twentieth century. One version of it—Marxism—is in serious trouble in most of the world. The other twentieth-century version of the concept of progress is *developmentalism*. That version is alive and well in most of the Third World and in relations between the industrialized Northern Hemisphere and the so-called developing countries. Institutions like the World Bank and the International Monetary Fund (IMF) are centrally involved in the doctrine of progress, precisely because they are involved in the ideology of developmentalism.

In this chapter we start from the premise that the doctrine of *progress* presupposes a concept of universalism. Both Marxism and developmentalism in the twentieth century have rested on teleological assumptions—and these in turn have been universalist in either scope or aspiration. Further, both Marxism and developmentalism have needed an image of an ideal society, a kind of role model. Marxism has regarded Western capitalism as a stage or two *before* the ideal society, but on its way there. Developmentalism has tended to regard liberal capitalism as the final fulfillment—what Francis Fukuyama has called "the end of history."[1]

We need hardly argue in this chapter that the choice of the West as the role model or ideal society is *ethnocentric,* while the idea that all societies are evolving toward the same destination is *universalist. The concept of progress is therefore a dialectic between the universalism of process and the ethnocentrism of destination.* In this chapter we are critiquing Western and Judeo-

---

1. See Francis Fukuyama, *The End of History and The Last Man* (New York: Free Press, 1992). In the book, Fukuyama goes beyond the thesis of his article "The End of History?" *National Interest* 16 (summer 1989): 3–18.

Christian teleological thought, partly from the perspective of the so-called developing world.[2]

I propose to argue in this chapter that Western theories of progress have been a meeting point of two universals, one religious and the other scientific. Universalism in Western religion has affected the normative foundations of theories of development and progress and sought to convert the world to Western culture. Universalism in Western science has transformed that cultural self-assurance into a technological expansionism. Theories of development in all the social sciences are a fusion of religious faith and scientific rationalism. This is part of what we mean by *the dual universalism of Western civilization*.

But if Western culture is so universalistic in scope, how can it be ethnocentric at the same time? The universalism is one of the causes of the ethnocentrism. The Jews taught the world about the one universal God—and then identified *themselves* as the chosen people. Similarly the West told the world about the universalism of both science and the gospel of Jesus—and then the white man of the West put himself forward as the chosen breed. He saw himself as the role model of humanity.

In the hands of Europeans, the Jewish concept of *the chosen people* was *racialized*. Without using the phrase itself, Europeans developed a racist concept of themselves as the chosen people. What had been a religious doctrine of Jewish ethnocentrism became a principle of arrogance in European racism. The concept of "the white man's burden" was born. Let us look at these historical developments more closely.

Westerners tend to trace their civilization to two cultural fountains, each of which is in turn mixed. These fountains are the Greco-Roman heritage and the Judeo-Christian tradition. If there is a division of labor between the two ancestries, it is one that makes the Greco-Roman legacy the ultimate mother of the scientific spirit and the Judeo-Christian tradition the mother of Western morality.

Both Western science and Western religion do indeed start from universalist premises. Western social science in the twentieth century has consciously modeled itself after the spirit, the method, and the universalism of natural science. But at least as profound an influence on Western social science is indeed the universalism of Western religion. It is often the religious universalism—rather than the scientific—that has fed Western theories of progress and of development at their most optimistic.

---

2. I have of course been a partial critic of Western theories of modernization over the years, including a presentation at the Mini-Planning Session on "A Global Political Theory," Section 4, XIV World Congress of the International Political Science Association, held in Washington, D.C., August 28–September 1, 1988.

Underlying the tendency has been the de facto Western self-conception as the new chosen people. Just as Western Christian missionaries believed that people of other faiths should be converted to the Christian gospel and "rescued" from "heathenism," so Western social scientists have often believed that Africans and Asians could be "rescued" from their cultures and converted to the Western gospel of development and progress.

"Development" especially has become the equivalent of a new religion rather than a new technology. What developmentalism shares with Christianity are the following characteristics:

1. They are both creeds that seek to convert the whole of humankind.
2. They have different interpretations of their own respective gospels ("The Gospel According to Matthew" or the gospel of Adam Smith).
3. On the other hand, they each have an underlying premise of a unilinear route to ultimate salvation.
4. Christianity and developmentalism are both deeply rooted in Western teleological culture and values.
5. The Western world is the global leader of both, with a disposition toward usurping the role of the chosen people.

## The Doctrine of the Chosen People

The idea that the Jews are the elect of God has been a recurrent theme in Jewish liturgy: "For you are a people holy to the Lord your God, and the Lord has chosen you to be a people of his own possession, out of all the nations that are on the face of the earth."[3]

Is "being chosen" a matter of superior moral qualities and "racial" sensibilities? Or is it, on the contrary, a matter of heavier burdens of responsibility and greater accountability? By being called upon to reveal, preserve, and transmit the word of God, were the Jews also called upon to aspire to higher standards of ethical and spiritual performance?

There have been Jews who have "modernized" the concept of the chosen people. They have made it a vehicle of *progress*. Nachman Krochmal is neo-Hegelian in his vision of the Jewish people as the bearer of the historical process. What Hegel saw in *Prussia* Krochmal saw in the *Jews*. But Krochmal added a cyclical dynamic to history. The Jews were the only nation to arise again and again, reinvigorated after every decline. The Jews alone had a direct link with the Absolute Spirit. The Jews were therefore a source of special creativity, for each ascent was to a higher level of self-realization. Moral

---

3. Deut. 14:2. King James Bible. Subsequent citations appear in the text.

progress was at work. Spiritual renewal and human creativity were the raison d'etre of the Jews as the elect of both God and history.[4]

Reform Jews in the contemporary era have de-emphasized nationality and have focused on the more positive aspects of the Diaspora. The concept of the chosen people has been demoted in the theology of Reform Judaism—but remains triumphant in more preponderant Conservative and Orthodox circles around the world. (Islam, on the other hand, it should be noted, does not regard the Arabs as a chosen people, although Arabic is considered the chosen language of God and has a special status and role in human communication with the Almighty.)

Perhaps the transfer of the concept of the chosen people to *Christians* began with St. Peter. He applied to Christians the Old Testament reference to *Israel* as "a kingdom of priests and a holy nation" (Exod. 19:6). St. Peter implied that the followers of Jesus were the new elect of God: "But you are a chosen race, a royal priesthood, a holy nation, God's own people."[5]

Peter did not know it, but he was setting the stage for what became nearly two millennia later, "The White Man's Burden." He was inaugurating the new era of *imperial christianity* dedicated to imperialism as an engine of progress.

The marriage between the Greco-Roman heritage and the Judeo-Christian tradition came with the conversion of Roman Emperor Constantine I (better known as Constantine the Great, A.D. 280–337). That constituted another major step in the universalization of Christianity. Was this a second stage in Christian "progress"? Over time it meant the conversion of much of the Roman Empire, and certainly most of Europe. A new de facto concept of the chosen people was being born—the supreme self-confidence of Europe.

Much later yet another stage in the universalization of Christianity was the settlement of the Americas by Europeans. This did win over the New World for the gospel of Jesus, seemingly for all time. Was this another step in "the pilgrim's progress"? Again it looked as if God had "chosen" Europeans to populate and control the New World.

The fourth major stage in Christian universalization was modern European imperialism, especially in Africa and Asia. This latest phase of Europe's role as the chosen people gave itself the slogan of "the white man's burden."

---

4. Convenient summaries of modern Jewish history and thought include Howard Morley Sachar, *The Course of Modern Jewish History* (Cleveland: World Pub. Co., 1958); Joseph Blau, *Modern Varieties of Judaism* (New York: Columbia University Press, 1966); and Nathan Rotenstreich, *Jewish Philosophy in Modern Times* (New York: Holt, Rinehart and Winston, 1968); Krochmal's own work on Jewish uniqueness was published posthumously in 1851 under the title *More nevukhe ha-zman* ("Guide for the perplexed of our time").

5. 1 Pt 2:9. For a less exclusivist application of Christian doctrine to global affairs, consult Alberto C. Coll, "Some Christian Reminders for the Statesman," *Ethics and International Affairs* 1 (1987): 97–112.

Europeans traversed the world in search of gold and glory—and to serve God. Africa was a particularly attractive area for Christian missionary activism. Was this yet another stage in "the pilgrim's progress"? Indigenous African creeds were not regarded as worth respecting, let alone saving. The crusade against African "heathenism" went unimpeded. African sacred belief systems were not called "religions" at all until the second half of the twentieth century.

Just as Black Africa had once been virgin territory for the spread of the Christian gospel, so it was later to be regarded as virgin area for experiments in developmentalism and modernization theories. The Gospel According to Matthew sometimes joined forces with the gospel according to Adam Smith. In postcolonial Africa the Gospel According to Mark sometimes gave way to a new gospel according to Marx. In all of them a basic dual universalism has persisted.

Somewhere between Mark and the Bible on one side and Marx and his successors on the other lies Charles Darwin, author of the momentous work *On the Origin of Species* and originator of an entirely new school of *the chosen species of* evolutionary teleology. In 1860 Karl Marx had written to Friedrich Engels after a month spent nursing his sick wife: "During my time of trial, these last four weeks, I have read all sorts of things. Among others Darwin's book on *Natural Selection*. Although it is developed in the crude English style, this is the book which contains the basis in natural history for our views." Marx elaborates this point elsewhere, arguing that in place of a war of nature he provided a theory of the "fierce strife of classes." And Engels in his funeral oration over Marx's grave in 1883 said: "As Darwin discovered the law of evolution in organic nature, so Marx discovered the law of evolution in human history." A new teleology had indeed arrived. And the dual universalism of Western civilization had entered a new phase.[6] The doctrine of *progress* was still unfolding.

## From Racism to Ethnocentrism

Charles Darwin's *Origin of Species* was published in 1859. It was soon to have long-term repercussions both for the study of biology and for the study of social science. Racists could now proceed to demonstrate, by the utilization of the theory of natural selection, that major differences in human capacity and human organization were to be traced to biological distinctions between races. To some extent this theory was much older than Darwin. What Darwin added

---

6. Cited in Edgar Hyman, *The Tangled Bank,* Universal Library ed. (New York: Grosset and Dunlop, 1966), 121–26. This part of the chapter is greatly indebted to my earlier work on political development and modernization. See especially Mazrui, "From Social Darwinism to Current Theories of Modernization: A Tradition of Analysis," *World Politics* 21, no. 1 (October, 1968): 69–83.

to it was the dynamism of converting mere classification of beings into a *process*. The static version of the theory was *religious* and went back to the ancient idea that God had so organized the world that the universe and creation were arranged in a "great chain of being"—that all creatures could be classified and fitted into a hierarchy extending "from man down to the smallest reptile, whose existence can be discovered by the microscope."[7] Those at the very top were the chosen people.

In other words, it was not just the lower species who were so classified. Even within the highest species created in the Almighty's image there were in turn other divisions. Theories of the great chain of beings assumed that the Almighty in his wisdom did not want a big gap between one type of creature and the next, so there had to be intermediate categories between orangutans and the white man. As early as 1713 naturalists began looking for the "missing link" between men and apes and apparently speculated on the possibility that Hottentots and orangutans might be side by side in the "scale of life," separated only by the fact that orangutans could not speak.[8]

What Darwinism helped refine into specific theoretical form was the element of *motion* in this process, the idea that the backward people might be on the move toward a higher phase, and those in front moving further still. *Progress* was activated at last.

The link between racism and ethnocentrism is not difficult to see. Even for the earliest racist theories there had been no difficulty about deciding where to place the white man in the chain of being. As Phillip D. Curtin puts it in discussing these early biological theorists:

> Since there is no strictly scientific or biological justification for stating that one race is "higher" than another, the criteria of ranking has to come from non-scientific assumptions. All of the biologists . . . began by putting the European variety at the top of the scale. This was natural enough if only as an un-thinking reflection of cultural chauvinism. It could be held to follow from the assessment of European achievements in art and science . . . it was taken for granted that historical achievement was intimately connected with physical form—in short, that race and culture were closely related.[9]

---

7. See Charles White, *An Account of the Regular Gradations in May* (London: C. Dilly, 1799), I. See also A. O. Lovejoy, *The Great Chain of Being* (Cambridge: Harvard University Press, 1936). Consult also Anthony Appiah, "The Uncompleted Argument: Du Bois and the Illusion of Race," *Critical Inquiry* 12, no. 1 (autumn 1985): 21–37.

8. Lovejoy, *The Great Chain of Being*, 233ff.; A. O. Lovejoy "Some Eighteenth Century Evolutionists," *Popular Science Monthly* 65, no. 4 (July, 1904) 238–51.

9. See P. D. Curtin, *The Image of Africa* (London: Macmillan and Company, 1965), 38–39. I am indebted to Curtin's book for bibliographical guidance and for some insights.

The dynamic element in ethnocentric theories of evolution inevitably led to assumptions about white leadership in the whole process of historical change. Progress was social selection if not natural selection. And within the white races themselves specific leadership was assumed to come from the "tougher" of the European stock. For example, in his inaugural lecture as Regius Professor of Modern History at Oxford in December, 1841, Thomas Arnold gave a new lease of life to the ancient idea of a moving center of civilization. Arnold argued that the history of civilization was the history of a series of creative races, each of which made its impact and then sank into oblivion, leaving the heritage of civilization to a greater successor. What the Greeks passed on to the Romans, the Romans bequeathed in turn to the Germanic race, and of that race the greatest civilizing nation was England.[10] In many cases this was seen as part of God's grand design. Emperors and kings were God's anointed.

Notions of leadership very often led to notions of the right to rule the less developed. Even that prophet of liberalism, John Stuart Mill, could still argue that despotism was "a legitimate mode of government in dealing with barbarians, provided the end be their improvement . . ."[11]

In Mill also there began to emerge the notion that Western democratic institutions constitute the ultimate destination of much of sociopolitical development. The capacity to operate democratic institutions was already being regarded as an index of political maturity and institutional stability. Mill even seemed to share some of the reservations held by current modernization theorists about the possibility of operating liberal institutions in multiethnic situations. To use Mill's own formulation, "Free institutions are next to impossible in a country made up of different nationalities."[12] Here, then, is the

---

10. See Thomas Arnold, *Introductory Lectures on Modern History* (New York: D. Appleton and Co., 1842), 46–47; consult also esp. Curtin, *Image of Africa,* 375–77. See also Arthur Penrhyn Stanley, *Life and Correspondence of Thomas Arnold* (London: Ward, Lock and Company, 1845), esp. 435, 438. This notion of a moving center of civilization is also discussed in my inaugural lecture *Ancient Greece in African Political Thought* (Nairobi: East African Publishing House, 1967).

11. J. S. Mill, *Representative Government,* ed. R. B. McCallum (Oxford: Basil Blackwell, 1946). Consult also Joseph Ike Asike, "Culture, Development and Philosophy," *Africa and the World* 1, no. 3 (April, 1988): 20–25.

12. Ibid. Carl G. Rosberg, Jr., for example, makes a similar point, when he argues that "The dangers to stability presented by ethnic and other parochialism are magnified in most African states by a lack of that fundamental of common values and widely shared principles of political behavior generally termed 'consensus.' Typically, the terms of a consensus prescribe that the pursuit of group interests be conducted peaceably and within established institutions of the constitutional framework." See Rosberg, "Democracy and the New African States," in *St. Antony's Papers on African Affairs,* No. 2, ed. Kenneth Kirkwood (London: Chatto and Windus, 1963), 26. Comparable arguments abound in the literature on democracy in new states.

essential assumption of some of the current theories of integration—a process toward the fusion of nationalities within a single territory into a new entity capable of sustaining the stresses of a more liberal polity.

At least one major approach in theorizing about political modernization in our own day has rested on what Robert A. Packenham describes as "the idea that political development is primarily a function of a social system that facilitates popular participation in governmental and political processes at all levels, and the bridging of regional, religious, caste, linguistic, tribal and other cleavages." Packenham goes on to argue that one form this particular approach has taken today is to assess the social correlates of democracy. Are these the new criteria of the chosen people? These correlates are supposed to include relatively high "scores" on such sociological variables as an open class system, literacy and/or education, high participation in voluntary organizations, urbanization, and communication system.[13] Much of this side of analysis assumes that the highest of modern institutions must inevitably be those that have been devised in the West. The Darwinian evolution toward modernity is evolution toward Western ways. Edward Shils seemed to be expressing as much his own view of the matter as of some members of the Afro-Asian elite when he said, "Modern means being Western without the onus of dependence on the West." And much of the rest of Shils's theorizing on the process of development bears the stamp of ethnocentric preference for "a regime of representative institutions" of the Western kind.[14] The concept of "the chosen people" has now been *democratized.*

There have been models of theorizing about development which have gone as far as to classify political regimes in the world in terms of first, the Anglo-American type; second, the continental European types; third, totalitarian types; and fourth, the types that one found in Africa and Asia.[15] The concept of the chosen people has found a liberal guise.

---

13. See Robert A. Packenham, "Approaches to the Study of Political Development," *World Politics* 17, no. 1 (October, 1964): 108–20. For subsequent additional insights I have benefited from conversations with Gwendolen Carter, the late William O. Brown, and the late James S. Coleman.

14. See esp. Edward Shils, *Political Development in the New States* (The Hague: Mouton and Co., 1965), 10 ff. See also David Easton, "Political Science in the United States: Past and Present," *International Political Science Review* 6, no. 1 (1985): 133–152.

15. Gabriel Almond has shared such a vision of political development, especially in his earlier work. A more cautious but related formulation is that of Eisenstadt, who says: "Historically, modernization is the process of change towards those types of social, economic, and political systems that have developed in Western Europe and North America from the Seventeenth Century to the Nineteenth and have then spread to other European countries and in the Nineteenth and Twentieth Centuries to the South American, Asian, and African continents." See Shmuel Eisenstadt, *Modernization: Protest and Change* (Englewood Cliffs, N.J.: Prentice Hall, 1966), 1. Consult also the series of books entitled *Studies in Political Development* sponsored by the Committee on Comparative Politics of the Social Science Research Council of the United States.

Evidently, this is ethnocentrism that has strong links with older theories of Anglo-Saxon leadership as a focus of a new wave of civilization. Again, theories of *evolutionary* change culminating in the preeminence of a single nation had major *philosophers* of the West among their disciples. Not least among these philosophers was Hegel, for whom the entire process of change in the universe had for its ultimate human culmination the emergence of the Prussian state and the Germanic genius. Hegel, too, was in a sense a pre-Darwinian social Darwinist, both in his notion of a creative tension between thesis, antithesis, and synthesis and in his notion of a powerful evolution toward the emergence of a high species.

More recently there have been *historians* who have seen human evolution in terms of a progressive rise to the preeminence of their own nation or group of nations. William H. McNeill in our own day—though by no means lacking in humility—had interpreted world history in such a way that he might easily belong to this tradition.[16] McNeill challenges in part the Spenglerian pessimism of a Western decline and the whole conception of history as a collection of separate civilizations, each pursuing an independent career. For McNeill human cultures have had a basic interrelationship—and their history has been leading to a global preeminence of Western civilization.

In the field of *sociology* Talcott Parsons has talked about "evolutionary universals" in terms that do indicate a belief that ultimately development is in the direction of greater comparability with the political systems of the Western world. Parsons argues that the existence of a definitive link between popular participation and ultimate control of decision making is so crucial for building and maintaining support for the political-legal systems as a whole and for its binding rules and decisions that, in so far as large-scale societies are concerned, the "democratic association" is an "evolutionary universal." In defense of this proposition against anticipated criticism Parsons prophetically declares:

> I realise that to take this position I must maintain that communist totalitarian organisation will probably not fully match "democracy" in political and integrative capacity in the long run. I do indeed predict that it will prove to be unstable and will either make adjustments in a general direction of elective democracy and a plural party system or "regress" into generally less advanced and politically less effective forms of organisa-

---

Of special interest as a study of value systems is Lucian W. Pye and Sidney Verba, eds., *Political Culture and Political Development* (Princeton, N.J.: Princeton University Press, 1965).

16. See William H. McNeill, *The Rise of the West* (Chicago and London: University of Chicago Press, 1963). For a more ambivalent work, see J. M. Roberts, *The Triumph of the West* (London: British Broadcasting Corporation, 1985).

tion, failing to advance as rapidly or as far as might otherwise be expected.[17]

A similar prophetic ethnocentrism is evident in the approach of J. Roland Pennock to the study of political development. Pennock enumerates principles such as "justice according to law," "the rule of law," and "due process" as among the political goods that are delivered when a society attains a certain degree of political development. Pennock declares in a long footnote:

> It might be objected that modern totalitarian dictatorships may not subscribe to the standards of justice according to law outlined above. Are we then to call them less "developed" than modern constitutional regimes? ... I would be quite happy to say that to this extent they are in fact less developed, less fitted to fulfill the needs of men and society.[18]

Later in the same article Pennock refers to other tendencies in the discussion of political development that bear the ethnocentric theme that the history of human evolution is toward the type of institutions and ideals cherished in the Western world. This is a new type of ethnocentric universalism. Pennock does not describe them as Western ideals; there is a tendency to refer to such things as "world culture." But the inclination to discern an upward movement of human evolution toward Westernism is recurrent in the literature. In the words of the concluding sentences of Pennock's article:

> It is common today to compare or rank states by the degree of party competition, or their adoption and use of the major devices of representative government, or their social mobilization. It is my suggestion that, to see a more nearly complete picture and to make more highly discriminating judgments, anyone who is concerned with political development in any way involving measurement of comparison should take full account of some of the measurable elements of the political goods of security, justice, liberty, and welfare.[19]

---

17. Talcott Parsons, "Evolutionary Universals in Society," *American Sociological Review* 20 (June, 1964): 356. See also in the same issue of the journal S. N. Eisenstadt, "Social Change, Differentiation and Evolution."

18. James Roland Pennock, "Political Development, Political Systems, and Political Goods," *World Politics* 18, no. 3 (April, 1966): 424.

19. Ibid, 434. Pennock cites an appendix in Gabriel A. Almond and James S. Coleman, eds., *The Politics of the Developing Areas* (Princeton, N.J.: Princeton University Press, 1960); and Phillips Cutright, "National Political Development: Measurement and Analysis," *American Sociological Review* 28, no. 2 (April, 1963) 253–64. Another discussion by Almond of some of these issues is in his article "A Development Approach to Political Systems," *World Politics* 17, no. 2 (January, 1965) 183–214.

By the time of our current theories of modernization and Fukuyama's "end of history," the racist element in theories of human development had considerably declined, at least within the ranks of scholarship. The racial component was what had given social Darwinism a continuing biological feature borrowed from the Darwin of the *Origin of Species*. In fact, in the heyday of racial theories it was by no means all that clear where biological Darwinism ended and social Darwinism began.

But in the modern theories of development and modernization Darwinism has been substantially debiologized. It is no longer pure racial bigotry that is being invoked to explain stages of political growth. What is now invoked is at the most mild racial arrogance or ethnocentric cultural pride, but on a universal scale.

### Evolution and Optimism

The shift from biological explanations of human backwardness to cultural explanations of that factor had important implications. Biological differences imply a slower rate of mutation of character. Africans, for example, thus could not help lagging behind for many generations simply because they could not help the biological traits they had inherited from their own subspecies. There is a quality almost of immutability, of being retarded, when a lack of development is attributed to hereditary characteristics within the race. But as ideas on social evolution took a turn more toward cultural determinism, the notion of a backward people catching up with more advanced people was at last brought within the bounds of feasibility.

The shift from biological determinism to cultural determinism had its transitional moments. Let us take W. R. Greg as a case of intellectual transition in this field of theorizing. Greg inherited the leadership of Anglo-Saxon ethnocentrism from Thomas Arnold, the Regius Professor of Modern History at Oxford. At any rate, upon Arnold's death Greg speculated further in the *Westminster Review* on the whole destiny of human evolution. He discussed Africa specifically. He noted that some "backward races" elsewhere were indeed becoming extinct. But the "Negro race" seemed to retain a striking resilience. Figures from North America indicated that blacks could continue in healthy persistence even when they were transplanted from Africa to the very different environment of North America and to the very different experience of constant contact with Europeans. Greg was indeed of the opinion that Africans were intellectually devoid of the possibilities of ultimate originality. But they had the one thing that was very important from the point of view of successful acculturation: Africans were endowed with a significant imitative genius. They could therefore assimilate what the West could bequeath to them. This had implications for the whole notion of progress. Greg was in fact to some extent a precursor of theories of "demonstration-effect." Human progress was possible because the more backward of the races had at least the ability to imitate. And European achievements could therefore be grafted unto the African stock.[20]

Some of these notions were to last well into the period of colonial expansion in Africa and of the legitimation of individual colonial policies consequent upon annexation. To some extent the whole paraphernalia of ideas of the French assimilationist policies in the colonies had direct intellectual contact with the kind of tradition to which Greg belonged—the perspective that conceded Africans the capacity to emulate without permitting them a capacity to innovate. The policy of attempting to Gallicize Africans was firmly within the flow of this historical stream of ethnocentric universalism. As independence came, theorists in the Anglo-Saxon world discussed for a while the feasibility of upholding some of the inherited institutions from colonialism. The argument of whether or not Ghana could sustain the "Westminster model" was also part of this argument on the potential imitative capacity of African political beings. But gradually theories of political development attained a sophistication that differentiated them more sharply than ever from simple biological explanations of whether or not there was an important emulative genius within the African subspecies. Ghanaian capacity to maintain the Westminster model, or the ability of Nigeria to cope with inherited federal and Westminster institutions, became now more firmly associated with varied constraints and preconditions that the Western world had already managed to cope with but which the rest of the universe had yet to evolve.

Nevertheless there was a firm conviction that the direction of universal change would be toward a greater approximation to Western achievements. Such conviction meant that progress was almost inevitable for the more backward societies. And the direction of that progress was toward greater similarity of values, norms, and structures of the Western world.

In discussing the processes of change explained in the varying contexts of the five geographical areas reviewed in his influential book *The Politics of the Developing Areas,* the late James S. Coleman asserted that the consequences were by no means uniform and yet "in general the changes have brought the countries concerned nearer the model of a modern society." And what is a modern society? Coleman's own view as expressed elsewhere is more detached and less ethnocentric. But in that early book he edited with Gabriel A. Almond, Coleman derived a definition of a "modern society" from Almond's introduction to the book and from Edward Shils's model of a "political democracy." The attributes of a "modern system" had thus been enumerated. A new chosen people was identified. On the basis of these systemic characteristics Coleman concluded that "it is clear from this list of attributes that the

---

20. W. R. Greg, "Dr. Arnold," *Westminster Review* 39, no. 7 (January, 1843), 1–30.

Anglo-American qualities most closely approximate the model of the modern political system . . ."[21]

But is the march of history in the former Soviet Union in that modernizing direction? Are Africa and Latin America democratizing afresh in a similar direction? Has political science intimations to convey to us about the future? And how do those intimations relate to religious prophecy on one side and scientific prediction on the other? Let us turn to these areas of convergence now.

## On Prophecy and Teleology

According to tradition Paul's conversion began with a sign on his way to Damascus. Emperor Constantine's conversion also involved a prophecy that he would win a war by the sign of the cross. And the whole career of Jesus was predicated on the prophecy of the Messiah.

Prophecy and foretelling the future were for a long time part of the validation of religion—especially among some Semites (Arabs and Jews). With the new social sciences in the twentieth century in the Western world *prediction* replaced *prophecy* as a measure of credibility. As the social sciences have claimed greater affinity to *science,* they have attempted greater proximity to predictive power. But once again what appears to be an effort to marry social studies to the scientific method is, at least in part, a case of resurrecting an older *religious* tradition. Predictive power as a validation of science is sometimes another version of prophetic power as a validation of religion. The social studies are caught in between.

This is a different kind of universalism—the universalism of *time,* as contrasted with the universalism of *space* that we have discussed so far. Spreading the gospel to different parts of the world is a conquest of space; identifying the future is a conquest of time. Western social science has claimed the universalism of time, as well as of space, while still remaining ethnocentric. Is the collapse of communism in the former USSR and Eastern Europe a vindication of the predictive power of Western social science?

In the earlier phases of classical political theory a major preoccupation was to validate the present by reference to the *past,* rather than forecasting the future by reference to the present. Thus, the state of nature in Thomas Hobbes and John Locke was partly derived from Genesis and the Garden of Eden. Hobbes preferred the idea of "original sin" and humankind's basic fallibility. Locke preferred the concept of man as Adam before the fall. Nevertheless, the

---

21. Conclusion in Almond and Coleman, *Politics of the Developing Areas,* 536, 533. In his introduction to *Education and Political Development* (Princeton, N.J.: Princeton University Press, 1965), Coleman defines political development more neutrally in terms of enhancing "political capacity"; see esp. 15–16.

whole tradition of the "social contract" as a basis of political obligation rested quite often on assumptions about the past of humankind. (It is true that later contractual theorists more systematically regarded the contract idea as a logical device rather than a historical assertion about people's first entry into society.)

On the other hand, the historicity of the social contract remained part of the debate in political theory for quite a while. When Hobbes equated the state of nature with the state of war he felt he had to defend himself against those who were skeptical of the reality of such a state. In Hobbes's own words:

> It may peradventure be thought, there never was such a time, nor condition of warre [of nature] as this; and I believe it was never generally so, over all the world; but there are many places, where they live so now. For the savage people in many places of *America,* except the government of small Families, the concord whereof dependeth on naturall lust, have no government at all; and live at this day in that brutish manner, as I said before. Howsoever, it may be perceived what manner of life there would be, where there were no common Power to feare; by the manner of life, which men that have formerly lived under a peacefull government, use to degenerate into, in a civill warre.[22]

Locke's concept of the social contract also had elements of historicity in its assumptions. And certainly the 1688 Glorious Revolution in England rested much of its philosophy on the presumed historical understanding between king and people. When later on Edmund Burke criticized the French Revolution, it was in part because the French Revolution was not adequately guided by a look into the past before attempting to push into the future. A lack of sensitivity to the past could, in Burke's estimation, lead to a reckless disregard of the real interests of future generations. For "people will not look forward to posterity who never look backward to their ancestors."[23]

Yet the move from theology and traditionalism in the evolution of political philosophy to the rationalism of the eighteenth and nineteenth centuries is in part a move from a backward-looking orientation of values to a futuristic orientation in norms. John Plamenatz, the late Oxford political theorist, asserted that man cannot help but see himself as a traveler, and cannot know that

---

22. Thomas Hobbes, *Leviathan* (1651). See Everyman's Library edition, edited by A. D. Lindsay (London: J. M. Dent, 1957), 65.

23. For an attempt to relate this to the problem of tradition and shifting loyalties in a new state in Africa see Ali A. Mazrui, "Edmond Burke and Reflections on the Revolution in the Congo," *Comparative Studies in Society and History* 5, no. 2 (January, 1963): 121–33.

he is alive, without looking back to a past and forward to a future, asking whether the journey is subject to *progress*. In Plamenatz's words:

> From the beginning the philosophical student of politics has been interested in the course of social change. Aristotle imagined the *polis* growing out of the village, and the village growing out of the family; and, since he called man a political *animal,* a creature whose nature it is to create a political community and to realise itself in so doing, he saw the movement from family to *polis* as a movement in a desirable direction, as progress. But he imagined nothing better than the *polis* and did not ask himself what might come after it to take its place.[24]

Liberalism as a tradition was perhaps intermediate between the older forms of political philosophy with their grounding in custom, religion, and history, on the one hand, and the militant scientism of some of the rationalist schools of political theory later in the nineteenth century, on the other hand. But liberalism itself was in the nineteenth century part of the whole phenomenon of widespread *belief in progress*. This was the belief that history was moving in a *desirable* direction, or could at least easily be helped to move in that direction. And the belief in progress was perhaps the real origin of the lure of prediction in some of the social sciences in the modern period. But was it different from the belief that history was moving toward the Second Coming—and the final opportunity for salvation?

The idea that history had a purposeful direction was older than the form it took in the eighteenth and nineteenth centuries. E. H. Carr has argued that it was the Jews, and after them the Christians, who made it a sound postulation of their thought that there was a goal toward which the historical process was moving—the teleological view of history. History was permitted to acquire a meaning and a purpose, but it was desecularized in the process. The attainment of the goal of history would automatically mean the end of history. Such a medieval view of history converted history into a theodicy. Carr goes on to assert, however, that the Renaissance restored the classical view of an anthropocentric (homocentric) world and of the primacy of reason. But for the pessimistic classical view of the future the Renaissance substituted an optimistic view derived from the Jewish-Christian tradition. Gibbon, perhaps the greatest of the enlightenment historians, found it possible to record what he called "the pleasing conclusion that every age of the world has increased, and

---

24. John Plamenatz, *Man and Society,* Vol. 2 (London: Longmans and Green, 1963), 409. See also Jacques Barzun, "Is Democratic Theory for Export?" *Ethics and International Affairs* 1, no. 1 (1987): 53–72. Consult also Ekkehart, "The Dominance of American Approaches in International Relations," *Journal of International Studies: Millennium* 16, no. 2, (summer 1987): 207–14.

still increases the real wealth, the happiness, the knowledge, and perhaps the virtue of the human race."[25]

Of the liberal exponents of the belief in progress Lord Acton also ranks high. He regarded history as a record of progress and the study of history as "a progressive science." For him history as the course of events was a continual expansion of liberty, though he was writing before the Afro-Asian struggles for independence:

> It is by the combined efforts of the weak, made under compulsion, to resist the reign of force and constant wrong, that, in the rapid change but slow progress of four hundred years, liberty has been preserved, and secured, and extended, and finally understood.[26]

Hegel brings us back to European images of the chosen people. He had an image of the *chosen state* rather than the chosen people. For Hegel the end of progress was indeed the emergence of the Prussian state. Marx, however, was more futuristic than Hegel. Marx's conception of the purpose of history and its direction bore a comparison with that of the liberal Acton. Both Marx and Acton in a sense looked at history as being in the direction of an ultimate maximization of human freedom. Their conceptions of intermediate freedom were vastly different, but their image of the ultimate freedom of the future had more in common.

Liberalism and Marxism have both shared a profound distrust of the state as an instrument of coercion. For Marx the state is basically an instrument of class oppression; for liberals it is all too often a threat to individual liberty. Yet the vision of the classless society in Marxism, projected into the future, does postulate a highly autonomous and functionally versatile individual, unencumbered by the state machinery or by the demands and constraints of economic need. This Marxist utopia is one in which the individual would at last be able to "hunt in the morning, fish in the afternoon, rear cattle in the evening, criticize after dinner . . . . without ever becoming hunter, fisherman, shepherd or critic."[27]

When normative political theory predicts certain forms of human behavior, there is often room for self-fulfilling prophecies. Marx believed neither in the chosen people nor in the chosen state; he believed in the *chosen class*.

---

25. Gibbon, *The Decline and Fall of the Roman Empire*, chap. 38; the occasion of the digression being his discussion of the downfall of the Western Empire. Cited by E. H. Carr, *What is History?* (London: MacMillan and Company, 1961), 104–5.

26. John E. E. D. Acton [Lord Acton], *Lectures on Modern History* (London and New York: Macmillan, 1906), 51.

27. Karl Marx and Friedrich Engels, *German Ideology*, ed. R. Pascal (1846; New York: International Publishers, 1963), 22.

Marx's predictions of proletarian or neoproletarian revolutions have sometimes approached fulfillment in situations where sufficient numbers of underprivileged people have believed in themselves as a revolutionary class. To act and behave as if Marx was right is sometimes a way of making Marx right. Marxist universalism—though also ethnocentric—has succeeded in producing rebels against other versions of Western hegemony.

Liberalism too has at times opened doors for self-fulfilling prophecies. An assertion, for example, that where elections are denied and freedom of expression suppressed, people will revolt could all too easily fulfill itself if enough people in such a situation believe in the inevitability of such a response. The American Declaration of Independence did in part rest on a belief that human nature revolted against illiberal regimes. Some of the agitation in modern Greece after the military coup in 1967 was an attempt to vindicate a view of the Greeks as a freedom-loving people. The patriotic British assertion that "Britons never, never, never shall be slaves," when it is believed by enough Britons, has been known to inspire them into resisting attempted repression or invasion.

Yet these are usually assertions that are colored by patriotic self-conceptions. On balance, British political culture has not been quite as convinced about the predictability of human behavior as have some of the less traditionalist and more rationalist cultures elsewhere. Teleology has been diluted in Anglo-Saxon conservatism. On balance, in fact, it might be said that the lure of prediction in normative theory is more characteristic of radical schools of thought than of conservative ones. The radical schools are closer to religion and to teleological theology. Indeed, it is almost a defining characteristic of conservatism to distrust the plannability of social change and political direction. The conservative normally distrusts faith in progress. In Michael Oakeshott's famous metaphor:

> In political activity then, men sail a boundless and bottomless sea; there is neither harbour for shelter nor floor for anchorage, neither starting-place nor appointed destination. The enterprise is to keep afloat on an even keel; the sea is both friend and enemy; and the seamanship consists in using the resources of a traditional manner of behavior in order to make a friend of every hostile occasion.[28]

## Progress and Laws of Regularity

In the more futuristic and rationalistic schools of normative political theory there has been a high component of determinism in the assumptions made.

---

28. Michael Oakeshott, An Inaugural Lecture delivered at the London School of Economics. See his *Rationalism in Politics* (London: Methuen and Co., 1962), 127.

Again the echoes of religious fatalism are strong. Determinism in turn presumes certain laws of causality. In Marxism there is an explicit doctrine of economic determinism placed within a broader conception of a materialistic system of causality. Sometimes there are echoes of John Calvin's doctrines of predestination.

Perhaps the most extreme form of determinism is that which is captured in the poet's words:

> With Earth's first Clay They did the Last Man's knead,
> And then of the Last Harvest sow'd the Seed:
> Yea, the first Morning of Creation wrote
> What the Last Dawn of Reckoning shall read.[29]

The determinism of Marx sometimes approaches the assertion that the final dawn of reckoning will inevitably be the first stage of real socialism, and this was predictable from the first morning of primitive communism in the cradle of history. And yet Marx in his totality is much less crude and naive than he sometimes sounds. For our purposes here what needs to be grasped is that determinism is the belief that, to use the words of the mathematician Laplace, "the present state of the universe [is] the effect of its antecedent state and the cause of the state that is to follow." Laplace himself believed that if one could comprehend that which is before one today, one could foresee what will happen tomorrow:

> An intelligence, who for a given instance should be acquainted with all the forces by which Nature is animated and with the several positions of the entities composing it, if further his intellect were vast enough to submit those data to analysis, would include the one and the same formula the movements of the largest bodies in the universe and those of the slightest atom. Nothing would be uncertain for him; the future as well as the past would be present to his eyes.[30]

Although scientific determinism has links with theological predestination, both can sometimes be greatly diluted or disguised in variant language. Arthur Stanley Eddington suggests that the basic wish of the determinist is to "base on our ordinary experience of the sequence of cause and effect a wide generaliza-

---

29. Edward Fitzgerald, *The Rubaiyat of Omar Khayyam of Naishapur.* (New York: Illustrated Editions Company, 1938).
30. Cited by Arthur Stanley Eddington, "The Decline of Determinism," in *Great Essays in Science,* ed. Martin Gardner (New York: Pocket Books, 1957), 246–47.

tion called the Principle of Causality."[31] The religious predeterminist believes in the laws of God; the scientific determinist believes in the laws of Nature.

A disguised form of neodeterminism might be a quest for regularities of human behavior that could then be attributed, either explicitly or by implication, to certain laws governing human responses to given situations. It is these subtle assumptions of regular patterns of human response that provided a bridge linking rationalistic normative theories such as Marxism, the scientific political theory of more recent times, and the approaches and methods of the natural sciences. David Easton, in itemizing the characteristics that go to describe one preeminent school of the new political science, cited as the first attribute the search for regularity. Easton defined this as an assumption that "there are discoverable uniformities in political behavior. These can be expressed in generalizations or theories with explanatory and predictive value."[32]

Mulford Q. Sibley takes the discussion further and argues that scientific prediction would appear to be as feasible in politics as in physics. In both realms the quest is for "scientific prediction: that is to say, we endeavor to state the several possibilities of future experience and the limits within which such alternatives must lie."[33]

Science can be looked to for information as to what *cannot* happen under specified conditions or, as Karl Popper puts it, the "lawfulness of phenomena" can be expressed by asserting that *such and such a thing cannot happen;* that is to say, by a sentence in the form of the proverb: "'You cannot carry water in a sieve.'"[34]

Sibley emphasizes categorically that *scientific* prediction is not to be confused with forecasting the future. That is more blatantly prophetic. He accuses Marx and Engels of having done the latter. He also cites Harold Lasswell as a modern analyst who often appears to confuse scientific prediction with overall forecasting. Nor was Lasswell alone in this. Several others associated with the behavioralist mode appeared to follow in this forecasting trend.[35]

---

31. Ibid., 256. Consult also Maurice Goldsmith and Alan Mackay, eds., *The Science of Science* (London: Souvenir Press, 1964).
32. David Easton, *A Framework for Political Analysis* (Englewood Cliffs, N.J.: Prentice Hall, 1965), 7.
33. Mulford Q. Sibley, "The Limitations of Behaviouralism," in *Contemporary Political Analysis,* ed. James C. Charlesworth (New York: Free Press, 1967), 60.
34. Karl Popper, *The Poverty of Historicism* (Boston: Beacon Press, 1957), 49.
35. Sibley, "Limitations of Behaviouralism," 64. The works he cites as illustrations of the tendency by modern social scientists to equate scientific prediction with forecasting include Harold Lasswell and A. Kaplan, *Power and Society* (New Haven: Yale University Press, 1950), Louis H. Bean, *How to Predict Elections* (New York: Knopf, 1948); Stuart Dodd, "Predictive Principles from Polls—Scientific Method in Public Opinion Research," *Public Opinion Quarterly* 15 (1951–1952), 23–24; R. A. Dahl, "The Science of Politics: New and Old," *World Politics* 7, no.

Sibley defines the distinction between scientific prediction and forecasting by saying that the behavioral scientific prediction is an *if-then* proposition and therefore hypothetical; whereas the forecast, insofar as it exists,

> must be unhypothetical or unconditioned, else it ceases to be a forecast. Thus, one can perhaps predict what Congress will do about a proposed piece of legislation under carefully assumed conditions and contingencies. But one cannot—at least scientifically—purport to forecast what it will do. One can conceivably predict what the population of the world is likely to be twenty years hence if trends *yex* continue under conditions *zoa* and *bbm*. But one cannot—behaviorally—forecast what the population of the world will be twenty years hence, period. Any forecast of this kind would be guesswork based on overall "hunches" and could never be classified as "scientific."[36]

According to the school of thought to which Sibley belongs, the boundaries of prediction, then, if they are to be regarded as scientific, lie within two areas of capability. First, scientific forecasting is feasible only negatively—to assert what *cannot* happen. This is like Popper's example of the proverb, "You cannot carry water in a sieve." What about a statement like, "You cannot sustain stability for long without democracy"?

The second area of scientific prediction may be positive, but *hypothetical.* It consists of *if-then* propositions. The behavioral scientist is thus expected to be able to suggest how, under precisely formulated conditions and circumstances, people *would* behave in the future, "and he will provide us with statements of limits beyond which, under a specified and controlled environment, they would probably not act."[37]

Perhaps one major difference between prediction based on observed regularity and a forecast based on prophetic vision is that the former lends itself more easily to conscious interference in order to *avert* what is forecast. Even for the determinist there has sometimes been an awareness that human consciousness could make a difference. Marx relegated human consciousness to the superstructure, arguing that it was the reflection of social factors more fundamental than itself. But Lenin, in reviving the role of ideology into a conscious instrument of change rather than a mere reflection of class awareness, reinstated human consciousness into the domain of active factors in history. Man can himself transcend his own original sin. The Supreme Being

---

3 (April, 1955): 479–89; and David Apter, "Theory and the Study of Politics," *American Political Science Review* 51, no. 3 (September, 1957): 747–62.

36. Sibley, "The Limitations of Behaviouralism," 64–65.

37. Ibid., 51. See also "Norms and Values: Rethinking the Domestic Analogy," *Ethics and International Affairs* 1 (1987): 135–62.

for Man is at last Man. The chains of predestination are at last broken. Yet not all ideologies are equally successful in practice. Human consciousness can sometimes be false. After all, Leninism failed in the land of its birth.

## Conclusion

I have attempted to explore in this chapter the interplay between Western ethnocentrism and the dual universalism of Western civilization in relation to progress and development. We have argued that Western social science is, to a large extent, a product of two universals—natural science and the Judeo-Christian tradition. But like the Jews who taught us about the universal God while proclaiming themselves the chosen people, Westerners have instructed the world about the universalism of both science and Jesus, while declaring the white man to be God's chosen breed. In other words, both the Jews and the Europeans revealed a genius for marrying genuine universalism to real ethnocentrism.

We have argued that Europe borrowed the Jewish religious concept of the chosen people and *racialized* it. The underlying ethnocentrism has affected Western academic paradigms.

Contemporary theories of development and modernization have been especially distorted by the conflict between Western ethnocentrism and the dual universalism of Western civilization. The scientific leg of the dual heritage entered a new phase with the biological findings of Charles Darwin and by their impact on social theories. The religious leg of the dual universalism was in turn profoundly affected by the ideological impact of Karl Marx.

Especially persistent in the theories has been a teleological tendency. There was a time when religion validated itself by demonstrating a capacity to prophesy. More recently branches of science have tried to establish their credentials by demonstrating a capacity to predict. The new methodology of the social sciences of the West has often been caught between claims of forecasting and claims of predicting. A look into the future has been one of the meeting points between religion and science in the history of the West. Mastering the future is a universalism of *time*. Conquering the world is a universalism of *space*. Doctrines of progress are often implicit in both.

It is by no means rare for major schools of intellectual analysis to have significant antecedents in earlier traditions. Perhaps that is what intellectual history is all about—a succession of waves or, alternatively, a long chain of moments of inspiration linked together in a tradition of thought. I have attempted to demonstrate that current theories of development and modernization do have ancestral ties with earlier notions of social evolution and Darwinism. There have been dramatic changes in many of the postulates of this line of intellectual analysis. In fact the change sometimes has been from racism to broad humanism. But it has often been a form of humanism that is animated by the self-confidence of ethnocentric achievement.

As a result, the idea of progress once justified classifying societies "from the primitive to the civilized." In the *name* of progress the slave trade was once defended as a method of propelling the industrial revolution. In the name of progress child labor has been exploited from factory to factory. In the name of progress Rudyard Kipling once celebrated race-conscious imperialism:

> Take-up the White Man's burden
> Send forth the best ye breed
> Go bind your sons to exile
> To serve your captive's need.
>
> Take up the White Man's burden
> the savage wars of peace
> Fill full the mouth of famine
> And bid the sickness cease
>
> The ports ye shall not enter,
> The roads ye shall not tread,
> Go make them with your living,
> And mark them with your dead.[38]

The doctrine of progress can all too easily turn Machiavellian—as harsh means are justified in pursuit of noble ends. In this light, developmentalism is one twentieth-century version of the doctrine of progress—sometimes justifying the harsh means of "structural adjustment" by reference to the noble end of "economic recovery."

As my summary verdict, I would conclude that Judeo-Christian universalism did indeed illicitly mate with Western ethnocentrism in history—and gave the world a bastard called "progress."

---

38. Rudyard Kipling, "The White Man's Burden," in *Rudyard Kipling's Verse* (Garden City, N.Y.: Doubleday, Doran, 1931).

# Denying the Holy Dark: The Enlightenment Ideal and the European Mystical Tradition

*John M. Staudenmaier*

It is time for electric lamps with a thousand points of light to brutally cut and tear your mysterious, enchanting and seductive shadows!
(Marinetti, Venice, 1910)

George Bush and his speechwriters were not the first to celebrate a thousand points of light. In 1910, Italian Futurist founder Fillipo Tommaso Marinetti so outraged Venetians with the speech from which this sentence is taken that a near riot, standard fare at Futurist extravaganzas, ensued.[1] One might easily dismiss the violent rhetoric of his attack on dark and enchanting shadows as flamboyance from the lunatic fringe of the Enlightenment tradition. Still, Marinetti frequently turns up as a notable influence on a respectable array of artists that includes John Dos Passos, Ezra Pound, D. H. Lawrence, Joseph Stella, and Hart Crane.[2] Marinetti's extremist rhetoric points to a mentality hardly limited to the Futurists. For more than two centuries it regularly colors the ritualized language of hymns, poems, sermons, celebratory speeches, and, more recently, advertisements: light liberates humanity from a darkness that oppresses, burdens, threatens, or imprisons. Thus, nearly two decades after the Venice manifesto, in the altogether more genteel venue of Henry Ford's "Light's Golden Jubilee" (1929: honoring Thomas Edison's first successful electric light bulb experiment), we find the following introduction to the banquet menu.

---

1. Fillipo Tommaso Marinetti, speech to Venetians in 1910, in *Marinetti: Selected Writings* ed. R. W. Flint, trans. R. W. Flint and A. A. Coppotelli (New York: Farrar, Straus and Giroux, 1971), 56. I prefer, and use here, the translation found in Thomas P. Hughes, *American Genesis: A Century of Invention and Technological Enthusiasm* (New York: Penguin, 1989), 326.

2. For an overview of Marinetti's influence, see R. W. Flint's introduction to *Marinetti: Selected Writings*, 3–36. On Dos Passos see Cecelia Tichi, *Shifting Gears: Technology, Literature, Culture in Modernist America* (Chapel Hill, N.C.: University of North Carolina Press, 1987), 204. On Pound and the Futurists, see David Harvey, *The Condition of Postmodernity* (Cambridge, Mass.: Basil Blackwell, 1989), 33. On Stella and Futurist influence, see Hughes, *American Genesis*, 327.

> Since the beginning, darkness has always pressed terrifyingly upon earth . . . driving men inward, closer towards the dying campfire, closer towards the ashes of the hearth, closer towards the guttering light of candles or of smoky oil. Danger walked always in darkness; and crime, disease, fear stalked in the dark lanes of congested cities.
>
> All of us remember some time and place where night-time brought a sudden end to the public activities of man, when humankind ran from darkness to take shelter behind thick walls. Who has yet forgotten torchlight processions trailing their brief, flickering yellow glow across the darkness of the town? Who can't recall some muffled lamplighter making his rounds at dusk, leaving pale dots of light on dangerous corners? How dark were the cellars, the rat-infested holds of ships, the terrible mines flooded with an almost palpable blackness? How long the dark, cold nights of winter seemed! How depressing the gloom of dark days!
>
> Into this darkness of fifty years ago, Edison, your guest tonight, flashed the spark which lighted the world![3]

Marinetti's dark is enchanting, seductive, and destined for brutal destruction. In the Edison invocation, night has no redeeming value; campfires are "dying"; candle light "guttering"; humans run for shelter; lamplighters are muffled. Were all street corners dangerous? Whence, one might ask, this unrelenting antagonism? We see here textual examples of the revaluation of the dark side of human consciousness that took hold in the West during the Enlightenment. The dark had long been understood as an ambiguous mix of experiences—some nourishing, some violent, some merely tedious. In the worldview represented here, these diverse understandings are all reduced to a single congeries of negativity.

I choose two opulent texts deliberately, hoping with the help of their provocative flavors to call attention to an elusive aspect of the idea of progress. The notion of progress rests on the central premise that new methods in science, technology, and business, rooted in a revolution of experimental method, precision measurement, and punctuality, and mediated by the enlightenment ideals of civility and objectivity, have set in motion a new historical force called "Progress." Progress dramatically improves the human condition in part because of the power of its methodologies and in part because these new methods work to overcome the darkness of superstition and magic.

---

3. Edison reenacted the original test over a national radio network. President Herbert Hoover graced the proceedings, with a host of America's industrial and financial elite. Banquet program and menu, original artifact from "Light's Golden Jubilee," October 21, 1929, Henry Ford Museum/Edison Institute Series: Box 2, File 14 Program (on page after Edison's portrait).

It is universally agreed that the Enlightenment marked the rise of rational method to preeminence in the West and that the cumulative influences of scientific research and technological innovation have resulted in what, by comparison with past cultures, are extraordinary human achievements. Since World War II, however, the Enlightenment's reputation has taken a fair beating on a number of fronts. The anti-Enlightenment movements stem in part from two World War II technical triumphs that came to be seen as heinous. Germany, epitome of scientific and engineering sophistication, used its expertise to build very efficient death camps; the United States constructed atomic bombs and dropped them on civilian targets. Building on this grim symbolic foundation, several social trends have coalesced in what some observers see as a crisis for the idea of progress itself. Since the mid-1960s ecological reformers have acquired significant political power. More recently, New Age believers and fundamentalist cults have attracted notable followings with the promise of escape from mainstream society. In the academy, radical deconstructionists dismiss the enlightenment project of rational achievement as illusory. These antimodernist movements notwithstanding, one need not look far to find very recent versions of progress talk in its crudest sense. Popular rhetoric—in contexts such as Disney's immensely popular EPCOT Center, advertisements using high-tech iconography, or congressional testimony on competitiveness—portrays a race toward the future in which Science and Technology shape and reshape reality with godlike inevitability.

In great part, popular ambivalence about progress comes from a longstanding elision of two ideas: first, that science and technology create progress in the sense that current research builds on prior research; second, that these cumulative processes constitute an inexorable transhistorical force that should not and cannot be challenged. When progress is used in the first sense alone, the communities of scientific and technological practitioners are seen to operate within a larger social context and, like all other forms of human behavior, are subject to influences from outside the expert community itself. Such an understanding, increasingly popular in recent research (e.g., the social construction of science and technology school), implies that science and technology are politically and culturally valenced. Understood in the second sense, however, science and technology take on a numinous quality that resists all outside critique defining it as obstructionism, the naive hankering for a romanticized past. True believers in the second sense lump all nonrational behavior together and see the light of reason standing against the darkness of sensuality, superstition, mysticism, witchcraft, aesthetic intuition, ignorance, disease, fanaticism, and ordinary crime. These two notions have bonded together so tightly in the rhetorical and mythic order that it is difficult to tease them apart.[4] Nevertheless, that is my purpose. By exploring the character and

---

4. For a more detailed analysis of the tendency for progress talk to slip from a notion of

some of the history of the Enlightenment's blanket antagonism toward a generalized "dark," I hope to help explain some of the antiprogress counterantagonism so evident today and to argue that the virtues of rationality do better when allied with the virtues of nonrationality than either do as hostile antagonists.[5]

Several cautions are in order. First, I use the light-dark dyad as a primary metaphor because it has so often been chosen in the past. The diurnal rhythm runs deep in human biology and culture, and both terms are laden with a host of overlapping connotations that tantalize and ultimately elude efforts to pin them down to a single clean definition. Nevertheless, since I mean to call attention to the elusive character of the concept of progress, light and dark may, by their multivalent character, help keep what follows from masquerading as a clean and tightly linked causal argument. If we are to attend to our mythic beliefs, we must learn to wait for them, catching glimpses that can make us thoughtful.

Second, I will use the handbook of mystical discipline written by the founder of the Jesuits, Ignatius of Loyola, as an exemplary case. I choose his *Spiritual Exercises* because my long familiarity with its history of use provides me with the sort of window into the transformation of Western understanding of the nonrational that is needed here, but my point is essentially secular. Mystical disciplines, themselves hardly limited to Roman Catholicism or to Christianity, represent Western traditions that have treated the dark with nuanced respect.[6]

---

cumulative science and technology toward the determinism described here, see my "Perils of Progress Talk: Some Historical Considerations," in *Science, Technology, and Social Progress,* ed. Steven L. Goldman (Bethlehem, Pa.: Lehigh Press, 1989), 268–98.

5. For a delicate rumination on darkness as positive, from a non-Western (Japanese) perspective, see Jun'ichiro Tanizaki, *In Praise of Shadows,* trans. Thomas J. Harper and Edward G. Seidensticker (New Haven, Conn.: Leete's Island Books, 1977). A recent study of Goethe's remarkable sensitivity to the play between light and dim is Julie A. Reahard, "'In her black eyes I read a genuine interest in me and in my life.' Black hole entropy: beyond the 'event horizons' of Goethe's *Werther* and *Wahlverwandtschaftern*" (paper presented at the annual meeting of the International Association for Philosophy and Literature, Pittsburgh, Pa., May 1993).

6. It should be noted, however, that my treatment of the *Spiritual Exercises* will be almost completely limited to the point in question, namely, to demonstrate that mystical disciplines of this kind interpret the "darkness" of individual emotional experience very differently from the mainstream of later Enlightenment thinking. I will not comment extensively on the larger theological worldview within which the *Exercises* operate. The mysticism found in the *Exercises,* then, should not be mistaken as an early version of late-nineteenth-century American liberal Protestantism after the manner of Henry Ward Beecher's preaching, where, as Richard W. Fox has recently observed, "the religious was not the transcendent, but the natural infused with passion and vitality." For Ignatius, passion was critically important in the mystical process, but the entire process was suffused with an understanding that the transcendence of God gives meaning to the human project rather than the other way around. See Richard W. Fox, "Intimacy on Trial: Cultural Meanings of the Beecher-Tilton Affair," in *The Power of Culture: Critical Essays in American History,* ed.

I will begin by describing the experience of the Jesuits with the *Spiritual Exercises* over the order's four-and-a half-century history as an example of Enlightenment amnesia. I will then consider evidence supporting the claim that the Enlightenment marks a radical breaking point in Western consciousness both because of the well-known revolutions in precision measurement, rationalized production, and scientific thinking and because of a novel antagonism toward mysticism and affective experience generally. To flesh out some implications of these changes, I will explore the emergence of standardization in the United States, first as a technological and later as a political ideal.[7]

### The *Spiritual Exercises:* A Case of Cultural Amnesia

In the early sixteenth century, the Basque petty nobleman Iñigo de Loyola retired from soldiering when a French cannonball shattered both his legs. From the beginning of his convalescence in 1521 until he settled at the University of Paris for graduate studies in philosophy and theology in 1528, he lived through a series of powerful mystical experiences. By his own account, the years 1522–23 in the tiny Catalonian village of Manresa were foundational. There, while living in a small cave at the edge of the town, the unwashed hermit followed an inner journey at one time so harrowing that he courted suicide and ultimately so joyous that from then until his death three decades later, his personal life was routinely punctuated with outbursts of merriment and extended periods of weeping. Ignatius was, for example, the first Jesuit to receive a dispensation from saying the daily breviary of the hours because, on his doctor's advice, he had to cut back or risk losing his eyesight. He would often weep softly for two to three hours at a time. He had entered what the Christian tradition had come to name a habitual mystical state.[8]

It is one of the ironies of historiography that this profoundly emotional man should turn up in the pages of later Western history as an archetype of calculating rational method. The tangled history of that metamorphosis from

---

R. W. Fox and T. J. Jackson Lears (Chicago: University of Chicago Press, 1993), 102–32. For a comprehensive study of the pertinent Ignatian theology, see Harvey D. Egan, *The Spiritual Exercises and the Ignatian Mystical Horizon* (St. Louis: Institute of Jesuit Sources, 1976).

7. Because most of my research deals with the history of U.S. technological style, I will stay close to the United States story and cite European material only where it helps explain related patterns in the United States. The first and most notable instance of European material follows immediately in my discussion of changes in the Jesuits' use of the *Spiritual Exercises.*

8. Some of the better known mystics of the late Middle Ages and early Renaissance period include Julian of Norwich, the anonymous author of the *Cloud of Unknowing,* Meister Eckhart, Theresa of Avila, and John of the Cross. For a comparative treatment that includes Theresa of Avila, the *Cloud of Unknowing,* John of the Cross, and Ignatius, see Harvey D. Egan, "Christian Apophatic and Kataphatic Mysticisms," *Theological Studies* 30, no. 3 (September, 1978): 399–426.

mystic to calculating strategist in the popular image of Ignatius is far too complex for this chapter, but it exemplifies the issue at hand. During his own life, Ignatius had to defend himself in 1526 and again in 1527, not from charges of excessive rationality but, rather, from accusations of pseudomystical Illuminism. Ignatius was suspect to the Inquisition in part because he taught a method for discerning God's will based on attention to affective experience.[9] Over the next several centuries, however, the method of *The Spiritual Exercises* underwent a transmutation, like its author's reputation, from mystical to rational; only very recently has it begun to be understood in its original mystical character. It is from the several centuries in which the *Exercises* were understood (by Jesuits themselves as well as others) as a series of standardized lectures on spiritual conversion that most popular accounts of Jesuits and their founder arise. The harrowing image of a Jesuit preaching hellfire and damnation to terrified adolescents in Joyce's *Portrait of the Artist as a Young Man* is apt for its period but a far cry, as we shall see immediately, from Ignatius's understanding of the role of director in the *Exercise*.

The *Exercises* are written as an instruction manual for one who directs a retreatant. Ordinarily they take place in solitude over approximately thirty days with the director and the retreatant meeting once a day when the retreatant recounts his or her affective experience over the day just ended and, with help from the director's observations, begins to understand what those experiences imply and where, again in light of those experiences, the retreatant chooses to begin on the coming day.[10] The director's main business is to help the retreatant interpret the meaning of each day's events. The introductory notes repeatedly admonish the director not to intrude in the process. A few examples show the flavor of the directions. The second annotation counsels brevity in proposing content for prayer ("for it is not *much knowledge* that fills and satisfies the soul, but the *intimate understanding* and *relish* of the truth"). The fifteenth annotation urges the director not to exert pressure on the retreatant

---

9. "In 16th Century Spain, the adherents of illuminism were called Alumbrados. The name identifies a group of pseudomystic Spaniards who claimed to act always under illumination from the Holy Spirit and independently of the means of grace dispensed by the Church" (*New Catholic Encyclopedia*, Vol. 7 [Washington, D.C.: Catholic University Press, 1967], 367). Ignatius was suspect both because he lived at the time after the manner of an itinerant preacher and because of the novelty of the *Spiritual Exercises* in which he directed various individuals. Both examinations by the Inquisition quarreled with his physical appearance, but neither condemned the *Exercises*. For one discussion, see Philip Caraman, *Ignatius Loyola: A Biography of the Founder of the Jesuits* (New York: Harper and Row, 1990), 62–65.

10. Note, however, that Ignatius encourages modifications based on the retreatant's circumstances. Because this adaptation for "one who is educated or talented, but engaged in public affairs or necessary business" occurs in Annotation 19, the increasingly common late-twentieth-century practice of nonclerical people making the *Exercises* over a six- to eight-month period is commonly called "the 19th annotation retreat."

("Therefore, the director of the Exercises, as a balance at equilibrium, without leaning to one side or the other, should permit the Creator to deal directly with the creature [i.e., the retreatant], and the creature directly with his Creator and Lord."). The fourth direction for the First Week insists that the pace of prayer be governed by the retreatant's affective experience ("I will remain quietly meditating upon the point in which *I have found what I desire* without any eagerness to go on *till I have been satisfied.*"). So important are personal affective movements as guides to the course of prayer that only once in the entire *Exercises* does Ignatius counsel the director to scrutinize the behavior of the retreatant because something might be going wrong with the process. The warning of potential trouble occurs if the retreatant "is *not affected* by any spiritual experiences, such as consolations or desolations, and that he is *not troubled* by different spirits" (¶6, my emphases).[11]

To say that the *Exercises* treat formal conceptual content as secondary and affective experience as primary is not to say that they lack an articulated methodology nor that they reduce religious experience exclusively to emotional impulse. Throughout the *Exercises* and especially in an appendix titled "Rules for the Discernment of Spirits," Ignatius elaborates a multifaceted method for interpreting feelings as they arise at different points over the whole thirty days. The rules are meant to help discern the character of diverse interior movements, learning which to follow and which to treat as distractions. To take a single example from many, one rule notes that disturbances can distract the retreatant "and may end in what weakens the soul, or disquiets it; or by destroying the peace, tranquillity, and quiet which it had before, may cause disturbance to the soul" (¶333). Rather than trying to manage the distraction, however, the rule suggests that the retreatant review "the whole course of the temptation" to find the point where the distraction began. The objective is to return to the place of origin because something in that experience is important for the retreatant. It is understood that one returns for further prayer at that point not yet knowing why it is important. Clarity will come later.

This sample from the rules for discernment suffices to show how the *Exercises* integrate purposeful rationality with mysterious emotion, in other words, what could be called "light" and "dark." On the most general level the *Exercises* presume a Christian understanding of God in relationship with the world and with the individual. As such they embody a rationally articulated

---

11. Ignatius uses a broad range of expression for affective experiences, such as: "inner motions," "disturbances," "intense feeling," "intimate knowledge," "inner relish," "consolation," "desolation," and others. For other noteworthy instances of the pattern of directing by attention to emotions, see ¶¶7, 8, 9, 10, 13, 14, 15, 16, 17, 62, 78 and the "Rules for the Discernment of Spirits" (¶¶313–36), which are themselves worth a complete article. My references to the text of the *Exercises* use the traditional paragraph numbering found in the translation by Louis J. Puhl, *The Spiritual Exercises of St. Ignatius* (Chicago: Loyola University Press, 1951).

theology that shapes the context for the *Exercises*. They are also intended to lead the retreatant to detailed self-knowledge about habitual affective patterns that influence the retreatant's choices and behavior. Balancing these several kinds of intellectual clarity, however, is the process that generates them. The method will not work unless the retreatant and the director are capable of following the retreatant's affective experiences without trying to know in advance where they will lead or even why they are important. In such a process emotions can neither be reduced to conceptual clarities, nor are they best understood as being "managed" by the rational self. They lead the process of discovery.[12]

In 1773 the Jesuits were juridically read out of existence by Pope Clement XIV and were not reestablished until 1814. As they struggled to reconstitute themselves they did so under the influence the powerful ideological forces at work in the mainstream of the Enlightenment. The historical accident of their 40-year suppression helps explain the Jesuits' extraordinary reinterpretation of the *Exercises* from the one-on-one affective direction we have seen to a program of group lectures offering theological and spiritual content that followed the conceptual outline found in the text. The revised *Exercises,* probably unnoticed by the Jesuits themselves, look remarkably like the commonplace nineteenth-century preference for conceptual clarity over unpredictable affectivity.[13]

The revision held for a century and a half. Thus, in my first long retreat after entering the Jesuits in 1957, the director gave five short lectures each day and we retreatants were expected to pray about what we had been told. The entire group followed a regimented program of considerations regardless of individual affective experience. Examples of the rationalization of the *Exercises* could be multiplied but one will suffice. Ignatius provided three methods for making an important decision (¶¶175–78). The first method involves a vision of God so powerful that ordinary discernment of affective states is not needed. Ignatius considered it a limit case based on scriptural accounts of the conversions of St. Paul and St. Matthew. The third method, to calmly weigh the pros and cons of one's alternatives "when the soul is not agitated by different spirits," falls outside the scope of the *Exercises,* which, as we have

---

12. The "Rules for the Discernment of Spirits" and their operation in the fully articulated process of the *Exercises* are far too complex for a complete treatment here. For a somewhat more thorough exposition see my "To Fall in Love with the World: Therapeutic Individualism and Self-Transcendence in American Society," in *Studies in the Spirituality of the Jesuits* 26, no. 3 (May 1994).

13. To my knowledge, no one has yet done sufficient historical research to track the Jesuits' revision of the *Exercises* from affective to rational program. It may well be that the influence of enlightenment consciousness began the process well before the French Revolution and the suppression of the order. What is clear is that somewhere during the centuries between the founding era (c. 1550) and the early nineteenth century, the revision became firmly established.

seen, guide the second method: "When much light and understanding are derived through experience of desolations and consolations and discernment of diverse spirits." Recent scholarship establishes what should have been obvious in the text, namely that "the second way, that of consolation and desolation, is superior to the third, for in it the person is guided 'by a better light than human reason.'"[14] Nevertheless, in the late 1950s the first and second methods were treated as suspect because of the delusions to which emotion was subject.

Jesuit revision of its foundational document provides us with an example of how powerfully European consciousness rejected emotion as a guide to mature decision making. The example, however, is remarkable only because we have such detailed access to its character. The same transformation of emotion's place in Western culture occurred throughout Western society.

Living with electric lights makes it difficult to retrieve the experience of a nonelectrified society. For all but the very wealthy, who could afford exorbitant arrays of expensive artificial lights, nightfall brought the works of daytime to a definitive end. Activities that need good light—where sharp tools are wielded or sharply defined boundaries maintained, purposeful activities designed to achieve specific goals, in short, that which we call work—all this subsided in the dim light of evening. Absent the press of work, people typically took themselves safely to home and were left with time in the evening for less urgent and more sensual matters: storytelling, sex, prayer, sleep, dreaming.[15] Well before efficient systems of electric lights, however, Enlightenment ideology began to treat dark behavior as suspect and to absolutize the precise virtues of clear lighting and the behavior it both symbolizes and makes possible. E. P. Thompson, in his seminal paper "Time, Work-Discipline and Industrial Capitalism," has charted some rhetorical benchmarks of the transition. Thus:

> By soaking ... so long between warm sheets the flesh is as it were parboiled, and becomes soft and flabby. The nerves in the meantime, are quite unstrung.
> (John Wesley, "On the Duty and Advantage of Early Rising," 1786)
>
> Thou silent murderer, Sloth,
> no more my mind imprison'd keep;

---

14. See John O'Malley, *The First Jesuits* (Cambridge Mass: Harvard University Press, 1993), 42. He quotes Juan Polanco, personal secretary to Ignatius during the final decade of his life.

15. Night rest was understood as something more than merely functional. Helen Luke calls attention to Dante's law of the mountain of purgatory. Those who climb the mountain toward paradise must rest where they are during the dark. Should they try to climb higher before dawn they will only find that they have been moved farther back down the mountain (Helen Luke, *Dark Wood to White Rose: Journey and Transformation in Dante's Divine Comedy* (New York: Parabola Books, 1989), 53.

Nor let me waste another hour with thee,
thou felon sleep.

(Hanna More, "Early Rising," 1831)[16]

It is not a compliment, in what later came to be called "the real world," to say, "You are an excellent sleeper" or "You are a dreamer."

To be sure, the West, like other cultures, manifests an ancient love of light; Jesus was hardly the first to observe that criminals love the dark because it hides their evil deeds, nor were the psalms the only hymns to praise the coming of the dawn as a manifestation of God's fidelity. For several thousand years, however, Western love of clarity and fear of chaos operated in the context of a balancing recognition that too much clarity is dangerous and that the uncertain dark is sometimes the necessary seedbed of life and of vision itself. Both the Jewish Job and the Greek Oedipus learn that some questions cannot or should not be answered. The Book of Job ends without concluding, its questions about the meaning of suffering finally silenced. Oedipus finds what he seeks but, seeing his history starkly revealed, puts out his eyes. Too much light can be destructive. Correlatively, the Western tradition of the holy dark, as the frightening place where visions are born and human purpose renewed, stretches from Abraham's vocational dream visions and Jacob's nighttime wrestling with the unnamed stranger to the *Cloud of Unknowing* and the dark nights of the medieval mystics such as Theresa of Avila, Julian of Norwich, or John of the Cross or again to Shakespeare's tender expression: "sleep that knits the ravell'd sleave of care."

Late medieval Christian theologians recognized a creative tension between light and dark. *Kataphatic* theology (literally, "that which can be articulated") addressed positive concepts of the nature of God, with particular emphasis on Jesus as Word. Negative, or *apophatic*, theology (literally, "that which is wordless") countered positive theology by emphasizing the inescapable limitations of all human conceptualization when dealing with the mystery of God. The mystical traditions were noteworthy in that they wove kataphatic and apophatic into a single back-and-forth discipline of prayer and practice.[17]

This long-standing intuition, that uncertainty must balance clarity and the ambiguous temper the purposeful, periodically collapsed over the centuries; occasional groups broke out in vicious fanaticisms such as Ferdinand and Isabella's ethnic cleansing of Jews and Muslims from Spain or the more violent

---

16. E. P. Thompson, "Time, Work-Discipline, and Industrial Capitalism," in *Past and Present*, no. 38 (December, 1967): 87–88.

17. See Egan, "Christian Apophatic and Kataphatic Mysticisms," and Michael J. Buckley, "Atheism and Contemplation," *Theological Studies* 40, no. 4, (December, 1979): 680–99. See also Simon Harak's study of Thomas Aquinas's integration of body and intellect and will in his theory of passions and virtues, *A Passion for God* (New York: Paulist Press, 1994), esp. chap. 4.

instances of Christian doctrinal enforcement. In such instances, love of clear boundary definitions drifted toward a savage lust for order.

Even during the worst excesses, however, the clarifying urge was held in check by a technological style that held precision measurement in only modest regard. However much one might long for the bright light of clean boundaries, the diurnal rhythm of day and night governed life. Medieval night prayers show both fear and suspicion of the dark ("Preserve us from violence and crises; keep our imaginations and passions in check") and affection for dimly lit times of storytelling and rest ("Into your hands, Oh Lord, we commend our spirits").[18] Daylight projects and strategies were themselves hampered by imprecise machines and instruments. To take one example from many, public clocks long showed only one hand, telling the hour but not the minute. In the course of the eighteenth century, however, improved clock escapements and temperature compensation enabled clock makers to improve best accuracy from an already remarkable ten seconds per day to one fifth of a second by 1800.[19]

The British industrial and the French political revolutions created an unusually powerful hiatus in European culture near the end of the eighteenth century. During the two decades spanning the turn of the nineteenth century the French revolutionary republic dismantled civic and religious structures only to be itself replaced by Napoleon's Empire. French engineers made remarkable strides toward their goal of gauge-measured interchangeable parts manufacture and industrialists began inviting British factory masters and skilled artisans across the channel to install the new system of manufacture. It proved a powerful mix; the traditions of the ancien régime died a violent death during

---

18. Several recent historians provide helpful accounts of the cultural transformation from dimly lit streets, where citizens locked their homes at night for fear of what might wander in the dark outside. As Wolfgang Schivelbusch observes, the gradual movement toward public lighting in the streets was part of the larger movement from the irregularities of an earlier Europe toward the passion for order that marks the rise of absolute monarchies and, eventually, the Enlightenment. Comparing the newly standardized design for street-paving stones in Paris in 1729 (nine inches on a side) to the monarchy's enforcement of its streetlight design, he observes: "The old paving stones bore the same relationship to the new ones as did the colorful, straggling armies of the Thirty Years' War to the regularly uniformed, standing armies of absolutism: in both cases, disorderly masses were transformed into neatly lined up, mathematically exact structures." *Disenchanted Night: The Industrialization of Light in the Nineteenth Century,* trans. Angela Davies (Berkeley: University of California Press, 1988), 85. See also David E. Nye, *Electrifying America: Social Meanings of a New Technology, 1880–1940* (Cambridge: MIT Press, 1990).

19. Tore Frängsmyr, J. L. Heilbron, and Robin E. Rider, eds., *The Quantifying Spirit in the Eighteenth Century* (Berkeley: University of California Press, 1990), 7; for dramatic improvements in measurement and quantitative thinking generally, passim. On one-handed clocks, see David S. Landes, *Revolution in Time: Clocks and the Making of the Modern World* (Cambridge: Harvard University Press, 1983), 104.

the years of the Revolution, and later attempts at restoration, particularly in church matters, were carried out under the powerful influence of industrial capitalism. Where factory masters tried to enforce precisely defined work rules, the church gradually turned to similarly detailed codes of doctrine and behavior. Boisterous politics, whether on the shop floor or in the Vatican, became increasingly suspect.

Recent scholarship has identified a striking instance of this phenomenon among the Sisters of St. Joseph in France. Eighteenth-century France was host to thousands of tiny congregations of Sisters of St. Joseph, typically five to 12 members. Communities in larger towns and cities differed dramatically from those in rural areas. Town houses conducted their financial affairs, chose their places and types of work, and governed their community lives with remarkable autonomy. The mostly illiterate women in the country houses, on the other hand, ordinarily operated under the tutelage of a town house sister with little autonomy. Both sorts of community were called by exactly the same name, "Congregation of the Sisters of St. Joseph," and both were considered independent organizations. Examples of similar nominal vagueness could be multiplied. To call these tiny groups by the same name required a tolerance for conceptual and behavioral ambiguity that did not survive the Revolution. When they recovered from their decimation during the Reign of Terror, their earlier pattern of amorphous cooperation among independent communities gave way to centralized government. Thus, by 1840, the Congregation of Lyon ran more than 200 separate houses from its central seat of governance. Communal life began to be regulated by detailed codes very like the factory work rules then transforming manufacturing.[20]

Gradually, while instrument makers and scientists revolutionized the world of precision measurement and quantitative analysis, religious and cultural leaders began to read the holy dark out of the Western canon.[21] Mysticism

---

20. Conversation with Patricia Byrne about work in progress, February, 1993. See also Marguerite Vacher, *Des "Régulières" dans le Siècle* (Clermont-Ferrand, France: Adosa, 1991). For another instance of blurred conceptual boundaries in prerevolutionary France, J. L. Heilbron notes the following confusion in units of measure: "The existence of French men and women around 1790 was made miserable by, among other things, 700 or 800 differently named measures and untold units of the same name but different sizes. A 'pinte' in Paris came to 0.93 liter; in Saint-Denis, to 1.46; in Seine-en-Montagne, to 1.99, in Précy-sous-Thil, to 3.33" ("The Measure of Enlightenment," in *Quantifying Spirit in the Eighteenth Century,* 207).

21. Theologian and historian Michael F. Buckley argues in this vein when he observes that "seventeenth century Catholic theologians ... Leonard Lessius and Marin Mersenne ... bracketed Christian religious experience as cognitively irrelevant to the issues of a putative atheism" ("The Rise of Modern Atheism and the Religious *Epoché,*" Presidential Address to Catholic Theological Society of America, in *CTSA Proceedings* 47 [1992]: 71). For his full argument, see his *At the Origins of Modern Atheism* (New Haven: Yale University Press, 1987).

went the way of playful ambiguity and sensuality; even Shakespeare's praise of sleep gradually became less acceptable than attacks on sloth.[22]

In his classic study of the industrial revolution, *The Unbound Prometheus,* David Landes caricatures all cognition that does not take a means-to-ends form as "superstition and magic."[23] Like many readings of the epistemological significance of the Enlightenment, he misses a key point about medieval and early Renaissance consciousness, namely, that the traditions that understood affective states as legitimate influences on human practice were at home with a very broad range of cognitive behavior that included rumor-based crazes cheek by jowl with subtle and discriminating disciplines such as the *Spiritual Exercises*. That state of affairs resembles the current mélange of science-based psychotherapy, New Age consciousness, pop psychology, astrology, postmodern deconstruction, and the revival of research into Eastern and Western mystical traditions. These recent trends suggest that the dark is making a comeback in many areas of popular thought and, as we observed at the outset, that the idea of Enlightenment progress is faced with a crisis of belief itself.

The story of how the Enlightenment project has come to the present crisis is too complex for comprehensive treatment here, but one important part of the story in the United States has to do with the emergence of standardization, first as a distinctively American technological style and later as a political ideal. For the classic eighteenth-century Enlightenment, "progress" in science and technology worked in active synthesis with republican political ideals, and both were rooted in a commitment to individualism. But as the United States moved toward standardization as its dominant technological style, the Enlightenment synthesis began to break down, replaced by a new social demography where technical experts managed large-scale systems while the larger population learned conformity with system constraints. Through the course of the nineteenth century, standardization evolved from a variety of societal trends, only some of which were overtly technological. Taken as a cluster of mutually influential cultural forces, they help explain how standardized systems began to replace the earlier ideal of republican politics with a new vision of efficiency and order. From the perspective of this chapter, the original Enlightenment ideal carried the seeds of its own troubles in its devaluation of the dark side of

---

22. It is noteworthy that Bartlett's *Concordance* of Shakespeare contains only six citations for *sloth* and 11 for *lazy* but requires four complete columns of citations for *sleep,* most of them positive. Bartlett's *Concordance* (London: Macmillan, 1894; St. Martin's, 1979).

23. "Rationality may be defined as the adaptation of means to ends. It is the antithesis of superstition and magic." David S. Landes, *The Unbound Prometheus: Technological Change and Industrial Development in Western Europe from 1750 to the Present* (New York: Cambridge University Press, 1969), 21. See the following pages for further examples of Landes's disjunction between rationality and other modes of consciousness, which are defined as defective by his dismissive, occasionally derisive, tone.

consciousness. The following discussion of standardization concentrates, therefore, on two characteristics of standardization: the shift from individualistic citizens to passive conformists and the replacement of negotiations with systems. Both changes, it will be seen, stem from the banishing of emotion from the domain of public decision making.

### Standardization as Technological Style and Political Ideal

An early sign of distaste for both spontaneous affect and sensuality in general appears in the remarkable popularity of etiquette books, beginning about 1830 and increasing through the century. Etiquette books taught aspirants to the middle class how to behave in public, a skill that Ervin Goffman and John Kasson call 'impression management.' The books proscribed staring, shouting, singing, or humming out loud. Civilized adults kept disorderly passions— sexual impulses, anger, grief, or joy—carefully in check. One neither wept nor exulted in the streets. In contrasting the etiquette world with what preceded it Kasson summarizes the research of Norbert Elias:

> [A] rising standard of emotional control is one of the most striking, if hitherto neglected, historical developments in modern northern European (and later, American) society. Before the seventeenth and eighteenth centuries, extremes of jubilant laughter, passionate weeping, and violent rage were indulged with a freedom that in later centuries would not be permitted even to children.[24]

In a society with little privacy it was understood that no one could sustain a consistent exterior persona. People managed their behavior to conform to

---

24. John F. Kasson, *Rudeness and Civility: Manners in Nineteenth Century America* (New York: Hill and Wang, 1990). See chapter 1 for his estimate that an average of three new etiquette books annually before the Civil War and rose to an average of five or six per year from 1870 through World War I. Erving Goffman, *Asylums: Essays on the Social Situation of Mental Patients and Other Inmates* (Garden City, N.Y.: Anchor Books, 1961). Norbert Elias, *The Civilizing Process*, vol. 1, *The History of Manners*, trans. Edmund Jephcott (New York: Urizen Books, 1978), cited in Kasson, *Rudeness and Civility*, 147. Kasson also calls attention to Carol Z. Stearns and Peter N. Stearns, "Emotionology: Clarifying the History of Emotions and Emotional Standards," *American Historical Review* 90 (October, 1985): 813–36. Stearns and Stearns argue that the history of emotion is only beginning to emerge from obscurity in the profession and that much of its early scholarship is marred by the excessive rationalism of its historians. Thus, for example, in critical response to scholars who correlate intense expression of anger in pre-Enlightenment Europe with a hostile relationship between parents and children, they observe: "Expressions of anger may have been more compatible with love for children than our modern values allow" (823–24). Finally, for the dramatically different view of theoretical understanding of human passions before and after the Enlightenment, see Harak, *A Passion for God.*

codes of conduct for specific events—dressing differently on holidays, for example—but ordinary life was spontaneous and, by present standards, often crude. Etiquette literature began to transform the meaning of civility from the citizen who actively engaged in political processes to the "civilized" person who could control spontaneous passions in public. In the process people learned to conform behavior to standards that had been codified with even greater detail than that found in factory work rules of the period.

A dramatic change in audience behavior after midcentury took the new civility into the theater and music hall. Early-nineteenth-century audiences, raucous throngs that included all social classes in the same building, routinely interrupted the musicians by cheering, shouting, and pounding the floor with their feet and sometimes demanding repetition of a well-liked passage of the music. Patrons booed, hissed, and threw rotten fruit or eggs at theatrical villains. Lawrence W. Levine offers the following description of audience reaction when a visiting Italian opera troupe cut the final scene of an 1837 performance of Rossini's *Semiramide* without prior announcement. According to the *New Orleans Picayune,* management's attempt to stop the uproar by darkening the hall and driving the audience out: "t'was the signal for the demolition of everything they could lay their hands on. . . . The drapery around the boxes was torn, the cushions in the pit ripped open, the seats broken, and chairs were flying in all directions." The next night, the chastened company performed "the last note that ever Rossini composed."[25] Audience-performer interaction was the norm, and few seemed surprised when public performance turned riotous. After the Civil War, however, a new discipline began to take hold. Thus, for example, noted conductor Theodore Thomas insisted on silent audiences, sometimes turning to stare them into submission before continuing a performance. By the turn of the century, audiences had sorted out along class lines into burlesque houses and saloons, where boisterous conduct remained acceptable, and orchestra halls and what came to be called "legitimate" theater. Middle- and upper-class audiences were domesticated even as they sharpened the boundaries separating them from their inferiors.[26]

While etiquette training highlights the Enlightenment's aversion to spontaneous affectivity, its relationship with technological standardization is only implicit. In a more obviously technological sphere, we find a similar transformation as methods of testing and measurement changed from craft to system. In the craft tradition of performance testing, a judge inspected a work sample and approved it. The principle was the same whether the work in question was

---

25. See Lawrence W. Levine, *Highbrow/Lowbrow: The Emergence of Cultural Hierarchy in America* (Cambridge: Harvard University Press, 1988), 91.

26. See Levine, *Highbrow/Lowbrow,* passim, and Kasson, *Rudeness and Civility,* chap. 7. Levine notes that the gradual disciplining of audience interaction was accompanied by the creation of separate establishments for upper-class and lower-class patrons.

student learning, as in the medieval disputation and subsequent traditions of oral examination, or a mechanical object such as a musket. Two characteristics of performance tests made them suspect for the Enlightenment mentality: (1) the judges had to wait until the process was complete to evaluate it; and (2) the tests involved subjective interaction between judge and judged, a seedbed over centuries for various abuses such as old-boy networks and racist double standards. Enlightenment thinking favored precision measurement that allowed prediction of performance in advance and created objective distance between the act of judgment and that which was to be judged.

Performance testing began to decline in the United States after the turning of the nineteenth century with the introduction of precision gauges in manufacture and quantifiable tests in schools. The movement toward gauge-measured production of standardized parts transformed the manufacture of metal parts equipment, first firearms and later sewing machines, typewriters, bicycles, and eventually automobiles and a host of consumer products assembled from predesigned interchangeable parts. In the handcraft tradition, skilled artisans judged the fit of each part with its working whole by eye and feel while fine tuning it with files. Ultimately, weapons were tested by proof firing. The new uniformity system meant determining a standard design for every part and constructing precision gauges so that parts could be measured before they were assembled into a final weapon. The more precise the gauges, the less necessary it seemed to proof test the weapons.[27]

School tests took the turn from performance to standard testing more gradually, beginning with the nineteenth century's adoption of numerical scoring and more dramatically with the early twentieth century's true-false and multiple choice formats. The changes eroded the communal sensuality of the teacher-student relationship inherent in oral examinations. When a student passes or fails a standardized test such as the SAT or GRE, she or he neither sees or meets nor can influence the judges. Those who designed the standardized questions, from among whose predesigned responses the student must select, remain anonymous.[28]

---

27. The definitive history of this development is David A. Hounshell's *From the American System to Mass Production, 1800–1932: The Development of Manufacturing Technology in the United States* (Baltimore: Johns Hopkins University Press, 1984). On the conflicts that attended the introduction of precision gauge measurement, see Merritt Roe Smith, *Harpers Ferry Armory and the New Technology: The Challenge of Change* (Ithaca, N.Y.: Cornell University Press, 1977) and "Military Enterprise and Innovative Process," in *Military Enterprise and Technological Change: Perspectives on the American Experience,* ed. M. R. Smith (Cambridge: MIT Press, 1985). On similar developments in eighteenth-century France, see Ken Alder, "Forging the New Order: French Mass Production and the Language of the Machine Age, 1763–1815," (Ph.D. diss., Harvard University, 1991).

28. See George F. Madaus, "Curriculum Evaluation and Assessment," in *Handbook of Research on Curriculum,* ed. P. Jackson (New York: MacMillan, 1992). Standardized, high-stakes

David Rothman and Michel Foucault, among others, have observed much the same pattern in judging criminals. The asylum prison system, popularized in late-eighteenth-century Britain as Jeremy Bentham's panopticon and in the United States as the Auburn (New York) and the Pennsylvania prison plans of the 1820s, abandons an earlier judicial focus on the criminal *act* (with its appropriate punishment) and concentrates on the *criminal* (and his or her need to be corrected). Judging the interior of the criminal and applying corrective remedies requires a defined exterior standard against which one is measured, and that in turn implies some person or group who gets to set the standard.

Performance testing, in retreats or academic settings or manufacturing shops, looks backward at completed activities; so does judging a criminal act and assigning the penalty due it. Testing to gauge looks to the future by defining standard norms and constructing gauges that will enforce them in the future. Standardized acceptance tests like the GRE predict the future behavior of potential admits according to a set of standardized norms in precisely the same way that precision gauges predict the behavior of a part before it has been assembled into a working artifact. In like manner, assessing the soul in therapeutic prison reform is aimed at future reform of inner behavior again according to standards defined by elite managers of the therapeutic system.

Nowhere, perhaps, is this shift in values more evident in the United States than in the Progressive era technocratic idea that expert system designers ought to replace political negotiation. During the Gilded Age and into the twentieth century the United States experienced two seemingly contradictory trends that together created a new national climate, at once very daring and very anxious. Americans thrilled again and again when they witnessed protean technological triumphs that promised to transform the burdens of what had been primarily a rough frontier life. Urban violence, however, frequently seemed to threaten all they held dear. Two decades of bloody confrontations between workers and management police were covered in lurid (and generally antiworker) detail in the national press. Still more unsettling, millions of immigrants from hitherto unfamiliar countries of eastern and southern Europe flooded the nation with what for many seemed to be hoards of disturbingly un-American strangers.[29]

---

tests such as the SAT can cause powerful conflicts when the testing company's algorithm for adjudicating raw scores judges that a particular student "probably cheated." For a case study of such a conflict, see Walter M. Haney, "Cheating and Escheating on Standardized Tests" (paper prepared for a symposium on cheating at the Annual Meeting of the American Educational Research Association, Atlanta, April 1993).

29. For an overview of scholarship on urban violence, see Paul Boyer's "'The Ragged Edge of Anarchy': The Emotional Context of Urban Social Control in the Gilded Age," in his *Urban Masses and Moral Order in America, 1820–1920* (Cambridge: Harvard University Press, 1978). On immigration patterns, see John Higham, *Send These to Me: Jews and Other Immigrants in Urban America* (New York: Atheneum, 1975) for a broad overview of legal and social resistance

Contemporary technologies stood out in stark contrast with these alarming symptoms of social disorder. New inventions—railroads, telegraphs, telephones, skyscrapers, electric light and power utilities—showcased experts who solved problems by designing seemingly miraculous systems. The fact that the systems required conformity from those who used them was less immediately obvious but equally significant. Gradually standardization supplanted the less efficient technological style rooted in hands-on negotiation among all concerned.

Examples abound. Historian J. L. Larson contrasts old and new railroad designs of grain-shipping facilities at St. Louis and Chicago in 1860. For the St. Louis depot, grain had to be bagged, loaded on train cars, off-loaded at the outer edge of the city (where, in typical antebellum fashion, the tracks ended), hauled by teamsters across the city, and loaded again onto riverboats. Chicago grain was bulk-loaded onto grain cars because the company-owned track ran through the city to the docks, where it was off-loaded onto grain boats. Larson concludes his description with the following provocative sentence: "If the Chicago system was a model of integration, speed, and efficiency, the St. Louis market *preserved the integrity of each man's transaction* and employed a host of small entrepreneurs at every turn—*real virtues in ante-bellum America*" (my emphases). St. Louis needed negotiation just to get the grain transported, but the more centralized Chicago system achieved greater efficiency, bypassing that "host of small entrepreneurs at every turn." About the same time, factory relationships between owner and worker were gradually changing from the sometimes respectful and sometimes tumultuous interaction of the earlier U.S. small shop toward the heavy-handed enforcement of work rules and the de-skilling of workers through increasingly automated machines.[30]

The older types of negotiation—skilled workers with owners or local businesses with national rail lines—were unpredictable and truculent, requiring political skill for technical results. The new standardized systems seemed to promise control over an unruly social order to match its obvious control of technical complexities. It is not surprising that those who feared social chaos

---

to immigration from 1870 through the draconian 1924 immigration act that marked the definitive end of the earlier open-door policy. On the origin and later history of the popular image of the melting pot see Philip Gleason, "The Melting Pot: Symbol of Fusion or Confusion?" *American Quarterly* 16, no. 1 (spring 1964): 20–46.

30. J. L. Larson, "A Systems Approach to the History of Technology: An American Railroad Example" (paper read at the Annual Meeting of the Society for the History of Technology, Philadelphia, October, 1982), 17. On changing labor-management relations in the nineteenth-century United States, see Herbert Gutman, *Work, Culture and Society in Industrializing America* (New York: Vintage, 1966) and David Montgomery, *The Fall of the House of Labor: The Workplace, the State, and American Labor Activism, 1865–1925* (New York: Cambridge University Press, 1987).

would look to scientific and technological expertise for answers. In 1898 sociologist Edward Alsworth Ross urged that "the right persons" (i.e., social scientists) undertake "the study of moral influences . . . for *the scientific control of the individual.*"[31] In the first decades of the twentieth century, technocrats such as F. W. Taylor proposed scientific management as the solution for the nation's problems through the application of "exact science," in factories, schools, and local governments, situations previously thought to require interactive negotiation.[32]

Pressure toward conformity appears over and over again in the period. The Ford Motor Company labor reforms of 1914 countered 1913's intolerable 370 percent worker turnover on the company's nearly complete assembly line. Ford doubled daily wages to five dollars and cut the workday from nine to eight hours. But the company also established a system of factory spies, home-visiting inspectors, and an English language school to produce Americanized workers for the company. Ford's mix of enforcement and paternalistic betterment programs was an early version of later control tactics seen in the Red Scare of 1919–20, the adoption of tear gas in 1923, industrial psychology, and welfare capitalism plans throughout the twenties.[33]

Substituting systems designed by expert elites for negotiation that had included the larger nonelite public takes its allure from the promise of doing things right and running public affairs more efficiently and fairly. Progressive era technocratic heros such as Thomas Edison, Charles Proteus Steinmetz, Frederick Winslow Taylor, or Henry Ford did not shrink, in speeches, autobiographical essays, or question-and-answer sessions with reporters, from making pronouncements about reorganizing society according to scientific or

---

31. Ross urged concealing such scientific secrets, for "to betray the secrets of social ascendancy is to forearm the individual in his struggle with society." Quotations from A. Michael McMahon, "An American Courtship: Psychologists and Advertising Theory in the Progressive Era," *American Studies* 13 (1972): 6.

32. On scientific management and its later spin-off, industrial psychology, see Edwin T. Layton, Jr., *The Revolt of the Engineers: Social Responsibility and the American Engineering Profession* (Cleveland: Case Western Reserve Press, 1971); and Samuel Haber, *Efficiency and Uplift: Scientific Management in the Progressive Era, 1890–1920* (Chicago: University of Chicago Press, 1964). For the biography of another of the major technocratic prolocutor of the period, see Ronald R. Kline, *Steinmetz: Engineer and Socialist* (Baltimore: Johns Hopkins University Press, 1992).

33. David Brody's *Workers in Industrial America: Essays on the 20th Century Struggle* (New York: Oxford University Press, 1980) provides a thoughtful analysis of welfare capitalism and the pre- and post-war labor-management context. For an interpretation focusing more on radical worker movements in the period, see James R. Green, *The World of the Worker: Labor in Twentieth Century America* (New York: Hill and Wang, 1980). On the introduction of tear gas into civilian police forces, see Daniel P. Jones, "From Military to Civilian Technology: The Introduction of Tear Gas for Civil Riot Control," *Technology and Culture* 19, no. 2 (April, 1978): 151–68.

efficient principles.³⁴ Thus, Steinmetz evolved a political philosophy he called "Corporate Socialism": "I look forward to the time when the corporation will be mankind, those times when all mankind will form a co-operative industrial organization which in its initial crude form is represented by the modern corporation." Ensconced as he was in General Electric, Steinmetz found the corporation the most suitable model for social justice. The Socialist party, he argued, "cannot be antagonistic to the corporation principle, since its ultimate aim, socialistic society, may be expressed as the formation of the industrial corporation of the United States, owned by all the citizens as stockholders."³⁵

Technocratic solutions were rooted in an elitism that routinely flavored their wisdom sayings. Henry Ford contrasts the design side and the conformity side of the moving assembly line:

> Repetitive labour—the doing of one thing over and over again and always in the same way—is a terrifying prospect to a certain kind of mind. It is terrifying to me. I could not possibly do the same thing day in and day out, but to other minds, perhaps I might say to the majority of minds, repetitive operations hold no terrors. In fact, to some types of mind thought is absolutely appalling. To them the ideal job is one where the creative instinct need not be expressed. . . .
>
> There is no reason why any one with a creative mind should be at a monotonous job, for everywhere the need for creative men is pressing. There will never be a dearth of places for skilled people, *but we have to recognize that the will to be skilled is not general. And even if the will be present, then the courage to go through with the training is absent.*³⁶

Attempts to inculcate conformity among the mass of ordinary citizens took perhaps their most sophisticated form in the full-service advertising agency that came of age immediately before, during, and after World War I. Apart from patent-medicine-style huckstering, most nineteenth-century advertisements presumed an essential equality between advertiser and buyer; sales were thought to result from discussion of the product's qualities, price, or availability. The First World War saw a new style emerge that focused on

---

34. Secondary literature on this point is abundant. See, for example, Kline on Steinmetz, Wachhorst on Edison, Haber and Layton on Taylorites. Tichi and Segal for overviews from literary perspectives.

35. Both quotations are from the same 1915 meeting and are cited in Kline, *Steinmetz: Engineer and Socialist,* 219; Steinmetz, "Response and Annual Address," *National Association of Corporation Schools, Proceedings* 3 (June 8–11, 1915), 54 and 839–42.

36. Henry Ford, in collaboration with Samuel Crowther, *My Life and Work* (New York: Doubleday, Page and Company, 1922), 103–4 (my emphasis).

product benefits. Advertisers perceived their targets as irrational and inept rather than decisive and adult. They designed ads aimed at changing citizens into "consumers" who needed help to make even elementary decisions and whose decisions were limited to the private domain.[37]

In their mature twentieth-century form, advertisements offer a mirror image of the *Spiritual Exercises.* For the *Exercises,* affective states lead through the darkness of uncertainty toward a slowly emerging clarity of purpose. For advertisements, affective states become "hot button" targets, which are psychologically analyzed and symbolically manipulated to achieve a predefined strategic purpose. Advertising agencies, of course, exploited and amplified the confusions and turmoil already at work in the country. In fact, the foregoing historical sketches understate the changing speed and scale of daily life. In the context of burgeoning urban growth, the new technical systems created an artificial landscape that defined the individual as a tiny figure against imposing, sometimes violent, and always dynamically changing forces. It is no surprise that the turning of the century was marked by hunger for inner meaning to counter the confusing pace of modernity.[38]

The fact that full-service ad agencies began hiring full-time psychologists about 1900, not long after the emergence of Freudian psychology, underscores the problem deciding whether the patient or client is primarily understood as an object to be studied and treated or as an active participant who leads the interpretative process. The unstudied rhetoric of those who claim the elite

---

37. In Michael Schudson's reading: "The satisfactions portrayed [in ads] are invariably private, even if they are familial or social; they do not invoke public or collective values." See his *Advertising, the Uneasy Persuasion: It's Dubious Impact on American Society* (New York: Basic Books, 1984), 221. The best study of these developments remains Roland Marchand's *Advertising the American Dream: Making Way for Modernity, 1920–1940* (Berkeley: University of California Press, 1985); on consumers as irrational, see 10, 68–69, and passim. See also Daniel Pope, *The Making of Modern Advertising* (New York: Basic Books, 1983) and Jackson Lears, *Fables of Abundance: A Cultural History of Advertising in America* (NY: Basic, 1994).

38. For an analysis of advertising as part of a larger social movement from a nineteenth-century Protestant ethic of productivity toward the twentieth-century therapeutic ethos, see T. J. Jackson Lears, "From Salvation to Self-Realization: Advertising and the Therapeutic Roots of the Consumer Culture, 1880–1930," in *The Culture of Consumption: Critical Essays in American History, 1880–1980,* ed. Richard Wightman Fox and T. J. Jackson Lears (New York: Pantheon Books, 1983), 1–38. William Barratt attributed the rise of the existentialist critique of the Enlightenment and the rise of depth psychology to the West's suppression of the nonrational: "It seems to me no accident at all that modern depth psychology has come into prominence in the same period as Existentialism and for the same reason: namely, that certain unpleasant things the Enlightenment had dropped into the limbo of the unconscious have begun to backfire and have forced themselves finally upon the attention of modern man" (*Irrational Man: A Study in Existential Philosophy* [Garden City, N.Y.: Doubleday Anchor, 1958], 245). In his provocative reading of the Aeschylus trilogy *Oresteia* from the mid-1950s, from which this quotation is taken, Barratt seems to me to be anticipating the postmodern critique of excessive Western rationality.

therapeutic status sometimes reveals the depth of contempt for those deemed in need of repair that is implicitly part of this social arrangement. Thus Karl Menninger writes:

> We, *the agents of society,* must move to end the game of tit-for-tat and blow-for-blow in which *the offender* has foolishly and futilely engaged himself and *us. We* are not driven, as he is, to *wild and impulsive actions.* With knowledge comes power, and with power there is no need for the frightened vengeance of the old penology. In its place should go a quiet, dignified, therapeutic program for the rehabilitation of *the disorganized one,* if possible, the protection of society during the treatment period, and his guided return to useful citizenship, as soon as this can be effected.[39]

The implied relationship of therapist and patient in texts like these echoes the perceived gulf between advertising professionals and the ordinary mass of humanity who were the targets of their creations. Roland Marchand's masterful study of in-house agency culture cites the firm of Ruthrauff and Ryan in *Printer's Ink* as follows:

> We must not forget that many things which are well-known to us are beyond the horizons of the multitude. In addressing the large audience, we cannot ignore . . . the mental and emotional limitations of the great mass. . . . Our choice of appeals, copy ideas, headlines, and illustrations must embody concessions to popular taste—whether we, as individuals, endorse that taste or not.[40]

The contrast between these crude, but high-status, forms of elitism and the tone set by Ignatius for the director-retreatant relationship is instructive when considered in terms of the standardization ideal. Menninger's therapist and the advertising professional analyze the emotional patterns of their inferiors with the intention of reprogramming their inner behavior, according to an already articulated theory of psychological normalcy, to achieve a prespecified new form of behavior. In the *Exercises,* both director and retreatant are led by the retreatant's affective movements as they find their way through the process of

---

39. "Therapy, Not Punishment," *Harpers Magazine* (August, 1959): 63–64 (my emphases). Menninger is quoted, together with Bertrand Russell, B. F. Skinner, and Benjamin Karpman to much the same effect in Herbert Morris, "Persons and Punishment," *The Monist* 52 (October, 1968): 480–81. Morris's essay has acquired the status of a classic critique of the therapeutic replacement of punishment. He roots his argument in the inherent dehumanization of the person when guilt is replaced by treatment: "In this [therapeutic] world we are now to imagine when an individual harms another his conduct is to be regarded as a symptom of some pathological condition in the way a running nose is a symptom of a cold" (480).

40. Marchand, *American Dream,* 70.

prayer. Since they must wait to see the outcome of such movements before evaluating them, their interaction is an instance of performance testing so common before the eighteenth century.[41]

The early twentieth century marks the maturation of a definition of progress that had been gradually transformed from the eighteenth-century notion to a standardized version. The unsettling character of the changes we have emphasized, a society dividing along the lines of designers and designed, wealthy and poor, alarmed some observers of the American scene. William Dean Howells, dean of American letters in the 1890s, already wrote in this vein in an 1888 letter to Henry James.

> I am not in a very good humour with "America" myself . . . but after fifty years of optimistic content with 'civilization' and its ability to come out all right in the end, I now abhor it, and feel that it is coming out all wrong in the end, unless it bases itself anew on a real equality. Meantime, I wear a fur-lined overcoat, and live with all the luxury my money can buy.[42]

The implications of the shift from a political ideal toward a technocratic one have not gone unnoticed in discussions of the idea of progress. Leo Marx contrasts an early Enlightenment commitment to "radical political liberation" with the later technologically driven notion found by the turn of the twentieth century. Merritt Roe Smith observes in like fashion that "belief in progress began to shift away from the moral and spiritual anchors of the revolutionary era toward a more utilitarian and hard-headed, business-oriented emphasis on profit, order, and prosperity."[43] Progress had come a long way from the found-

---

41. Psychotherapy and psychological counseling are sometimes described in the language of standardized therapeutic reform seen in the previous Menninger quotation and sometimes in language much closer to the director-retreatant language of the *Exercises*. My personal favorite example of the latter is Joanne Greenberg, *I Never Promised You a Rose Garden* (New York: Holt, Rinehart and Winston, 1964). It should be noted as well that Ignatius and other early directors of the *Exercises* presumed a basic mental health on the part of retreatants. Caution was to be observed about indiscriminately inviting people into the full dynamic of the retreat.

42. In John Kasson, *Civilizing the Machine* (New York: Grossman Publishers, 1976), 223–24. See also Daniel T. Rodgers, *The Work Ethic in Industrial America, 1850–1920* (Chicago: University of Chicago Press, 1974), esp. his epilogue "Charles W. Eliot and the Quest for Joyful Labor," 233–42.

43. Leo Marx, "On Heidegger's Conception of 'Technology' and its Historical Validity," *The Massachusetts Review* 25, no. 4 (winter 1984): 644–45. Merritt Roe Smith, "Technology, Industrialization and the Idea of Progress in America," *Responsible Science: The Impact of Technology on Society,* ed. Kevin Byrne (San Francisco: Harper and Row, 1986), 4. In a recent and as yet unpublished paper, Marx explores the gradual replacing of expressions such as "mechanic arts" by the word *technology* in the same late-nineteenth-century period: "The Idea of 'Technology' and the Tenor of Postmodern Pessimism" (paper delivered at the International Workshop on Technological Pessimism, Modern Societies and Their Environments, Tel Aviv and Jerusalem, January 1992).

ing fathers' Enlightenment confidence in the capacity of human beings to transform nature for their benefit while negotiating a liberating political order. By the first decades of the twentieth century, *Progress* implied passive conformity in the face of twin gods Science and Technology. Nowhere, perhaps, has the new relationship been more aptly encapsulated than in the boldfaced motto found in the guidebook of the 1933 Chicago Century of Progress Exposition. Here, in three two-word sentences, the relationships between science, industry (a conflation of business and technology) and human beings receive blunt treatment indeed: "SCIENCE FINDS. INDUSTRY APPLIES. MAN CONFORMS."[44]

## Conclusion

Was it inevitable that the Enlightenment would give birth to standardization as so pervasive a shaper of the twentieth-century United States? The patterns I have traced into the early decades of the century continue into the present. Distaste for unpredictable interactions continues to motivate research into preemptive systems. If anything, the late twentieth century is much more heavily standardized than the period we have considered here when it emerged as a dominant cultural ideal. The power of computer algorithms to manage very large accumulations of discrete information dramatically enhances the allure of precision measurement and standardized enforcement we traced earlier. Algorithms routinely irritate those who are judged by them—students judged by standardized tests, adults whose ability to take out a loan depends on computerized credit ratings, phone operators whose time per call and time between calls are monitored on a second-by-second basis, airline pilots governed by automated flight plans, recipients of targeted telephone marketing appeals—the list seems endless. Despite considerable evidence to the contrary, intrusive systems demanding conformity are routinely legitimated by the argument that enhanced information management improves efficiency over older hands-on methods.[45] The sweet promise of a world uninterrupted by the messy

---

44. Chicago Century of Progress International Exposition, *Official Book of the Fair* (Chicago: A Century of Progress, Inc., 1932) 11.
45. Complex computer algorithms increasingly control manufacturing and design processes. It turns out that engineers frequently treat the algorithms as black boxes, turning the crank without breaking open the algorithm to assess the validity of its governing assumptions for current conditions. Engineer George E. Smith calls attention to the problem as follows: "The economic advantages of such a practice are obvious. Yet it has drawbacks. The user often has only a limited understanding of many of the programs in the overall package. He knows input conventions and calling sequences, but not much about assumptions made in the programs. Consequently, he is not in a good position to critically assess many of the outputs, and has little choice but to take them at face value" (George E. Smith, "The Dangers of CAD," *Mechanical Engineering* 108 [February, 1986], 60). Shoshanah Zuboff (*In the Age of the Smart Machine* [New York: Basic Books, 1988]) analyzes repeated instances in which computerized algorithms are used in decision-making roles to

unpredictabilities of disagreements, unhindered by the need to negotiate with persons unlike oneself, a world cleansed and desensualized and programmable, maintains a powerful presence at the structural level of contemporary society.

I write in the wake of the cold war's collapse, a period deeply troubled by vicious outbreaks of religiously and tribally motivated violence such as the current Serbian ethnic cleansing. Weeks before finishing this chapter, David Koresh's cult, the Branch Davidians, brought home the horror of cults who match the fanatical emotion of their inner life with the sharp edges of their boundaries against the outside world. A more unpropitious time to invoke and encourage the holy dark, it would appear, could hardly be imagined. Indeed, what seems needed most is a renewal of Enlightenment civility, the dream that human beings from very different backgrounds could learn to converse across lines of belief and feeling with temperate voices.

This chapter is written in the spirit of that hope. I have argued here, however, that the civilities of rational conversation and thought cannot be sustained for very long by pretending that belief and passion and ordinary moods can somehow be objectified into nothing more than programmable instruments for achieving goals that have already been defined. Where it has thrived as a subtle discipline of discernment, the holy dark has worked to moderate and relativize the human projects that have already been set in motion by one or another advocacy group. Disciplines of affectivity are meant to help find goals worth working for. They teach human beings when it is time to focus toward a perceived goal and when it is time to wait, expecting to find the way toward a still mysterious purpose.

The modernist ideal of progress through enlightenment has come under increasingly severe assault in the past several decades as previously marginalized voices claim a place at center stage and radical deconstruction acquires popular academic currency. Ecological crises, population pressures, and tribal, religious, and urban conflict all combine as a set of public events providing credence to postmodern criticism. Such critique is helpful, it seems to me, insofar as it calls attention to the imbalances of the modernist project, and no help at all when it drifts into nihilism: the rejection of the possibility of positive content in human discourse, the denial of a larger reality that transcends and gives meaning to the competing strategic rhetorics so aptly analyzed by methods of deconstruction.[46] To engage postmodern criticism and at the same

---

maintain hierarchies of power—this despite repeated experiences, often in the same companies, that an open-access approach to computerized data systems, an approach that dramatically increases the possibility of negotiation among all levels of the work force, improves productivity, efficiency, and profitability; see especially chapters 6, 7, 9, and 10.

46. My position here agrees more-or-less completely with David Harvey's interpretation of the relationship between modernism and postmodernism. See especially chapter 6, "POSTmodernISM or postMODERNism?" in Harvey, *Condition of Postmodernity,* 113–18.

time respect the modern tradition of scientific discourse and technological sophistication requires, I am thinking, a retrieval of the West's ancient understanding that light indeed liberates, but in the final analysis it liberates only when tempered and nourished by the dark, the imprecise, and the blessedly ambiguous.

> Here come more stars to character the skies,
> And they in the estimation of the wise
> Are more divine than any bulb or arc,
> Because their purpose is to flash and spark,
> But not to take away the precious dark.
> We need the interruption of the night
> To ease attention off when overtight,
> To break our logic in too long a flight,
> And ask us if our premises are right.
> (Robert Frost, "The Literate Farmers and the Planet Venus")

# The Domination of Nature and the Redefinition of Progress

*Leo Marx*

There is no mystery about the waning of the belief in Progress in our time. Much of that loss of collective optimism is attributable, as we note in the introduction, to the catastrophic events—and disheartening trends—of the century now approaching its end. Perhaps nothing has contributed more to the gathering pessimism than the marked heightening, beginning some three decades ago, of public awareness of the grave damage that modern industrial societies inflict upon the global environment. The increasingly plausible idea that the institutions and practices of modernity are inherently damaging to the global ecosystem, and that much of the damage they inflict may be irremediable, strikes at the conceptual heart of the progressive belief system. After all, the modern concept of Progress, from the time of its definitive formulation during the Enlightenment, has derived much of its credibility from the steady increase, and the manifest benefits, of humanity's perceived dominion over nature.

But if that perception still has merit, does it follow that future progress requires the unlimited extension of human domination?[1] My aim here is to reassess the idea of the increasing dominion over nature as a reliable gauge of progress and to conclude with Thomas Jefferson's unconventional, historically precocious, essentially negative answer to the question just posed. In arguing against the development of U.S. manufactures at the outset of the industrial era, he tacitly enunciated the guiding principles he would have the young republic apply in setting limits to its economic growth and—by extension—to the transformation of the natural world. Although firmly committed to the larger Enlightenment project—above all to scientific rationalism, republicanism, and the advance of knowledge and the arts (both fine and mechanic)—Jefferson nonetheless was dubious about the need for, or the desirability of, the limitless expansion of human power over the natural world. For a moment, indeed, he

---

1. For an explanation of my use of the capitalized and uncapitalized forms of the word *Progress/progress,* see note 7.

tacitly endorsed a modification of the emergent, soon to be all but universally accepted doctrine of Progress—a modification that in retrospect has become immensely appealing. To appreciate the distinctiveness of Jefferson's vision, however, it is first necessary to recognize the extent to which the credibility of Progress is bound up with an exultant awareness of humanity's rapidly expanding power over nature.

**Progress as the Domination of Nature**

The modern belief that history is a record of continuous improvement—of Progress—is Western culture's most popular, comprehensive, and compelling boast about its eventual triumph over "nature." Nature, in this view, represents the totality of the nonhuman—all that exists independent of humanity and its works.[2] Ever since it was definitively formulated, during the eighteenth-century Enlightenment, the full-blown modern concept of Progress has been routinely justified by citing evidence of humankind's steadily increasing knowledge of—and power over—the forces of nature. The socioeconomic motor of this triumphant expansion of human power has been industrial capitalism; its primary intellectual resource has been science, and the equipment required to achieve the kind of serial improvement called Progress has been provided by technology, that is, by innovations in the mechanic arts.

Before the onset of industrialism no society ever had dared promise a future of continuously enhanced material well-being. As Ernest Gellner puts it, the industrial capitalist societies of the West are (or were until recently) the only kind "ever to live by and rely on sustained and perpetual growth, on an expected and continuous improvement. Not surprisingly, . . . [they were the first] to invent the concept and ideal of progress, of continuous improvement."[3]

---

2. Today this popular meaning of nature often is criticized by environmentalists as a misleading vestige of a now discredited Cartesian dualism; from a sophisticated post-Enlightenment, post-Darwinian, postmodern viewpoint, it is said, humanity and its works should be seen as parts of—as "belonging to"—nature conceived as one seamlessly related set of biophysical processes. From the viewpoint of a cultural historian, however, the significant fact is that in common parlance nowadays educated adherents of Western culture simultaneously credit the validity of (at least) two radically incompatible meanings of the complex word *nature*. The continuing popularity of the dualistic, excessively anthropocentric, but phenomenologically accurate concept of nature as the "Not-Human" or the Other testifies to humanity's continuing commitment, in the modern era, to the continuing effort to effect a technological transformation of its habitat. That we also are willing, when reminded, to credit the truth value of the opposed, monistic (Darwinian) concept suggests the depth of the ambivalence that figures in our relations with the environment.

3. Ernest Gellner, *Nations and Nationalism* (Ithaca, N.Y.: Cornell University Press, 1983), 22.

A culture's belief in Progress, put differently, derives from (and refers to) that distinctively modern kind of social change made possible by acquiring *from* the realm of nature the unprecedented power to establish a steadily increasing domination *of* nature.

A precondition for diffusing this belief was the increasing awareness, in early modern Europe, of an accelerating rate of benign change. Only when significant segments of the populace were able to discern a marked trend of improvement—when they compared their own lot with that of their parents and their children—did this unprecedented belief become credible. This shift in consciousness was bound up with another unique set of events: the transformation of relatively small and localized, static, hierarchical, predominantly rural-agricultural and barter-based ways of life to larger, nation-state size, dynamic, urbanizing, market-based, commodity-producing and -exchanging capitalist societies.

The transition to capitalism was accompanied by a shift in attitude toward the natural world. The traditional medieval view of nature as a divinely ordained, gloriously unified, but spiritually vacant creation, to which (potentially) immortal humanity was temporarily bound, gradually was supplanted by an increasingly secularized sense of the natural world as an objectified, resistant, knowable, inescapable habitat and body of resources susceptible to being understood, controlled, improved, and used by enlightened humanity.

Nature, thus redescribed, comported with the distinctively, aggressively analytic, probing, instrumentalist treatment accorded it by modern science and technology. To be sure, ancient precursors of the narrative of Progress—the myth of Prometheus comes to mind—had conveyed more than a little antagonism toward nature. But the degree of aggressive intervention and transformative processing implicit in the impersonal, analytic, rational, reconstructive approach to nature favored by the eighteenth-century narrative of science-based improvement was without precedent.

So was the speed with which the idea of Progress gained widespread credence. Within 200 years, roughly from 1550 to 1750, the long-standing, hitherto lopsided power relations between an awesome nature and our relatively impotent species had begun to seem reversible. The late-eighteenth-century Enlightenment was the intellectual culmination of this reversal, for it affirmed an exhilarating sense of humanity's new intellectual capacity to penetrate the most remote, elusive, or obscure recesses of the cosmos—a sense of the power of knowledge famously captured by Alexander Pope (in his epitaph for Isaac Newton):

Nature and nature's laws lay hid in night;
God said, "*Let Newton be!*" and all was light.

By the end of the nineteenth century the attainment, by Western societies, of these hitherto unimaginable forms of knowledge and power had issued in: (1) the creation of immense new wealth; (2) a manifest improvement in the prevailing conditions of everyday life for large parts of the population; (3) the gradual spread of less authoritarian, republican, political institutions; and (4) the achievement of something like global geopolitical hegemony. With these seemingly solid accomplishments in view, the idea of Progress itself acquired the status of a verifiable, self-evident, historical fact.

Half a century later, however, in the aftermath of Hiroshima, it became obvious that this optimistic view of history was rapidly losing credibility. In retrospect, indeed, it was evident that the process had begun decades earlier. Instead of introducing an era of peace and plenty, as had been repeatedly predicted, the nineteenth-century "Age of Machinery," as Carlyle had named it,[4] had been followed by a century of worldwide warfare, genocide, totalitarian tyranny, unmatched material devastation, and—though its scope has been significantly reduced—continuing mass poverty. Today, as the century is ending, even the engine of economic progress, identified with increased productivity and consumption, may be losing momentum.[5] But the most revealing aspect of this total reversal of expectation, to say it again, is the extensive despoilation, unprecedented in geographical scope and gravity, inflicted upon the biosphere in recent decades by means, ironically enough, of the very science-based inventions that had been extolled as the primary motive force of Progress. Leaving aside all the other reasons for skepticism, this turn of events makes it difficult—many would say impossible—to imagine a future marked by continuing improvement in the prevailing conditions of human life.

To say this, however, is to raise an intriguing set of questions. If the belief in the idea of history as a record of the progressive growth of human power over nature is illusory, does that mean that it should be completely abandoned? Or can it be modified and salvaged? If we abandon it, what do we then say about all those aspects of modernity that seem to ratify the idea? But the difficulty we have in imagining an alternative suggests another line of speculation. To think of Progress as a particular "idea" may be misleading, and indeed it resembles what Alfred North Whitehead once called the "philosophy of an epoch"—a philosophy that rests, he explained, on assumptions that adherents of all the variant systems within the epoch "unconsciously presuppose" and that appear "so obvious that people do not know what they are assuming

---

4. In his seminal 1829 essay, "Signs of the Times," in *Critical and Miscellaneous Essays* (Chicago: Beford, Clarke, and Co., n.d.), 5–30.

5. For a recent analysis claiming to establish the end of economic and material progress, see C. Owen Paepke, *The Evolution of Progress: The End of Economic Growth and the Beginning of Human Transformation* (New York: Random House, 1993).

because no other way of putting things has ever occurred to them."[6] In more current language, it might be described as a pervasive "collective mentality."

## Progress as Collective Mentality

To think of the belief in Progress simply as a commitment to another "idea" among countless others is to trivialize it. The ideologically prolific culture of modernity generates myriad ideas, but few, if any, have gained as powerful a hold on the collective consciousness as the identification of history with Progress. To understand the centrality of that belief in the culture of modernity, it is necessary to distinguish between two distinct meanings of the word *progress*. The first is a relatively straightforward, everyday meaning: when we say that a person or group has made progress within a specific practice, one with a clearly bounded scope and a more-or-less obvious purpose, we simply mean that they have moved closer to their goal. This sense of the word is especially clear when it refers to advances within an explicitly demarcated, institutionalized practice, such as a scholarly inquiry in physics, biology, or mathematics, or in any other field that is inherently sequential, incremental, or cumulative, where the manifest aim is to reach a better understanding and control of the matter under study. Under those circumstances, there can be little doubt about what it means to make progress, or about its value. Progress so conceived is incontrovertibly appealing. None of the writers represented in this volume seems to have any doubts about the existence, or the desirability, of such clearly bounded forms of progress.

But there is a different meaning, or set of meanings, conveyed by the word *progress* that is anything but simple, straightforward, or self-evident. The difference resides in the greater complexity and scope of whatever entity is thought to be making progress. When we refer to the progress of groups—professions, organizations, communities, nations—compelling reasons for skepticism immediately arise. There is a close correlation, it seems, between the limited scope and boundedness of the allegedly progressing entity, or practice, and the credibility of the claim that it can achieve, or already has achieved, progress. Hence the problematic character of the belief in Progress that evolved in the West during the onset of modernity. Far from referring to a distinctly bounded practice, this modern notion of Progress refers to nothing less, finally, than history itself. It would be hard to imagine a putatively progressing entity of greater scope or complexity. History so conceived becomes a record of the more-or-less steady, continuous, cumulative (some also might say

---

6. Alfred North Whitehead, *Science and the Modern World* (New York: Macmillan, 1925), 71.

preordained) improvement in the overall conditions of human life.[7] To call such a belief an "idea" is no more adequate, in conveying its historical efficacy, than to call Hellenism or Christianity or Marxism "ideas." Between 1750 and 1950 (roughly) the belief in Progress exercised a growing and largely unrivaled dominion over the secular thought of the West.

The modern conception of history as a record of Progress eventually became the fulcrum of an all-encompassing collective mentality. There is no need, for present purposes, to assign this belief to a particular category of collective mentality (such as ideology, myth, ethos, *mentalité*[8]), but it is important to notice that in the naturalistic (or secular) cultural climate of modernity, distinct conceptions of history are capable of doing cultural work very much like that once done, in traditional premodern cultures, by religious myths of origin. Thus the belief in Progress has provided a temporal matrix for—a way of ordering and assigning priorities to—a large portion of modern society's shared meanings, values, and purposes.

Perhaps the contrast between bounded and unbounded concepts of progress—and the particular efficacy of the latter when extended to history itself—is most obvious in the outlook of such radical republican adherents of the Enlightenment as Turgot, Condorcet, Priestley, Paine, Franklin, and Jefferson. They spoke for the revolutionary generation that initially theorized the possibility of comprehensive, or universal, human Progress. (As they saw it, Progress was closely bound up with a belief in "the perfectability of Man.") In a sense they arrived at this notion of *boundless* Progress by means of extrapolation. By the eighteenth century the markedly increasing incidence of progress in the *bounded* sense—progress *within* many, indeed virtually all, the arts and sciences—had become incontrovertible. The obvious next step was to extend the idea to the overall sequence of events, which is to say, to history. Thus Condorcet's generation invented the blustery story of Progress, a metanarrative that served to impart direction, meaning, and purpose—a controlling teleological theme—to the ostensibly linear, upward, inchoately purposeful course of human affairs.

The ultimate goal implicit in the narrative is the supplanting of ignorance by knowledge and of chronic vulnerability to the natural world's cruel, often

---

7. Some writers reinforce the distinction by using the lower case (*progress*) for the bounded examples and reserving the upper case (*Progress*) for this comprehensive, virtually unbounded sense of the word, and I have adopted that practice.

8. In the vast literature on the subject, there probably have been instances of assigning the idea to each of the subordinate kinds of collective mentality: myth, ideology, worldview, *mentalité*, episteme, belief system, ethos, utopia, and metanarrative—the list could be extended. But there is no reliable scholarly consensus about the distinctions among these terms, and since it is not vital to my argument, I will simply rest with the notion that the idea of progress has served as the nucleus of a widely held modern worldview.

terrifying constraints by the power to understand, manipulate, eliminate, and dominate them. The colonial expansion of Europe, especially the westward migration to the Americas, provided tangible geopolitical evidence of the power of (Western) civilization to "conquer" vast expanses of raw, undeveloped nature. By helping to create and distribute vast new wealth, and by making possible the upward socioeconomic mobility of a large segment of the population, Europe's worldwide territorial expansion nurtured a credible illusion that the fact of Progress had been made visible—had been verified.

Although the idea of history as Progress became the nucleus of a secular collective mentality, it was sufficiently abstract—and imprecise—to blend with quite different, in some cases logically incompatible, metaphysical or religious beliefs. (Logical coherence is not a conspicuous feature of myths, worldviews, or other collective mentalities.) Obvious affinities thus made possible the coexistence, sometimes the actual blending, of the secular idea of Progress and the faith in a Second Coming held by various evangelical Protestant sects. In the United States the optimistic, future-oriented, millennial tenor of those sects (probably the most characteristic—and popular—strain of Christianity in nineteenth-century United States) matched the dominant secular rhetoric of the era, with its credulous assumptions about the forward (and upward) course of human events. Although strict secularists looked forward to a consumers' utopia, and religionists to a millenium ruled by Jesus Christ, both anticipated a redemption from such age-old constraints of nature as scarcity, disease, and even mortality.[9]

It is a commonplace of modern historical writing to link the belief in Progress with the contemporaneous "rise of the bourgeoisie." Yet this progressive view of history was no mere rationale for the status of a privileged class. Indeed, there are few better demonstrations of the virtual universality of the nineteenth-century belief in Progress than the fact that it was as fondly embraced by both the most hostile critics and the most ardent exponents of industrial capitalism. Marx and Engels, who developed the most systematic and influential critique of capitalist society, probably were even more deeply committed to the idea of history as a record of cumulative material progress than were most bourgeois apologists for that regime. In Marx's view, the critical factor in human development—counterpart in the history of the human species to Darwinian natural selection in the history of nature—is the continuing growth of humanity's productive capacity.[10] To be sure, the Marxists added

---

9. James Ward Smith and A. Leland Jameson, *The Shaping of American Religion* (Princeton: Princeton University Press, 1961), 396–401 passim; Sydney F. Ahlstrom, *A Religious History of the American People* (New Haven: Yale University Press, 1972), 478–81 passim.

10. A belief in the centrality of humanity's increasing productive power as a historical agent also was congenial to the classical economists and other exponents of capitalism; another vital distinction (also most clearly set forth by Marx and Engels) between the economic "base" of

a decisive political stipulation, namely, that capitalism constitutes both a stage in and an obstacle to the realization of economic progress, and that the working class must seize power before humanity can hope to realize the inherent promise of its increasing knowledge of—and control over—nature. Marxism, along with social democratic and other left-liberal political persuasions, claimed that the presumed agenda of Progress required the supplanting of capitalism by socialism and, eventually, by the communitarian utopia, communism.

## Mapping Progress onto the History of Nature

No branch of knowledge did more to extend the scope of the belief in Progress during the nineteenth century than evolutionary biology. The era's most innovative science, as formulated by Darwin and interpreted—or misinterpreted—by many others, served to fuse the history of nature and the history of culture into a single, unbroken continuum of improvement. Thus Progress, in Herbert Spencer's immensely popular version of the doctrine, had begun with the very first manifestations of the process of evolution from simple to complex—from lower to higher—organisms. In *Progress, Its Law and Cause* (1857), Spencer extends this universal principle to the development of the individual, whom he describes as also evolving from a homogeneous to a heterogeneous state. Spencer, along with his followers and imitators, in effect projected this cherished nineteenth-century idea back to the most remote origins of life on Earth.

Although the affinity between the Darwinian concept of human origins and the belief in Progress has often been noted, the significance of this decisive convergence is not generally recognized. In place of the biblical idea of a divine creation at a fixed date in the relatively recent past, the new doctrine posited the emergence of life as the result of an evolutionary process extending over some two billion years. Most of Darwin's contemporaries, ignoring his own reluctance to do so, interpreted the sequence of developmental stages from microorganisms to the "lower" animals to present-day humanity as a further, self-evident corroboration of the universality of Progress.[11] By expanding the

---

society, to which causal primacy was accorded, and the "superstructure" of extra-economic institutions also was endorsed by many capitalists and various apologists for industrial capitalism.

11. It is next to impossible, even in our more skeptical age, for most people to conceive of the Darwinian history of nature without investing it with some anthropocentric connotations of upward or forward motion, improvement, or, in a word, progress. This tendency to map the belief in Progress onto the history of nature and biological theory is a striking and consequential instance of our culture-bound and perhaps inescapably anthropocentric way of reading (or misreading) Darwin's argument, but it has received relatively little attention as compared with that given to the more obvious misapplication of evolutionary theory to human behavior known as social Darwinism, especially as developed by Spencer and his idea, so resonant in the milieu of a competitive market economy, of the "survival of the fittest." Darwin, it should be noted, did not use the phrase.

idea to embrace the parallel (or consecutive) operation of these two disparate sets of impersonal, deterministic forces (biological evolution and capitalist productivity), Spencer and his followers (and imitators) were able to metaphysicalize Progress: to give it the aspect of an all-embracing teleology. When the combined biological and cultural process, Evolution/Progress, was projected back to the inception of all life, it in effect became the supreme law of the cosmos.

But the astonishingly rapid, widespread dissemination of this belief during the nineteenth century can only be explained by the fact that it was represented by things as well as words. This was especially true of the United States, where the technological transformation of the "wilderness," a process made possible and dramatic by the virtually undeveloped terrain of North America, inculcated the message of progress directly, topographically, imagistically, wordlessly. Of course this remaking of the landscape by Europeans had begun much earlier, in the age of exploration. By the nineteenth century, however, a sense of rapidly accelerating, technologically powered improvement was implicit in many, perhaps most, directly perceived and represented images of the landscape.[12] The eyes of the American people, said Tocqueville, are fixed on only one sight: "its own march across these wilds, draining swamps, turning the course of rivers, peopling solitudes, and subduing nature."[13] To become a believer in Progress in a geophysical setting so pregnant with meaning, one did not have to know anything about the advance of knowledge in physics, biology, or the sciences generally; nor, for that matter, did one need to have encountered an explicit version of the idea of Progress itself. "The mere visible fruits of scientific progress," John Stuart Mill noted apropos of Tocqueville's views on the outlook of Americans, "carry the feeling of admiration for modern, and disrespect for ancient times, down even to the wholly uneducated classes."[14] The most telling evidence of the pervasiveness of these feelings, indicating the material tangibility and visibility of Progress, is to be found in the record of the visual arts and of popular culture generally.[15]

---

12. See Susan Danly and Leo Marx, eds., *The Railroad in American Art: Representations of Technological Change* (Cambridge: MIT Press, 1988); Barbara Novak, *Nature and Culture: American Landscape and Painting, 1825–1875* (New York: Oxford University Press, 1980).

13. Alexis de Tocqueville, *Democracy in America*, 2 vols. (New York: Vintage, 1945), 2:78.

14. John Stuart Mill, "M. de Tocqueville on Democracy in America," *Edinburgh Review*, October, 1840, reprinted in *Dissertations and Discussions: Political, Philosophical, and Historical*, 2 vols. (Boston: William V. Spencer, 1865), 2:148.

15. For an analysis of nineteenth-century U.S. rhetoric of progress, see Leo Marx, *The Machine in the Garden: Technology and the Pastoral Ideal in America* (New York: Oxford University Press, 1964), 190–226; for the technocratic imagery of progress, see Merritt Roe Smith, "Technological Determinism in American Culture," in *Does Technology Drive History? The Dilemma of Technological Determinism*, ed. Leo Marx and Merritt Roe Smith (Cambridge: MIT Press, 1994).

As the appealing belief in Evolution/Progress became more widely diffused, however, its tenor became increasingly technocratic. By the late nineteenth century the old distinction between the means and ends of progress, as initially conceived by the Enlightenment philosophers, had lost much of its force. Condorcet and his colleagues among the philosophes had regarded advances in science and technology as constituting only the *means* of achieving political and social *ends:* a liberation from monarchic, aristocratic, and ecclesiastical tyranny, and the creation of more just, less hierarchical, peaceful, republican institutions. But the nineteenth-century inheritors of the idea, partly because they assumed that the political goals had been (more or less) achieved, or could easily be achieved as soon as the building of the economic "base" had been completed, regarded the sensational advances of science-based technologies, along with the success of industrial societies in creating new wealth, as sufficient warrant for believing in the approaching triumph of humanity in its "conquest of nature." The rapidly mounting rate of technological innovation was increasingly accepted as the primary motor, as well as the most reliable gauge, of Progress. By the early twentieth century this technocratic conception, as embodied in such ancillary doctrines as Fordism, Taylorism, and technocracy, and in the work of the painters, sculptors, architects, and writers of the high modernist movement (c. 1900–1930), seems to have become the prevailing Euro-American version of Progress.[16] Or, put differently, by this period the belief in Progress was in large measure embodied in a pervasive set of assumptions, like that described by Whitehead, that adherents of all the variant contemporary systems of thought unconsciously presupposed. If there is a tacit "philosophy" of the industrial epoch, its keystone is the belief that humanity is destined to prosper by steadily enlarging its dominion over nature.

**Progressivism in Crisis**

Although the belief in Progress has waned since it won all but universal credence within the culture of modernity, it would be wrong to imply that it has disappeared. Indeed, the Enlightenment sense of history as a record of continuous improvement has retained some of its hold on the general public and on many, perhaps most, intellectuals with a secular cast of mind; this is especially true, no doubt, of scientists, engineers, and other professionals with technical skills. Granted that today's increasingly contested, amorphous idea of Progress no longer elicits anything like the enthusiasm of intellectuals that it once did, it

---

16. Many writers have explored the connection between the modernist movement in the arts, technological innovation, and the belief in progress. See Lewis Mumford, *Technics and Civilization* (New York: Harcourt, Brace, and Co., 1934); Siegfried Giedion, *Mechanization Takes Command,* (New York: Oxford University Press, 1948); Thomas Hughes, *American Genesis* (New York: Viking Press, 1989).

nonetheless continues—if only for lack of a compelling alternative—to shape their thinking. That is especially true of most who subscribe to a naturalistic world view, the so-called secular humanists and other academic practitioners of the humanities and the social sciences (fields of inquiry in which the narrative of progress recently has come under concerted attack) and the shrinking but still influential minority of politically oriented intellectuals with left-liberal convictions. The latter, with their legacy of Jacobin-Marxist progressivism, have not lost all hope for the organized political power of working people to effect change in basic social arrangements—to make them more just, more democratic. As Robert Heilbroner recently has written:

> Since the early nineteenth century, progress has been perceived as the movement of Western society "leftward" along an imaginary line that began in the feudal past, ran through early, middle and late capitalism, and ended—or at least pointed toward—the dimly perceived social formation called socialism, and far beyond that, communism.[17]

In recent decades, however, a powerful wave of anti-Enlightenment thought, reinforced by the far-reaching implications of the political upheavals of the 1960s and 1989, has seriously eroded those convictions. (Stalinism, like most offshoots of Marxism, had included its own strong version of Progress.) Indeed, all totalizing ideas about history became a particular target of the new post–1960s, post–New Left critical theories. Exponents of deconstruction and other poststructuralist, postmodernist doctrines have attacked such large explanatory ideas, with their deceptive, ungrounded claims to universality, as misleading "metanarratives" that embody the hidden values of powerful, privileged, oppressing elites. Thus the metanarrative of Progress is widely regarded as serving the purposes, often masked to be sure, of the West's expansionary, colonizing system; on this view, indeed, progressivism continues to provide ideological support for the drive of neocolonialist, Eurocentric (white male) elites for world domination. The destructive results of that drive are most vividly exhibited by today's rapidly accelerating, and frightening, despoliation of what formerly was called "nature," but is now more likely to be called "the global environment." In the words of Fredric Jameson, "postmodernism is what you have when the modernization process is complete and nature is gone for good."[18]

In recent decades the growing anxiety about the "end of nature" has helped make the optimism of progressive thought seem illusory. In this context

---

17. Robert Heilbroner, "Does Socialism Have a Future?" *The Nation* (September 27, 1993), 312. This essay was excerpted from his book *21st Century Capitalism* (New York: W. W. Norton, 1993).

18. Fredric Jameson, *Postmodernism, Or the Cultural Logic of Late Capitalism* (Durham: Duke University Press, 1991), viii.

the notion of the end of "nature" as an independently existing entity has a dual significance: in a literal material or environmental sense, it refers to such phenomena as the human penetration and transformation of the earth's atmospheric envelope; in an abstract conceptual sense, it refers to the weakening of the concept of "nature" as an independent locus of ultimate values and meanings. In any case, an informed awareness of the damage created by humanity's vaunted domination of the natural world has made it increasingly difficult to credit the identification of history with Progress. Even if we ignore the views of the more apocalyptic alarmists, in and out of the scientific community, and heed only the current consensus of moderate opinion about: (1) the recently determined pattern of climate change (global warming); (2) the existence of unprecedented gaps in the ozone layer; (3) the projected growth of the human population; and (4) the extensive weakening of Earth's biological stability due to the accelerating rate of species extinction—even then it remains difficult to accept the complacency nurtured by the progressive worldview. Indeed, these credible forebodings about the deterioration of the biosphere as a human habitat have palpably influenced reigning assumptions about the essential character of the relations between modern industrial societies and nature. The fundamental long-term shaping power of such assumptions—as Emerson put it, "the views of nature held by any people determine all their institutions"—cannot be overstated.[19]

Since the Enlightenment, many adherents of Progress have represented nature as little more than an objectified realm of resources, whether conceptual or material (indeed "raw material") to be "worked up" in the service, ultimately, of economic prosperity.[20] In reacting against that view, postmodernist historians and critics regard the despoliation of the environment as in part at least a consequence of the Enlightenment's grand theory of Progress: its epistemic content, they would argue, rests on essentially the same dubious foundationalist premises that have characterized the mainstream of Western rationalistic philosophy as it flowed from Plato to the twentieth-century positivists. The advance of knowledge, as conceived by most thinkers in that mainstream, is a process of acquiring greater access to a timeless, objective, context-free

---

19. Ralph Waldo Emerson, *English Traits, Works,* 11 vols, (Philadelphia: John D. Morris & Co., 1906), 2:46. See Caroline Merchant, *The Death of Nature: Women, Ecology, and the Scientific Revolution* (New York: Harper Collins, 1983); Bill McKibben, *The End of Nature* (New York: Random House, 1989).

20. Both historians of religion and historians of science have argued that the historical roots of these attitudes lie deep in the monotheistic Judeo-Christian heritage, the world religion that ostensibly creates the widest gulf between humanity and nature. See Mircea Eliade, *Cosmos and History: The Myth of Eternal Return* (New York: Harper, 1959); and Lynn White, Jr., "The Historical Roots of our Environmental Crisis," in *The Subversive Science; Essays Toward an Ecology of Man,* ed. Paul Shepard and Daniel McKinley (Boston: Houghton Mifflin, 1964), 341–51.

foundation for a single incontrovertible truth. The accessibility of that foundation is the chief philosophic premise on which the faith in endless Progress ultimately rests. All of which suggests the need, if we are to salvage a tenable version of the progressive worldview, to reconsider the illusory notion of humanity's endlessly expanding domination of nature.

### Jefferson's Choice: A Modified Version of Progress?

During the winter of 1783–84, while engaged in writing his *Notes on Virginia*, Thomas Jefferson momentarily caught a glimpse of an appealing—and perhaps still tenable—modification of the emergent concept of Progress. It should be said, to be sure, that this was not his purpose. He entitled "Query XIX" of the *Notes* "The present state of manufactures, commerce, interior and exterior trade?" In effect he was posing a fundamental question about the long-term socioeconomic development of the young American republic. Would it be best, he asked, for most of its citizens to continue being farmers or for half of them to be "called off" the land to work in manufacturing and the handicraft arts? The particulars of his famous reply, "Let our work-shops remain in Europe," need not concern us here. For one thing, his political opposition to the introduction of manufactures in the American states proved to be short lived, and for another, the pertinent aspect of his answer for us is what it reveals about his long-term vision of the new society and about the guiding principles he would use in choosing the social policies designed to realize that vision. The chief point here is that Jefferson's choice prefigures a significant alternative to what already was coming to be regarded as society's one—the only possible—available route to modernity.

Jefferson frames his answer to Query XIX with a stark, oversimplified, and finally invidious contrast between two ways of life. In one, the typical citizen is an independent yeoman farmer ideally represented as a "noble husbandman," and most people live on the land—"close," as we say, to nature. In the other, most people live in towns or cities with market economies and thus depend for their subsistence not on their own soil and industry, but on the "casualties and caprice of customers." Within this tendentious framework, a well-established convention of eighteenth-century writing in the pastoral mode, Jefferson develops what he later would acknowledge to be a politically impractical argument against introducing manufactures in the American states. On the basis of this contrast between two ideal types, a rural-agricultural and an urban-commercial society, Jefferson proposes a long term socioeconomic policy that implicitly sets limits to development and, by extention, to economic progress.

> [F]or the general operations of manufacture, let our work-shops remain in Europe. It is better to carry provisions and material to workmen there, than bring them to the provisions and materials, and with them their manners and principles. The loss by transportation of commodities across the Atlantic will be made up in happiness and permanence of government. The mobs of great cities add just so much to the support of pure government, as sores do to the strength of the human body. It is the manners and spirit of a people which preserve a republic in vigour. A degeneracy in these is a canker which soon eats to the heart of its laws and constitution.[21]

This oft-cited statement routinely is dismissed as an expression of Jefferson's "agrarianism"—his deep commitment to the values presumably nurtured by agricultural economies. So, in one sense, it is. In its local, immediate, practical import, Jefferson's choice surely expresses a bias in favor of an agricultural life, but to stop there is to miss the more fundamental, far-reaching implications of that choice. The covert influence of principles whose import far transcends agrarian economics is signaled by his failure to rest his case against manufactures, as eighteenth-century exponents of agrarianism typically did, on the presumed *economic* superiority of agricultural societies. (Agriculture, in that widely accepted view, provides the most stable, productive base for a national economy.) Jefferson rests his argument, however, on quite different extra-economic considerations.

He is so vehemently opposed to the development of large-scale manufactures, and to the kind of society they entail, that to avoid it he is willing to pay a high—arguably exorbitant—price. He is willing to have the young republic suffer the potentially immense economic loss incurred by shipping the raw materials it produces across the ocean and thus having to buy them back in the form of manufactured goods. Why? What would compensate the American states for such a severe self-imposed penalty? Jefferson's astonishing answer, which embodies the cardinal assumptions of his pastoral vision, deserves the closest attention. "*The loss*," he writes, "*by the transportation of commodities across the Atlantic will be made up in happiness and permanence of government.*"[22]

But, again, it is important to situate this surprising argument in the context of Jefferson's ardent support for the larger agenda of the progressive Enlightenment. Had he urged an uncompromising resistance to the advance of scientific rationalism—to the coming of modernity as a whole—his argument would not

---

21. Adrienne Koch and William Peden, eds., *The Life and Selected Writings of Thomas Jefferson* (New York: Modern Library, 1944), 280–81.

22. My emphasis.

be as noteworthy. But a policy of limiting economic growth is not, as he sees it, incompatible with his wholehearted commitment to the advance of knowledge of—and power over—nature, a power derived from the latest discoveries in the natural sciences and the mechanic arts. In his view, indeed, those achievements of applied rationality were closely bound up with the spirit of 1776 and with the prospect of the universal triumph of republicanism. Yet here, in Query XIX, he unequivocally opposes the application of an innovation that is widely assumed to hold the promise of enhanced economic efficiency and productivity or, as a Hamiltonian Federalist would have said, of national wealth and power. The new system of manufactures, already operating in England, was generally regarded as the logical next step in the forward march of Western civilization.

But not by Jefferson. In retrospect, what is most striking about his willingness to limit economic growth is his tacit refusal to endorse—his marked unresponsiveness to—the Enlightenment concept of history as a record of a steady, incremental, continuous, cumulative process called Progress. Though he enthusiastically approves of the various *bounded* forms of contemporary progress, as manifested by advances in, say, celestial mechanics, instrumentation, zoology, geography, and engineering, he is not impelled to endorse the putative chain of steps—a metaphysical or deterministic logic—ostensibly leading humanity toward the realization of Progress. He therefore reaches beyond the economic considerations raised by the immediate question—whether or not to introduce the new system of manufactures—to invoke principles central to his vision of the future republic.

These principles derive from the ancient tradition of pastoralism, a view of life that leads Jefferson, as I have argued elsewhere, to conceive of the new American nation in the image of an ideal republic of the "middle landscape."[23] It is a landscape that symbolically combines the most desirable features of advancing European "civilization" with the most desirable features of the undeveloped North American continent—of raw nature. In Query XIX, in other words, Jefferson in effect translates that pastoral view of the United States into socioeconomic principles more specifically applicable to the American case at hand. Though he later changed his mind on the particular issue of developing manufactures, he never repudiated the more general principles he drew from the pastoral tradition.[24]

The first and most concrete of those principles is implicit in Jefferson's refusal, in Query XIX, to invoke the standard argument for the economic

---

23. Marx, *Machine in the Garden,* 116–44.
24. His changing views may be traced in a series of letters he wrote between 1785 and 1816, but in his final letter on the subject (to Benjamin Austin, January 9, 1816) he is still saying, with reference to the question he had raised in Query XIX, "The former question is suppressed, or rather assumes a new form." It assumes a new form because, he implies, the principle at issue is largely the same. See Marx, *Machine in the Garden,* 139.

superiority of agriculture. Not only does he reject that particular argument, but in accepting the economic losses that would follow from his policy, he clearly rejects the primacy of *all* economic criteria in choosing long-term social goals. Such criteria are, in his view, of secondary importance in framing social policies, and he would subordinate them to criteria based on what now would be called the "quality of life." What matters most, for Jefferson, is the republican character of the polity, and the degree of fulfillment—of happiness—the citizenry enjoys. Thus he unequivocally rejects, in advance as it were, what would become the standard calculus of Progress in the West over the next two centuries. In doing so he anticipates the posture of late-twentieth-century environmentalists. They too insist on the subordination of economic criteria of social policy to such indices of the "quality of life" as drinkable water or breathable air. It is striking that as early as the 1780s, Jefferson was anticipating the recurring need of late-twentieth-century society to compare, and to make choices among, economic and environmental costs, economic and environmental benefits.

The second principle implied by Jefferson's choice affirms, as the chief aim of society's economic activity, the ideal of equitable sufficiency. In a pastoral society, where striving for wealth, status, and power is disdained, people require only that degree of material wealth necessary to enjoy the satisfactions of love, leisure, art, and music. Here, again, Jefferson adopts a measure of economic well-being—sufficiency—wholly at odds with that commonly accepted in Western capitalist societies of the nineteenth and twentieth centuries, namely, their relative capacity to maximize national wealth, productivity, and consumption—or material standard of living. In effect, then, Jefferson's choice would replace the stock notion of economic progress as requiring a continuously growing, expanding economy, with something like the idea of a low-growth, steady state economy. He willingly accepts the kind of trade-off that today's environmentalists often face: the possibility that a reduced level of collective productivity and wealth may be the price of maintaining, or recovering, such intangible "qualities of life" as "happiness" or "permanence of government."

The third, and perhaps the most significant, of Jefferson's principles affirms the need for society to accommodate its institutions and practices to the imperatives of—the opportunities and constraints inherent in—the natural world. This principle, in other words, is grounded in the essential underlying relationship between society and nature. But the idea of nature derived from the pastoral tradition is in many respects premodern. Pastoralism, which after all has its origin in antiquity, long antedates modernity, and the construction of that dominant modern conception of nature as the realm set over against—and upon which humanity exercises—its science-based technological power. In the narrative of Progress, nature is the subordinate Other. Oddly enough, the pastoral view of the natural is in several respects more consonant than the prevailing modernist view than with the antimetaphysical strain in postmodernism.[25] The pastoral view comports with the postmodern historicist assumption that the concept of nature, like any other, invariably is a social construct—a product of particular peoples in particular times and places. Thus the decisive locus of nature for Jefferson is neither the wild, unspoiled, primitive nature that Americans identified with the Western frontier, nor the overcivilized nature of the gardens at Versailles. Rather, it is a landscape of reconciliation, a human construct whose origins are traceable to the ancient yearning for "harmony" between humanity and the environment. Jefferson, like modern environmentalists, recognized the unattainability of Arcadian or Edenic fantasies—fantasies of achieving perfect "harmony" or "balance" or "stable equilibrium" with nature—but he also recognized that they serve as idealized long-term goals, and that it is possible to achieve a significant measure of accommodation between society and the natural world.

It may seem odd to invoke pastoralism, widely regarded as a merely romantic, nostalgic, sentimental mode of thought and expression, as the basis for a modification of the serious belief in Progress. It surely is the case that pastoralism derives much of its imaginative energy from the ancient yearning for harmony with nature. But it should be noted that most metanarratives are woven around a core of fantasy and that the waning belief in history as a record of Progress is no exception. It too revolves around a futuristic dream, but unlike the unaggressive pastoral vision; it is a dream of gaining total control over nature. A nice example is the familiar "Star Trek" vision of life aboard a self-sustaining space vehicle. In this wholly built habitat, where virtually all materials undergo continuous recyling, most ties with organic nature have been severed. Such fantasies of Progress have as their ultimate aim total control over—hence complete escape from—the natural. They are indeed more fantastic, less attainable, and finally more dangerous than pastoral dreams of harmony with nature. But in any event, fantasy is a vital component of these rival mentalities, and far from constituting grounds for dismissing their significance, its presence indicates the depth from which they arise in the collective imagination.

Granted that neither the pastoral nor the progressive vision is achievable, only one of them points toward a future society that could maintain life-

---

25. On the current significance and usefulness of pastoralism, see Leo Marx, "Pastoralism in America," in *Ideology and Classic American Literature,* ed. Sacvan Bercovitch and Myra Jehlen (Cambridge: Cambridge University Press, 1986), 36–69; "The American Ideology of Space," in *Denatured Visions: Landscape and Culture in the Twentieth Century,* ed. Stewart Wrede and William Howard Adams (New York: Museum of Modern Art, 1991), 62–78; "Does Pastoralism Have a Future?" in *The Pastoral Landscape,* ed. John Dixon Hunt (Washington: National Gallery of Art, 1992), 209–225.

enhancing relations with the natural environment. Jefferson's vision of the middle landscape is a useful guide to modifying the prevailing belief in Progress and to counteracting the heedlessly aggressive attitude toward nature that it fosters. In place of a concept of Progress measured by the degree of human domination, we require one that is measured by the degree of achieved accommodation with biophysical nature.

# Contributors

**Jill Ker Conway**
Visiting Professor
Program in Science, Technology, and Society
Massachusetts Institute of Technology
Cambridge, MA

*The Road from Coorain* (Alfred A. Knopf, 1989)
Ed., *Written by Herself—Autobiographies of American Women: An Anthology* (Vintage Books, 1992)
*True North—A Memoir* (Alfred A. Knopf, 1994)

**Zhiyuan Cui**
Assistant Professor of Political Science
Massachusetts Institute of Technology
Cambridge, MA

*Sustainable Democracy,* with Adam Przeworski et al. (Cambridge University Press, 1995)
Currently at work on book on institutional alternatives to the neoliberal program of economic and political reform in China

**Leon Eisenberg, M.D.**
Maude and Lillian Presley Professor of Social Medicine
and Professor of Psychiatry, Emeritus
Harvard Medical School
Boston, MA

"Human Ecology in the Repertoire of Health Development." *World Health Forum,* 1988, 9:564–68.
"From Circumstance to Mechanism in Pediatrics during the Hopkins Century." *Pediatrics,* 1990, 85:42–49
"Medicine—Molecular, Monetary, or More than Both?" *Journal of the American Medical Association,* 1995, 274:331–34

## Contributors

**Robert Heilbroner**
Norman Thomas Professor of Economics, Emeritus
Graduate Faculty
The New School for Social Research
New York, NY

*The Crisis of Vision in Modern Economic Thought,* with William Milberg (Cambridge University Press, 1996)
"Do Machines Make History?" and "Technological Determinism Revisited," both in Merritt Roe Smith and Leo Marx, eds., *Does Technology Drive History?: The Dilemma of Technological Determinism* (MIT Press, 1994)

**Gerald Holton**
Mallinckrodt Professor of Physics and Professor of History of Science
Harvard University
Cambridge, MA

*Science and Anti-Science* (Harvard University Press, 1993)
*Einstein, History, and Other Passions* (American Institute of Physics Press, 1995; reprint, Addison-Wesley, 1996)
*Thematic Origins of Scientific Thought,* 2d ed. (Harvard University Press, 1988)

**Leo Marx**
William R. Kenan Jr. Professor of American Cultural History, Emeritus
School of Humanities and Social Science
and Senior Lecturer, Program in Science, Technology, and Society
Massachusetts Institute of Technology
Cambridge, MA

*The Machine in the Garden: Technology and the Pastoral Ideal in America* (Oxford University Press, 1964)
Ed., with Susan Danly, *The Railroad in American Art* (MIT Press, 1988)
Ed., with Merritt Roe Smith, *Does Technology Drive History? The Dilemma of Technological Determinism* (MIT Press, 1994)

**Bruce Mazlish**
Professor of History
Massachusetts Institute of Technology
Cambridge, MA

*The Fourth Discontinuity: The Co-Evolution of Humans and Machines* (Yale University Press, 1993; reprint, 1995)
*A New Science: The Breakdown of Connections and the Birth of Sociology* (Oxford University Press, 1989; reprint, Penn State Press, 1993)

## Ali A. Mazrui
Albert Schweitzer Professor in the Humanities
and Director, Institute of Global Cultural Studies
Binghamton University, State University of New York at Binghamton
Albert Luthuli Professor-at-Large in the Humanities and Development Studies
University of Jos in Nigeria
Senior Scholar and Andrew D. White Professor-at-Large, Emeritus
Cornell University, Ithaca, NY

*A World Federation of Cultures: An African Perspective* (Free Press, 1976)
*Cultural Forces in World Politics* (James Currey and Heinemann, 1990)
*The Africans: A Triple Heritage*—a television program jointly produced by the BBC and the Public Broadcasting Service (WETA, Washington) in association with the Nigerian Television Authority

## Alan Ryan
Professor of Politics
Princeton University
Princeton, NJ;
Warden-elect of New College, Oxford University, England

*John Dewey and the High Tide of American Liberalism* (W.W. Norton, 1995)
*Bertrand Russell: A Political Life* (Hill & Wang, 1988)
Ed., *John Stuart Mill, On Liberty and Other Essays* (1996)

## John M. Staudenmaier, S.J.
Professor of History, University of Detroit Mercy
and Editor of *Technology and Culture* (International Quarterly of the Society for the History of Technology)
Detroit, MI

*Technology's Storytellers: Reweaving the Human Fabric* (MIT Press, 1985)
"Rationality vs Contingency in the History of Technology," in Merritt Roe Smith and Leo Marx, eds., *Does Technology Drive History? The Dilemma of Technological Determinism* (MIT Press, 1994)
"Science and Technology: Who Gets a Say?" in Martin Bakker and Peter Kroes, eds., *Technological Development and Science in the Industrial Age* (Kluwer, 1992)

## George W. Stocking, Jr.
Stein-Freiler Distinguished Service Professor, Department of Anthropology
University of Chicago
Chicago, IL

*Race, Culture and Evolution* (Free Press, 1968)
*Victorian Anthropology* (Free Press, 1987)
*After Tylor: British Social Anthropology, 1888–1951* (University of Wisconsin Press, 1995)

**Richard White**
Professor of History
University of Washington
Seattle, WA

*The Organic Machine* (Hill & Wang, 1995)
*Land Use, Environment and Social Change: The Shaping of Island County, Washington* (University of Washington Press, 1980)
"Discovering Nature in North America." *Journal of American History* 79 (December 1992)

# Index

Acton, John (lord), 168
Addams, Jane, 115
Agriculture
   Jefferson's argument for, 214–16
   widely accepted eighteenth-century view, 214
Alland, D., 55
Almond, Gabriel, 164
*Ancient Society* (Morgan), 69–70
Anderson, P. W., 25
Anonymous, 55
Anthropology
   changes in (1890s to 1920s), 72–74
   crisis of, 78
   ethnographic, 69–70
   evolutionary and racial view, 68–71
   neoevolutionary, 76–77
   post–World War II, 77–78
   primitivism, 73–76
   questions about nature of inquiries, 80
   refocusing of, 79
   *See also* Civilization, European; Cultural relativism
*Anthropology* (Kroeber), 76
"Antispengler" (Neurath), 24
*Apollinian spirit* (Spengler), 16–17
Archer, G. L., 58
Aristotle, 109
Arita, I., 51
Arnold, Thomas, 159

Bacon, Francis, 9
Barinaga, M., 53
Battle of ancients and moderns, 30, 33
Baudelaire, Charles, 2, 27
Becker, Gary, 85

Benedict, Ruth, 74–75
Bentham, Jeremy, 30
Berkowitz, R. L., 58
Berlin, Isaiah, 95
Berman, Marshall, 3, 27n.1
Biodiversity, 129–30
Birth control
   medical advances related to, 117–19
   women's rights, 116–17
Blendon, R. J., 54
Bloch, A. B., 55
Blumenberg, Hans, 142–43
Boas, Franz, 71–72
Bookchin, Murray, 137
Botkin, Daniel, 139
*Brave New World* (Huxley), 100
Breman, J. G., 51
Brower, David, 137
Buffon, G. L. L., 122–23
Bunyan, John, 30
Burke, Edmund, 103, 107, 166
Bury, J. B., 9, 11
Bush, Vannevar, 12

Canguilhem, Georges, 37
Capitalism
   history of, 90–91
   transition to, 203
Carr, E. H., 167
Carson, Rachel, 129
Castelli, W. P., 52
Castoriadis, Cornelius, 145–46
Causality
   probability and quantum, 19–20
   of Spengler, 16–18

223

Centrism, Western, 141–46. *See also* Eurocentrism
Chen, Martha, 146
Children, 114–15
Chivian, E., 58
Chosen class concept (Marx), 168–69
Chosen people concept
  development of, 154–60
  of Hegel, 168
  identification of new, 164–65
Christianity
  characteristics shared with developmentalism, 155
  concept of chosen people, 156–57
  universalization of, 156–57
"City of Ladies" (de Pizan), 112
Civilization
  ethnocentrism of Western, 154–62
  European
    issue of progress, 66–67
    in racial terms, 68–70
    transition from culture to (Spengler), 16–17
    winter phase (Spengler), 17
Class, 108–9
Coleman, James S., 164–65
Commoner, Barry, 137
*Communist Manifesto, The,* (Marx), 3
Comte, Auguste, 31, 115
Condorcet, M. J. A. N., 30, 45–46, 112, 210
Constant, Benjamin, 107–8
*Control of Nature, The,* (McPhee), 133
Cook, E. F., 52
Cooperative systems, 151–52
Cornoni-Huntley, J., 54
Cosmic Religion (Einstein), 23
Coughenour, M. B., 59
Cultural determinism, 163
Cultural relativism
  criticism of, 146–47
  formulation of, 76–77
  in idea of progress, 74–75
Culture
  conquering nature, 126–27
  emphasis on male-female differences, 116–17
  evolution of, 128
  as explanation for human backwardness, 163
  modern pluralistic and relativistic concept, 71–72
  races arranged in order of, 70
  transition to civilization (Spengler), 16–17
  Western insensitivity to Third World, 144–46
*Culture: Concepts and Definitions* (Kroeber and Kluckhohn), 77
Curtin, Philip D., 158
Cycle theory (Spengler), 14–20
Cyclicist school
  view of science and progress, 14–20, 28

Darwin, Charles, 31, 39, 157–58
*Decline of the West, The,* (Spengler), 15
Degérando, Joseph, 67
de Gouges, Olympe, 112–13
de Kruif, Paul, 47
de Pauw, Cornelius, 123
de Pizan, Christine, 112
Derrida, Jacques, 34
*Descent of Man, The,* (Darwin), 39
Determinism
  of normative political theory, 169–70
  religious, 171
  scientific, 170–71
  *See also* Forecasting, scientific; Neo-determinism; Prediction, scientific
Devall, Bill, 137
Developmentalism
  characteristics shared with Christianity, 155
  as concept of progress, 153
  in the Third World, 153
Dewey, John, 98–100
*Discourse on the Origins of Inequality* (Rousseau), 103–5
Douglas, Mary, 132

DuBois-Reymond, Emile, 11
Dubos, J., 49
Dubos, Rene, 49, 56
Dyson, Freeman, 132

Easton, David, 171
Ecologists, deep, 136–37
Ecology
  as mass popular movement, 138
  present scientific emphasis, 139–40
  as science, 140
*Economic Approach to Human Behavior, The,* (Becker), 85
Economic progress, 92–93
Economics
  Keynesian, 88
  neoclassical
    definition of new, 84
    definition of original, 84
    definition of progress within, 88, 89–90
    as progressive scientific research program, 85–86
    science-related aspect of, 85
  non-neoclassical
    aim of, 88–89
    definition of progress within, 88–89
    emphasis on historicity, 87, 90
    identification of, 87–88
    significance of state intervention, 90
Eddington, Arthur Stanley, 170–71
Einstein, Albert, 20–24
Eisenberg, C., 59–60
Eisenberg, L., 50, 54, 56, 57, 58
Eisenstadt, Shmuel, 145
Ekirch, Arthur, 121, 124
Emerson, Ralph Waldo, 124–25, 212
End-of Science movements, 19
"End of the Modern Era, The," (Havel), 10–11
Engels, Friedrich, 3, 157
Enlightenment, the
  anti-Enlightenment thought, 211
  concept of progress formed during, 1, 201–2
  equality of women in thought of, 112–13, 117
  history as record of continuous improvement, 203–4, 210
  idea of progress in, 30–31
Environment, natural
  modern scientific thinking about, 139
  relation to progress, 122
Environmentalism
  morality argument of, 135–37
  proper management argument, 137
  quality of life argument, 216
  relation to progress, 133–37
  *See also* Ecologists, deep
Environmental issues
  closed space doctrine, 128
  defenders of progress related to, 131–33
  doomsayers, 131–32
  price of progress, 129
  progress used as pejorative term, 128–29
Epstein, A. M., 54
Equality of women
  in Enlightenment thought, 112–13, 117
  in feminist thought, 111
  granted by underground resistance groups, 113–14
  progress in, 119–20
  progress in view of Oneida Community, 114
  Shaker belief, 113
Ethnocentrism
  Boas's criticism of, 71
  in concept of progress, 153
  link to racism, 158
  theories of evolution, 159
  of Western culture, 154
Eurocentrism, 35. *See also* Centrism, Western
*Europe and the People Without History* (Wolf), 79
Evolution
  idea of chosen species, 157
  idea of progress in, 158

Evolution (*continued*)
  ideas of social, 163
  ideas used by advocates of progress, 138–39
  issues in anthropology, 80
  as progress, 127–28
Evolutionary theory
  Boas's criticism, 71
  human progress in, 69–71
  influence on belief in progress, 208–10
  relation to progress, 31
Ewigman, B. G., 58

*Fable of the Bees* (Mandeville), 103
Farmer, P., 56
Faustian spirit (Spengler), 16–19
Feldman, J. J., 57
Feminism
  in early modern society, 112
  effect of post–1960 agitation, 118–19
  during the Enlightenment, 112–13
  relation to technological change, 115–16
  thought related to ideal future, 111
Ferguson, Adam, 66
Fischl, M. A., 55
Flegal, K. M., 57
Ford, Henry, 194
Forecasting, scientific, 171–72
Foucault, Michel, 34
*Fragility of Goodness, The,* (Nussbaum), 38
Frazer, James, 71
Frost, Robert, 200
Fryxel, J. M., 59
Fukuyama, Francis, 153

Geddes, Patrick, 115
Geertz, Clifford, 77
Gellner, Ernest, 202
*Genealogy of Morals, The,* (Nietzsche), 108
Gérando, M. Joseph de. *See* Degérando, Joseph

*German Ideology, The,* (Marx and Engels), 92
Gibbon, Edward, 167–68
Giddens, Anthony, 35–36
Gilman, Charlotte Perkins, 115
Glassroth, J., 49, 50
*Global 2000 Report to the President,* 131
God
  Einstein's idea of, 23–24
  postmodernist perception, 33
Goffman, Ervin, 188
Goldman, L., 52
Goldsmith, Edward, 139
Gould, Stephen, 138
Grant, J. P., 50
Greg, W. R., 163–64
Grey, Thomas, 149
Gruenberg, E. M., 50
Guilford-Davenport, M., 57
Guyer, B., 51

Habermas, Jürgen, 35–36
Hardin, Garrett, 135–36
Harding, Sandra, 13
Havel, Václav, 9–11
Havlik, R. J., 54
Hays, Samuel, 133, 134
Hegel, G. W. F., 161, 168
Heilbroner, Robert, 211
Herskovits, Melville, 76
Hesse, Mary, 12
Hirshleifer, Jack, 85
History
  of capitalism, 90–91
  Comte's laws of, 31
  different perceptions of, 167–68
  identification with progress, 212
  Marxist conception of, 3
  as progress, 1, 130
  as a record of progress, 206–7
*History of Astronomy* (Smith), 30
Hobbes, Thomas, 100–102, 105, 107, 165–66
Howells, William Dean, 197
Huebner, R. E., 55

Hughes, H. Stuart, 15–16
Human progress
　issues of, 68–69, 75–76
　link of race to, 69–71
Human self-assertion
　concepts of universal and infinite in, 141–44
　institutional innovation to support, 147–52
　relation to progress, 142–43
Hume, David, 103
Huxley, Aldous, 100

Idea of progress, 6–7
　belief in, 28
　influence of modernity on, 31–32
　opposing views of, 32
　origins of, 29–30
　parts comprising, 35
　weakened, 1–2
*Idea of Progress, The,* (Bury), 9, 11
*Ideas and Opinions* (Einstein), 23
Ignatius of Loyola, 178–80
Illich, Ivan, 46
Industrialization, Chinese rural, 147–48, 151–52
Industrial revolution
　Emerson's perception, 125
　labor of women and children with, 114–15, 118–19
Innovation
　shareholder-cooperative system in China, 147–52
　technological, 210
Intuition (Einstein), 22

Jackson, J. B., 130
Jacoby, G. A., 58
James, William, 125–26
Jameson, Fredric, 211
Javitt, J. C., 54
Jaynes, Julian, 40
Jefferson, Thomas, 124, 201–2, 213–14
Jorm, A. F., 53
Judaism, 154–56

Kahn, Herman, 131–32
Kames (lord), 65
Kant, Immanuel, 96
Kasiske, B. L., 54
Kasson, John, 188
Keynes, John Maynard, 84, 92
Kipling, Rudyard, 174
Kluckhohn, Clyde, 76–77
Knox, R. A., 53
Krochmal, Nachman, 155
Kroeber, A. L., 76
Kuczmarski, R. J., 57
Kuhn, Thomas, 80, 98
Kumanyika, S. K., 57

LaCroix, A. Z., 54
Lakatos, Imre, 85–86
Landes, David, 187
Landrigan, P. J., 50
Laplace, Pierre, 170
Larson, J. L., 192
Lasch, Christopher, 122, 129
Latour, Bruno, 12–13
Lederberg, J., 59
Lederman, Leon, 17
Lee, Mother Ann, 113
*Legitimacy of the Modern Age* (Blumenberg), 142–43
Leibniz, Gottfried Wilhelm, 22
Lenin, V. I., 172–73
Leopold, Aldo, 136, 137
Levine, Lawrence W., 189
Liberalism, 167
Life expectancy
　improvements, 52–54
　of women, 119
*Limits of Growth, The,* (Club of Rome), 128, 131
Locke, John, 102, 165–66
Lovelock, James, 137
Lyotard, Jean-François, 34

Maine, Henry, 68
Malcolm, A. H., 53
Malthus, Thomas, 122–23, 135
*Man and His Works* (Herskovits), 76

*Man and Nature* (Marsh), 125
*Man and Technics* (Spengler), 19
Mandeville, Bernard, 103
Mann, J., 55
Marchand, Roland, 196
Marinetti, Fillipo T., 175–76
Marsh, George Perkins, 125
Marshall, Alfred, 84
Marx, Karl, 9, 91–92, 157, 168–70, 172
Marx, Leo, 125, 197
Marxism
  as concept of progress, 153
  discrediting of, 2
  doctrine of economic determinism, 170
  modernism of, 2–3
  perception of progress, 208
Material progress, 42
  effect on environment, 134–35
  Hardin's solution to check, 135–36
McKeown, T., 49
McKibben, William, 130
McLennan, John, 68–69
McNeill, William H., 161
McPhee, John, 133
Mead, Margaret, 74, 75–76
Meade, James, 151
Medawar, Peter, 27
Medicine
  criticism of (Illich), 46
  as a determinant of health, 56–59
  faith in (Condorcet), 45–46
  improvement in women's life expectancy with, 119
  progress in, 46–50, 56
  science in, 50
Menninger, Karl, 196
Mentality, collective
  of history as record of progress, 206–7
*Microbe Hunters* (de Kruif), 47
Mill, John Stuart, 92, 95, 159, 209
Millennarians, 29
*Mind of Primitive Man, The,* (Boas), 71
Modernism
  antimodernism in, 32
  critique of, 2
  of Marx, 2–3
  postmodernism as continuation of, 33–34
  progress equated with, 33
Modernity
  with idea of progress, 30
  influence on idea of progress, 31–32
  meanings of progress in culture of, 205–10
Modernization
  critique of, 2
  political, 160
Modern period, 30, 33
Montesquieu, C. L. de Secondat, 30
Morality
  not cumulative or progressive, 38–39
  of progress, 135–37
Moral progress
  of Boas, 72
  definability, 42
  issues of, 37–39
  possibility of, 39–40
More, Hannah, 118
Morgan, Lewis Henry, 69–70
Mortality rates
  declines for specific diseases, 47–49, 51
  rise in specific disease, 49–52
Mumford, Lewis, 126
Mysticism
  of Christian theologians, 184, 186–87
  in place of idea of progress, 33
  as replacement for scientific truth (Spengler), 19

Nash, Roderick, 136
Nature
  end of, 211–12
  Jefferson's perception, 217–18
  as measure of progress, 127
  perception with transition to capitalism, 203
  relation to progress, 122–26, 137
  *See also* Ecology; Environment, natural

Needham, Joseph, 146
Neodeterminism, 171
Nesbit, Robert, 13
Netter, T. W., 55
Neurath, Otto, 24
Nietzsche, Friedrich, 34, 108
*Notes on the State of Virginia* (Jefferson), 124
Nussbaum, Martha, 38

Oakeshott, Michael, 169
Oaks, S. C., 59
Odum, Eugene, 58
Oersted, Hans Christian, 25
*On Liberty* (Mill), 95
*Opus Majus* (Bacon), 9
Order
   ordering of time, 28
   races arranged in order of, 70
   in theories, 2
*On the Origin of Species* (Darwin), 157
Ormerod, W. E., 59
Owen, Robert, 114–15

Packard, R. M., 56
Packenham, Robert, 160
Parsons, Talcott, 161–62
Pastoralism of Jefferson, 215–18
*Patterns of Culture* (Benedict), 74–75
Pearson, M. L., 55
Pennock, J. Roland, 162
*Pilgrim's Progress* (Bunyan), 30
Pisa, Z., 51
Plamenatz, John, 95, 166–67
Political progress
   concept of, 96
   conditions for sustaining, 101–2
   Hobbes's conception, 100–102, 105
   lack of, 96–100
   in relation to class and gender, 108–9
   of Rousseau, 103–5
Politics
   of antiquity, 107–8
   contrast between modern and ancient, 109

   of Rawls, 106
   two assessments of, 106
*Politics of the Developing Areas, The,* (Coleman), 164
Pope, Alexander, 203
Popper, Karl, 88, 171
Positivism, 31
Postmodernism
   criticism of modernism and modernization, 2
   criticisms of idea of progress, 32–35
   critics of, 33
   progress as despoiler of environment, 212
   skepticism of, 2–3
Prediction, scientific, 171–72
Pre-established harmony theory (Leibniz), 22
Prichard, James Cowles, 68
Progress
   as actuality, 7
   Adam Smith's conception of, 91–93
   belief in, 1–2
   Boas's conception, 71–72
   cyclicist school of, 15–20
   defined within branches of economics, 88
   of European civilization, 66–68
   failure of Marxist version of, 3
   justification of concept of, 202
   Marx's conception, 91–92
   notions of possible and inevitable, 142
   signs of, 43–44
   waning belief in, 2–3
   Western theories of, 154
   *See also* Economic progress; Human progress; Idea of progress; Material progress; Moral progress; Political progress; Scientific progress; Social progress
*Progress, Its Law and Cause* (Spencer), 208
*Progress for a Small Planet* (Ward), 129

Property
  bundle of rights view, 149–51
  consolidated and disintegrated, 148–51
Putnam, Hilary, 24

*Quiet Revolution, A,* (Chen), 146

Race
  distinct species with unequal capacities, 68
  link to progress, 70
Racism
  in context of evolutionary theory, 157, 163
  development of European concept of, 154–63
  link to ethnocentrism, 158
Rationalism
  of the Enlightenment, 117–18
  Havel's criticism of, 10–11
Rationality
  of Einstein, 23
  integrated with emotion, 181–82
Raup, Hugh, 139
Rawls, John, 106
Reason, as matter of faith, 27, 37
Redfield, Robert, 75, 77
Reductionism (Einstein), 21
Regularity, 171–72
*Reinventing Anthropology* (Hymes), 79
Religion
  during the Enlightenment, 113
  lack of conflict with science (Einstein), 23
  link to science, 20, 23, 32
  in place of idea of progress, 33
  universalist premises of Western, 154–55
  *See also* Christianity; Judaism
*Religion of China* (Weber), 144
*Representative Government* (Mill), 95
*Resourceful Earth, The,* (Simon and Kahn), 131–32
Rettig, R. A., 58
Revolutions
  French, 31
  industrial, 31
  political, 29
  scientific, 29, 30
Ricardo, David, 92
Rice, D. P., 54
*Rights of Women, The,* (de Gouges), 112–13
Robins, A. G., 49, 50
Roosevelt, Franklin D., 12
Rorty, Richard, 108
Rosen, G., 57
Ross, Edward Alsworth, 193
Rousseau, Jean-Jacques, 103–5
"Rust of Progress, The," (Nesbit), 13

Sahlins, Marshall, 83
Samuelson, Paul, 84
Sapir, Edward, 73–74
Sarton, George, 12
Sartorius, N., 58
Schoolcraft, Henry Rowe, 68
Schumpeter, Joseph, 92
Science
  as aspect of medical practice, 50
  as continuous paradigm, 36–37
  cyclicist view of, 14–20
  deep ecologists' claims to, 137–38
  divergence from linearist and cyclicist models, 25–26
  Einstein's prediction, 21
  Einstein's view of doing, 20–21, 23
  Havel's criticism of, 9–11
  hierarchical structure theory, 25–26
  linearist view of, 14, 20–24
  pluralism theory, 25
  as self-constructing enterprise, 24
  Spengler's predictions for, 16–19
  universalist promises of Western, 154
  used in service of power, 35
*Science in Traditional China* (Needham), 146
Scientific progress
  anthropologic views, 80
  cultural consequences, 80
  linearist theory, 20–24

outcomes, 41
  perpetual revision in, 37
  question of limits to, 13–14
  views of, 11–13
Scientific revolution (medicine), 50–51
Secular thought, 206
Sessions, George, 137
Seward, William, 127
Shareholding-cooperative system, China, 142
Shareholding systems, 151–52
Shils, Edward, 160, 164
Shope, R. E., 59
Sibley, Mulford Q., 171–72
*Silent Spring* (Carson), 129
Simon, Julian, 131–32
Sinclair, A. R. E., 59
Singer, Joseph, 150
*Sketches of the History of Man* (Kames), 65
Slevin, M. L. H. Plant, 54
Small, P. A., 55
*Small is Beautiful* (Schumacher), 134
Smith, Adam, 30, 91–93
Smith, Merritt Roe, 197
Snider, D. E., 49, 50, 55
Social contract
  Hobbes's concept, 166
  Locke's concept, 166
Social progress, 101–2
Social science
  economics in, 85
  founding of, 30
  universalism of time and space, 165
  Western, 173
Sociology, 31
Solow, Robert, 89
Sommer, A., 54
Spencer, Herbert, 11, 208–9
Spengler, Oswald, 15–20
*Spirit of the Laws* (Montesquieu), 30
*Spiritual Exercises* (Ignatius of Loyola), 178–83, 187, 195, 196–97
Stalinism, 211
Standardization, 187–88
Steinmetz, Charles, 193–94

*Structure of Scientific Revolutions, The,* (Kuhn), 80, 98
St. Simon, Claude, 115

Tarantola, J. M., 55
Taylor, F. W., 193
Technology
  effect on nature and environment, 130–33
  implications for women with changes in, 114–16
  innovation as gauge of progress, 210
  Spengler's prediction related to, 19
  *See also* Industrialization
*Theory of Justice, A,* (Rawls), 106
Thompson, E. P., 183–84
*Time and the Other* (Fabian), 79
Tocqueville, Alexis de, 121, 209
Tomes, N. J., 49
Truth in idea of progress, 35–37
Turner, Frederick Jackson, 128
*Two Treatises of Government* (Locke), 102
Tylor, E. B., 70

Uemura, K., 51
*Unbound Prometheus, The,* (Landes), 187
Unger, Roberto, 143–44, 146
Universalism
  dual nature of Western civilization, 154, 157
  ethnocentric, 162
  of Marx, 168–69
  of process in concept of progress, 153
*Untergang des Abendlandes, Der* (Spengler), 15

Veblen, Thorstein, 115
Villarino, M. E., 55
*Vindication of Natural Society* (Burke), 103
Virchow, Rudolph, 57
von Helmholtz, Hermann, 11, 17

Walras, Leon, 86
Ward, Barbara, 129, 134, 137
Weber, Max, 38, 144
Wenneker, M. B., 54
White, E. B., 129
White, Leslie, 77, 121–22, 126–28
Whitehead, Alfred North, 204–5
Wildavsky, Aaron, 132
Wilkinson, R. G., 57
Wilson, J. F., 57
Wilson, L. G., 49
Wolf, Eric, 77–79
Wolfson, Harry, 143, 145

Women
    education in nineteenth century, 118
    implications of technological change for, 114–16
    in industrial work force, 114–16, 118–19
    life expectancy, 119
    political views of rights of, 108–9
    rights related to birth control and fertility, 116–17
    scope of work opportunities, 119–20
    *See also* Equality of women